i

Also by Ray O'Brien …

*Fulford, Québec, The Changing Geography
of a Canadian Village*

*American Sublime, Landscape and Scenery
of the Lower Hudson Valley*

*Bucks County, A Journey Through Paradise,
From the Peaceable Kingdom
to the Suburban Dream*

The Story of
BUCKS COUNTY

ISBN 978-0-578-17069-5

Aberystwyth-Hilltown Press

The Story of
BUCKS COUNTY

Ray O'Brien

For my wife Debra

The Harvest Field – Buck County

Pennsylvania Beautiful by Wallace Nutting,
New York: Bonanza Books, 1924 (p. 69)

The primordial things are commonplace, frog voices in the pond, crickets, a bull bellowing, the sun climbing up out of the bracken ... it is in these things that God and the devil were born and where they live ... I do not mean that either of these creatures is here or there or anywhere. They are within us, but to identify them is the whole purpose of life.

–William Wood, A History of the Devil, 1973

CONTENTS

APPENDICES

BIBLIOGRAPHY

ILLUSTRATIONS

CHAPTER 3:

CHAPTER 4:

CHAPTER 5:

CHAPTER 14:

*(Unless otherwise indicated,
all illustrations are either created by the author,
or are part of the author's collections)*

In the pale moonlight ... a frightful sight
on the old settling ground.

*(After Raphael Tuck & Sons, Post Cards Series
160, Circa 1900)*

Preface

Home is always the impossible subject,
multilayered and maddening.

– Paul Theroux, *Smithsonian,*
May 2012

Bucks County is one of 3,143 counties (including Louisiana's parishes and Alaska's boroughs) in the United States. It is one of sixty-three counties in the state of Pennsylvania. And it is the one and only "Bucks." It was created in 1682 and named for Buckinghamshire in England, the ancestral home of the Penn family. Places speak; they have stories to tell, if we but listen. Listen and you will hear the sometimes sad, sometimes humorous, but always captivating story of Bucks County. But this is not a novel. No, definitely not.

Which is odd because there is, in fact, a lead character. Let me explain. In 1943 the geographer Ralph Brown wrote *Mirror for Americans, Likeness of the Eastern Seaboard, 1810*[1] In it, he created the imaginary "Mr. Thomas Keystone, Esq." of Philadelphia and employed him as a gentleman traveler to observe the America of his day. This was very effectively done and the work was (and is) known far and wide among historical geographers, if not the reading public. Similarly, I conjured up the devil to tell the story of Bucks County in the 1988 *Journey Through Paradise.* And did I have hell to pay! "College Professor Stalks the Devil," blared the headlines (*Bucks County Courier Times).* It was Satanism run amok; black magic gone wild in God's backyard – the *Peaceable Kingdom* of the Pennsylvania Quakers. But critics and most commentators entirely missed the point. The point is that the devil was being used as a literary vehicle (much as

---

[1] Ralph H. Brown, *Mirror for Americans, Likeness of the Eastern Seaboard, 1810,* New York: American Geographical Society, 1943.

Mr. Keystone) to help better understand and illustrate the county's past and present.

Johann Wier (1515–1588) is regarded by some as the father of modern psychiatry; this claim rests, at least in part, on his explanation for witches' abnormal behavior – just "sick" people he said, Renaissance-age psychotics, but not possessed by the devil. When not studying witches or sorcery in Africa, Doctor Wier also calculated "without any possibility of error" that there were 7,409,127 devils in Satan's legion. One of these many devils helps tell the story of Bucks County. The devil (a devil) has been an abiding presence in this land of gently rolling hills and valleys since European settlers first arrived (and probably before). Folkloric in origin, his later day presence (or absence – and here there is much controversy) reflects the feelings people have about their county as well as peoples' relationship with the land, the landscape, the whole natural world. Is evil present in the world today? And if so, what form, what guise does it take here in Bucks County?

An attempt to answer these questions was made by the moviemaker M. Night Shyamalan in two Bucks County films (*Signs*, 2002 and *Lady in the Water*, 2006). These films also helped further the county's national profile. Space aliens in the corn fields? Water fairies in an apartment complex pool? A sense of wonder and a disconnect between nature and modern society? Who knows. It did put Bucks on the big screen, though *Signs* failed to capitalize on one of the county's greatest assets: fall foliage, fields of pumpkins and scarecrows, the thrill and the chill of the Halloween season when the county absolutely bathes in the glory of autumn and fall tourism.

Hayrides and haunted houses generate a wealth of money in just one month while the county's positive and pleasing image generates hundreds of millions of dollars in year round tourism. *Dream Destinations* (a *Life* magazine publication) rated Bucks as one of the top one hundred vacation spots in the entire world: "Bucks County …

could compete with any upcountry hamlet in a Currier and Ives contest."[2] What's called "marketing" the county has, of course, been good. And yet ...

Sometimes the county's notability stems from its notoriety. Throughout the latter chapters and in Appendix D, those who live here (not the tourists) express their displeasure with the land of "McMansions" and question whether the occupants of a 4,000 square foot gated mega home are any happier than the Levittowners who moved into their more modest Ranchers a half century ago ("No, they're not" the consensus seems to be). This, and the continuing loss of open space and farms and the worsening congestion of potholed roads and crumbling bridges, reflects a locally diminished quality of life that becomes a new "Mirror for Americans" for national trends.

Philadelphia magazine said it like this: "Bucks County: Once an Eden, Now 'Devastation'."[3] The *International Business Times* headlined: "Bucks County, Pennsylvania: A Microcosm of America's Post-War Suburban Sprawl."[4] The article details "the gradual and perhaps irreversible destruction of Mother Nature" and quotes Douglas Kane, professor of environmental design at Delval University in Doylestown: "The things we praise about Bucks County, we are destroying because of development." Mark Arbeter, county resident and Standard and Poor's strategist, says:

> I don't really know exactly when the beautiful landscape started to get gobbled up, but it has transformed and scarred a lot of the county forever ... some call it progress, I call it devastation.

---

[2] As reported by Crissa Shoemaker DeBree, "Bucks Trip a 'Dream Destination'." *The Intelligencer*, April 19, 2008. It was pointed out however that "the dream" referred only to the upper county and not the Philadelphia-like lower county.

[3] www.phillymag.com/realestate/neighborhood-news/bucks-county, September 5, 2013.

[4] Palash Ghosh, www.ibtimes.com/bucks-county-pennsylvania-microcosm, September 4, 2013.

The good and the bad of it, the benefits that tourism and self-promotion bring (more people and more business) along with the downside (too many housing tracts and malls, too much traffic). It was all made jarringly clear on Sunday, October 18th, 1987. It was a memorable date in county history. On that beautiful autumn afternoon with the leaves in full color (and with the NFL on strike and nothing to watch on TV) everybody from New York to Philadelphia decided to drive through charming Bucks County. The result was what the local news reporters called "Rural Gridlock." Parks and historic sites filled up and their entrances barricaded, the roads were bumper-to-bumper with no place to park or stop, and people couldn't exit their own driveways. The county literally choked on its own success (or was it excess?).

Of all the counties in America, few have powerful enough name recognition to be spoken of on a first name only basis: Dade (Florida), Cook (Illinois), Marin (California), Fairfax (Virginia), Lancaster (Pennsylvania), along with a handful of others. Some counties become infamous because they're stigmatized by poverty (Harlan and Owsley in Kentucky). Some become famous because of literary associations: Mark Twain's Calaveras in California, William Faulkner's (fictitious) Yoknapatawpha in Mississippi, and Aldo Leopold's Sand County (actually Sauk County) in Wisconsin. And then there's Brooklyn (Kings County); everybody knows Brooklyn.

Bucks is just Bucks. It's renowned because of its closeness to national media outlets in New York City and because of its longstanding artistic, literary, and theatrical associations. Name recognition is further enhanced by popular tourist attractions like Sesame Place, Washington Crossing, Peddler's Village, and the village of New Hope. At one time there was even a restaurant in New York City named for it. When a developer placed advertisements in several national magazines for retirement properties in South Carolina, the sales pitch (naturally) featured Bucks: "Imagine Bucks County with 60-degree winters!" And imagine finding "the things that (make) Bucks County so special" in the Sunbelt. The things that make Bucks County so special were never itemized or explained; presumably, they were thought to be widely and commonly known.

Online auction sites list a great variety of "Bucks" or "Bucks County" collectibles. Few other counties can match Bucks in the wealth of items made in or named for it: pottery from Morrisville and Quakertown produced from local clays, Mercer tiles from Doylestown, traditional and impressionistic landscapes in oil or water color (some on barn boards) that range in price from hundreds to tens of thousands of dollars. There's even a "Ralph Lauren Collection" of Bucks County bed skirts, comforters, shams, and duvet covers featuring "gorgeous Bucks County country patterns."

**Department 56
"Snow Village"
Series**

BUCK'S COUNTY

"...a legendary place known as Buck's County. Here, life passes at a leisurely pace under the big skies and a million twinkling stars. The county stretches across acres of prized land ... Buck's County offers the best in country living ... Hard days in the field harvesting this year's crop ... After chores are done, night draws to a close with a hayride through the south forty ... Take a ride in a pickup or on your favorite horse along the back roads and beyond Main Street."

[Note: Packaging boxes incorrectly use an apostrophe in Bucks ("Buck's")].

**The Abandoned Gas Pump
#55121**

**Yesterday's Tractor
#52869**

As part of its "Snow Village" series, Department 56 created a number of Bucks County-themed ceramic collectibles. These wintery scenes included a farm house, horse barn, horse trailer (This **is** Bucks County), water tower, abandoned gas pump and country store, and "Yesterday's" farm tractor (*See above illustration*). "Legendary" Bucks County is described in a highly sentimental way on the packaging, making it sound like Norman Rockwell or Grandma Moses might have lived and painted here. The gas pump, set amid a debris field of old tires and automotive junk, last sold gas for twelve cents a gallon. The "Willmark" farm tractor has a flat rear tire and busted front grill and is backed against a dead tree. These miniature scenes of rural abandonment and depopulation evoke an elegiac sadness for the Bucks that was, but is no more. For the America that was.

I've lived half my life in Bucks County, and prior to that the other half in the Bronx (County). Beauty and the beast. Two extremes and no comparison. But not so fast. Despite vast differences in poverty rates, diseases, income levels, population densities, etc. etc. there is surprisingly much common ground. Both were populated by Lenape tribes and were visited early on by Dutch and Swedes who planted grain and brewed beer. Both developed a successful iron industry (Jordan Mott in the Bronx and the Morris family at Durham Furnace in Bucks). Morris family members became wealthy landowners in both locales. Lewis Morris proposed that the Bronx (Port Morris) be the nation's capital, while Robert Morris offered the Congress the sale of his "high ground" near Morrisville, Bucks County as a site for the capital. Neither made a convincing enough argument. Both the "Beautiful Bronx" and charming Bucks attracted artists and poets to record their natural treasures. Later film makers set up studios and took full advantage of the unparalleled rural scenery in the silent era.[5] Both the Bronx and Bucks evolved a "Little Italy," a colony of Italian immigrants with a partiality for stonework and masonry. (*See: A Closer Look* in Ch. 6). Both counties share parts of a common infrastructure: historic Route 1 (The Boston Road) and Interstate-95. And, I'm sure there are many more such comparisons between the counties that could keep an army of history majors writing theses for years to come.

While living in the Bronx my family and I moved every couple of years from neighborhood to neighborhood to stay one step ahead of the blight and crime, the fires that consumed the South Bronx block

---

[5] In Bucks County, a segment of *The Perils of Pauline* (1914) was filmed on the tracks of the New Hope and Ivyland Railroad. The location used is still called "Pauline's Trestle."

by block. The moving was always "up," north through the county. Ironically, my life in Bucks has followed much the same geographical progression – moving "up" north through various townships and boroughs. Of course, address changing in Bucks lacks the urgency, the near desperation it had in the Bronx. Yet fundamentally, it's been an attempt to escape the blight ... the blight of development and overcrowding. An attempt to live in green(er) surroundings with a dark(er) night sky above. Recently, when a severe winter storm dropped three inches of snow and ice per hour on the upper county, a barn roof came crashing down (in Milford Township). "Barn collapses on Cows" read the headline. But people cared and volunteers and friends rescued the cows (a bit shaken up and bruised). It was newsworthy and it ended happily. In the upper county barns are considered to be the very "essence" (Audubon Society) of the land and barn tours are popular. Things rural elicit interest and caring ... at least here and at least for a while.

When I first arrived in Bucks County in the late 1970s there was much to like and appreciate despite the ongoing post-Levittown growth spasms. Quirky crossroads hamlets with names now gone, probably twice as many fields and farms and semi-paved roads as today, and stone houses with damp and musty-smelling basements ... in fact, an entire village that had that not unpleasant smell. I never experienced the old(er) Bucks personally, but there were bits and pieces of that tattered fabric still in place. There was "pleasure driving" on weekends, barn sales and flea markets ... the flea markets unhappily replaced by outlet shops, restaurants featuring the latest nouveau cuisine, and even a gambling casino. At night, tucked away and neglected graveyards where soul lights darted and danced over the moldering earth. Now, open houses at the newest subdivisions are advertised outside the cemetery gate. "Move up to Bucks ... move up to the 'Elegantly Appointed Estate Homes'" the realty signs proclaim. The *New York Times* announces "stores galore" for Bucks; malls, mini-malls, and always more and more of everything. It takes its toll.

So, are these just bittersweet reflections on the passing years? A negative and depressing diatribe on the way the county has changed? Things change, places change, accept it and move on. Must the story be so gloomy? No upbeat ending? That's for the reader to decide.

At the time I wrote the first version of *Bucks County* in the 1980s I was reading a lot of Kurt Vonnegut and Tom Robbins. These writers appealed to me because however serious their themes, they told their stories with humor, with a playfulness of words (not flippancy) that entertained and drew the reader on. (Parenthetically, I'm still reading Tom Robbins latest; e.g., "…nothing the human race has ever invented is more cool than a book. I still believe that today.").[6] Similarly, John Fraser Hart (b: 1924), the distinguished American geographer, encouraged students to pursue their studies with a sense of enjoyment, to explore the world with sensitivity and sympathy … and to have fun doing it.[7] I've tried to achieve a balance and combine the playful with the serious in studying this slice of the American landscape. Savor the clownishness and tomfoolery of the folk world; nail-biting nightmares come with the modern world.

What to title it then? When the earlier *Bucks County* was published in 1988 (*See Illustration*), it was subtitled *"A Journey Through Paradise, From the Peaceable Kingdom to the Suburban Dream."* Symbolically, the cover photo showed the last days of a dairy farm outside of Newtown … with a housing development sneaking up in the distance. The same scene can be seen today in parts of the upper county where sprawl remains a nasty reality and where municipalities are growing at 8-9% per decade … that's faster than the central and lower areas of the county.[8] Themes of sprawl and "development" are

---

[6] Tom Robbins, *Tibetan Peach Pie*, New York: HarperCollins, 2014, p. 35.

[7] John Fraser Hart, *Presidential Address*, 77th Annual Meeting of the Association of American Geographers, Los Angeles, Cal., April 21, 1981.

[8] This is a faster percentage increase with 8,000 more residents arriving between 2000-2010. The mid or central area of the county grows faster in absolute numbers, adding more than 18,000 population in that decade. Lower Bucks was actually stagnant, losing a small number of people. *(See Appendix B)*. Overall, population growth has dramatically slowed; the local press (*The Intelligencer*) observing that in 2014: "(Bucks') 54 boroughs and towns collectively added just enough people to fill a local TGI Friday's."

persistent and remain at the core of both the earlier and this newer edition.[9]

BUCKS COUNTY
A JOURNEY THROUGH PARADISE

*From the Peaceable Kingdom
to the Suburban Dream*

by
Raymond J. O'Brien

---

[9] Mostly, this edition is not just a newer or "second" edition, but rather an (almost) entirely new work. Between eighty and ninety percent of the content has been re-written and updated. The maps have been re-drawn and new illustrations added. The 1988 edition was a period piece in that some of the words and expressions used were influenced by the popular culture of the 1970s-80s. This has been left intact.

Again, what title to use? "Bucks County: Going Through the Changes"? "Then and Now"? "Top to Bottom"? "Bucks County Revisited"? "Bucks County, The Journey Continues"? How about we keep it pure and simple: *"The Story of Bucks County."* And to understand the county's story, you have to go back, far back to the very beginning ...

"The Oldest House in Bucks County" The Lacey Homestead in Wrightstown. It was built in 1705-06 of oak and cedar logs with a great chimneystack. *"This venerable dwelling was taken down on a Saturday afternoon in the spring of 1877 ... after it had been laid low, a lunch was served."* W. Davis, *History of Bucks County*, 1884, Ch.17.

Acknowledgments

I am grateful to the many people who, over the years, have contributed to this project by sharing their time, and especially their ideas, opinions, and feelings about this county we all call home. My colleagues at Bucks County Community College in Newtown were most helpful in their areas of expertise, and were always there to impart confidence in this work ... and friendship too. Among them were Mart Sutton, Lyle Rosenberger, Tony Wolf, Mitch Bunkin, Bob Stout, and Bill Wheeler. Kingdon Swayne and Bob Frazier gave freely of their knowledge of and insights into Quaker History and the "Friends" way of life. Librarians on the college campus and at libraries throughout the county were helpful in the utmost. Thanks as well for the assistance rendered by the library staff at the Mennonite Heritage Center in Harleysville and at the Schwenkfelder Library-Museum in Pennsburg. Though their names are far too numerous to mention, students in my Geography and History courses at the college were invaluable for their input into Appendices C ("Old Stereotypes") and D ("County Survey and Postcard Project"). Other individuals I'd like to thank are Mr. Robert Ford and Carol Ford for their always interesting recollections of Levittown and the lower county. Carol also helped with the editing, as did Tina Vine. My thanks to Peter Osborne for sharing his knowledge of book publishing and printing. And to Joanne Ford and Chuckie Henneberg for their help with the mysteries of the word programs. And last, but certainly not least, my wife Debra for the typing and for all the miles and hours of fieldwork we did together in the county ... our county.

CHAPTER I

ORIGINS: BOTH DEMONIC
AND TRIASSIC

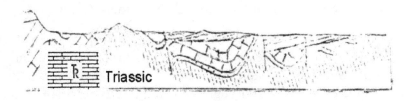

*For the land there is both good and bad,
both hills and vales.*

– George Haworth, writing to friends in
England (1701)

*We devils are the very quintessence of the
world, the earth, matter. Do you understand?
We form the bond, as it were, between you and
the earth. And we make sure that this bond is
not broken.*

– The "Benevolent Devil" in P.D. Ouspen-
sky's *Talks With a Devil*, 1972

Origins

Long, long ago, a fallen angel tumbled to earth somewhere in Mesopotamia. His long tumble through the firmament and his collision with the earth gave him a crumpled and badly misshapen body. Forevermore, he would limp through this world. He picked up his misshapen self, shook the stardust from his clothes, and, hitchhiking his way west, decided to see Europe before the tourists ruined it.

Like many a good artist, and a con artist he was, his formative years were spent on the Continent. But in 1165 this archfiend was reported riding a great black steed amid a mass of gray clouds that swept across the cliffs of Scarborough; he had arrived in England. Down below, locked in the DNA of the Yorkshire folk huddled asleep in their hovels on the moors and in the dales were the future settlers of Bucks County. They would all meet in a future time and place.

For the next several centuries "Old Boots" or "Hornie,"as the English affectionately called him, appeared to yeoman as they plowed their fields and threshed their grain. Taking the form of a goat, tree, dog, and sundry other rural commonplaces or just being his old mischievous self - - he wheeled and dealt with them, sometimes winning and sometimes losing. He was accepted as a natural enough part of life itself, and even received an honorary title from the Crown: "Prince of Darkness." He received the even greater honor of having a pub on London's Fleet Street named after him: "The Devil." All across Britain, from Cornwall to Scotland, and from Wales to Yorkshire, he became the "titular landlord" of places named after him: the Devil's Nostrils, Throat, Elbow, Ladder, Slide, Frying Pan, Cauldron, Beef Tub, Kettle, and Punch Bowl.

Around this time, in an ancient abbey in the shire of Buckingham on the outskirts of London, several wealthy and perverted gentlemen founded the Hellfire Club(s); what was inscribed above the abbey's door, *"Fais ce que tu voudras,"* described the bill of fare within. "Do What Thou Wilt" they did, invoking the devil to preside over black masses and drunken orgies.

Years before, and in this same shire of "Bucks," the devil had taken possession of "a young maid of lovely innocent beauty." He spoke from the hollow of her belly in a guttural voice, and further caused her "to bark like a Dog, bellow like a Bull ... (in) a wonderful frightful manner." Discretely down the road from these goings on, rows of plainly-dressed men and women sat on worn wooden benches in a worn brick meetinghouse and silently meditated. Protectively surrounded by "an infinite ocean of light and love," they absolutely rejected carnal practices and worldly ways. Blacksmiths, shoemakers, farmers, butchers, and housewives gathered together in "the fellowship of the Spirit." They were a "Society of Friends" and they and the devil would all meet again.

In the great world beyond this green and pleasant shire of Buckingham the calendar pages and almanacs of human history were turning faster. Whole continents had been discovered and were being peopled, a new trans-Atlantic civilization was in the making. For "Old Boots," duty called. In a world of dualities and dichotomies, it wouldn't do that all the ships heading for America carried only preachers, holy books and hymnals, and good intentions. God ordered him to book passage for the six-week crossing, even paying for his ticket. Not stowed below deck with the livestock and indentured servants (the cattle and chattel), and not in the ship's hold with the cartons and crates labeled "cultural baggage." The devil came first class – up front with the weapons, tools, Bibles, and religious predilections of the ragtag and diverse recruits from Tudor and Stuart England, from Wales, and from the German Palatinate and Black Forest, and Swiss Alps.

In this New World, all things organic, whether animal or plant, grew bigger and became more wholesome than in the stale and tired air of Europe; and all things inanimate such as mountains and mountain storms were naturally grander and bolder as well. Or so the more scientific of our Founding Fathers argued! Transplants moreover grew much bigger, grander, and bolder, though not necessarily more wholesome. In other words, the devil flourished here. What Hawthorne described as "the dark-visaged stranger" whose "eyes glowed with a redder light than that of the bonfire" preyed ravenously upon the hills and townships of New England. In a land where people were said pray a lot and do good deeds, his best friends (i.e., his clients) included church deacons, small town politicians, and a majority of the Great and General Court.

With a vigor that would put the best of election eve, baby-kissing politicians to shame, he was everywhere from Boston Bay to Burlington on Lake Champlain. The New England coastal plain along Long Island Sound was conceded to be the "Devil's Belt." He was busy as a fiddler's elbow, he and his fan club of witches. Shaking hands and making contracts, entering names and phone numbers in his black book, he carefully wrapped up souls in cloth and placed them in boxes he found discarded in back of shoe and boot factories. Little oblong boxes for souls rather than soles! He thrived in the Puritan state, and like a drive-in-movie monster took power from that which tried to destroy him. Indeed, the Puritan theocracy symbiotically thrived on him. The Puritans, being a dull enough crew to begin with, really had no excitement in life, no evil to expunge, no witches to burn, no hellfire and brimstone to cringe before without old "Mr. Scratch" as he came to be known locally.

Perhaps puffed-up with all this success and recognition, perhaps having become too contented when the Puritan ethic disintegrated, he left himself open to one mistake. He had been and would be involved with politicians too numerous to mention; politics was in fact his most fertile stalking ground. But high up in the ancient hills that gave shape to the state borders of Massachusetts, Vermont, and New Hampshire he met his match. Daniel Webster, who should have been out working on the Missouri Compromise, used the tricks of the lawyer's trade to sweet talk, beguile, and confound "Old Scratch." In fact, as recounted by Stephen Vincent Benet and later documented on film and on stage, it can be seen that any self-respecting betting parlor would pick the devil as the underdog. For this dramatic confrontation, the soft-spoken "Scratch" appeared devilishly debonair: his grave and decent attire included polished boots, sparkling white teeth, and natty black mourning coat. Webster, by contrast, was true to his legend: a "steam engine in trousers" fortified by mighty swigs of home-distilled whiskey. It was no contest. Webster's oratorical thunder prevailed and, more embarrassed than hurt, the grotesque and cloven-foot figure in high crowned hat was sent reeling by a powerful kick to the butt through the hideous and gloomy woods of western New England. With his collection box under his arm and trailing a blue mist of evil, the "Lord of Evil," like many a New England outcast, followed the terrain toward regions more religiously tolerant.

The Route of Evil

Look at a map of the eastern United States that shows landforms such as mountains and valleys, and you will quickly see it. Gaze for a moment and see the mountains rise as if in a 3-D popup book. Technically, they're called the Reading and Manhattan spurs of the New England upland. But, if geology truly is a fountain of metaphor as John McPhee said, then these spurs might better be thought of as a two-pronged pitchfork, its handle in the mountains of western New England (Berkshires and Taconics), its shorter prong having a terminus on the lower part of Manhattan Island, and its longer prong (the Reading spur) pointed towards, and indeed poked into, the rolling flesh of good farmland in southeastern Pennsylvania. This longer prong juts diagonally across the Hudson Valley and then northern New Jersey (the Ramapo Mountains and Musconetcong Hills) and consists of venerable hard rocks, the very bones of the earth. These crystalline granites and gneisses are of a billion or more years in age ... so far back in the shrouded mists of deep time that geologists once referred to the period of their creation as "Cryptozoic," i.e., hidden or buried so profoundly that the record of their birth may never be fully known. "Basement" rock of pink, gray, and green; banded, streaked, and speckled. Rock older and harder than the devil.

These primordial hills in the Reading Prong are shot through and through with veins of metallic ore: copper, silver, and gold are there ... but pipedreams have burst and daydreams have faded because none of it ever proved concentrated enough to be commercially valuable. The real Eldorado was found in short parallel veins of ore that surfaced on ridge sides, discoloring the granitic host rock. This was iron, "magnetic iron ore of tolerable purity." For a while, this range of hills that stretched from western Connecticut to Copake and Dover on the New York State line, and southwest to Ringwood in the New Jersey Ramapo Mountains and then west to the Delaware River was the center of the nation's iron industry. Long before the devil came this way, this hilly spur was studded with blast furnaces, limekilns, charcoal pits, and forges and foundries. By the early 1800s most of it was already derelict, the structures

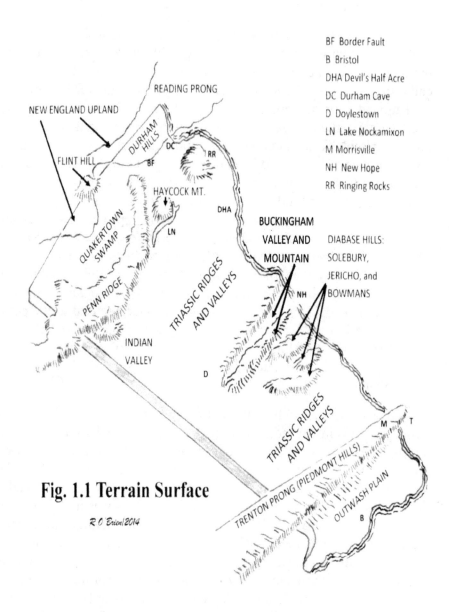

BF Border Fault
B Bristol
DHA Devil's Half Acre
DC Durham Cave
D Doylestown
LN Lake Nockamixon
M Morrisville
NH New Hope
RR Ringing Rocks

READING PRONG

NEW ENGLAND UPLAND

DURHAM HILLS

FLINT HILL

DC

RR

BF

HAYCOCK MT.

DHA

BUCKINGHAM
VALLEY AND
MOUNTAIN

DIABASE HILLS:
SOLEBURY,
JERICHO, and
BOWMANS

QUAKERTOWN
SWAMP

LN

TRIASSIC RIDGES
AND VALLEYS

NH

PENN RIDGE

INDIAN
VALLEY

D

TRIASSIC RIDGES
AND VALLEYS

M   T

TRENTON PRONG (PIEDMONT HILLS)

OUTWASH PLAIN

B

Fig. 1.1 Terrain Surface

R O'Brien/2014

abandoned and the workers gone. The hills and forests had become a boom and bust backwater where the sands of time got stuck in the neck of the hourglass.

One thing further about this long hilly spur: its lower (or southern) side is a geologic divide, a scar where the rocks are visibly sheared. Nearby rocks indicate movement through their slick and shiny and polished surfaces. Here, the hard metamorphosed rocks of the spur lie uneasily against a region of softer sedimentary rocks, loose sediment, and red mud. This meeting ground is a fault – not the awesome, headline-grabbing California magnitude fault, but a real straight-line fault nonetheless. It's been given names: the Ramapo Fault in New York and New Jersey, and the Triassic (or Monroe) Border Fault in Bucks County. This fault was actually given "National Natural Landmark" status in 1980 because it gives a "better understanding of man's environment." Unfortunately, it's inaccessible to the public and sits on private land and thus has no souvenir shops with t-shirts that say *"Greetings from the fault."* The fault is not to be taken too lightly though. It lives. Again, not with the earth-wrenching, highway re-aligning, and dam-bursting strength of a San Andreas Fault; but from time to time it is nasty enough to spill the pills from medicine cabinet bottles, to slop tea from dainty cups and trembling hands and onto the laps of little old ladies, to cause the recorder needle to palpitate on the seismograph at Princeton. Not quite an earthquake, but rather an earthshake, a dirtquake. With a sound like that of a sonic boom, it's just the earth settling in, the red rock being forced westward, infinitesimally but relentlessly. When the devil's venom drips into Fire God's face, this causes both him and the earth to shudder and tremble. When this happens, as it occasionally does, it at least makes the local news.[10]

"Old Scratch" followed this long mountain and fault system southwest from New England and into Pennsylvania. Banished and bruised by the boot of the great Daniel Webster, the devil skedaddled along the longer spur of the pitchfork, traveling the mountain trails by night and squeezing and squirming his way down along the fault line fissures and cracks by day. He thought the subterranean blackness and

---

[10] For a more detailed description of the Monroe Border Fault, See: Kathryn Finegan Clark "National Treasure in Durham," *Bucks County Herald*, July 30, 2015.

warmth actually quite refreshing and quite Freudian in that the dark and inward heat of the earth was like the mother womb for the lusty spirit of earth and fertility.

Considering the possibility of a new life along the Hudson, the demon found the valley already overstaffed with the ghastly gallery of apparitions conceived of in the mind of Washington Irving: storm gods, headless horsemen, ghosts of Dutch sailors, little people, and other un-canny critters. No room here for ordinary devils! Hudson Valley folk-lore does relate that he sojourned one night in a hill town; he was the stranger who won every penny in a card game, leaving behind only "the unspoken question as to his identity" – the dirty mark of a cloven hoof beneath the card table. He had pocket money to continue his journey.

Further along, New Jersey too offered no repose. Even at this early date, it had developed a rather unfair reputation for blandness, the vacuousness of an "empty barrel," and terminal insipidness … a repu-tation that would in much later times be immortalized in one-liners by stand-up comics and on TV sit-coms. Moreover, the territory had al-ready been staked claim to by a native-born son, the Jersey Devil (a.k.a. "the Hookman"). The cursed thirteenth child of a South Jersey woman, he had roamed the pine swamps since the early 1700's, causing com-motion and panic among the populace.

So, "Old Scratch" followed the fault still further, forced still deeper into the narrow eternal silence of some still deeper, long dormant fault beneath a fault as he crossed far beneath the rushing waters of the Delaware River. Cool white water was up above a zillion grains of com-pacted sand that hadn't sparkled on sunlit beaches in a million, million years. Through that earth darkness and dankness he scurried, with light far ahead. Leaving the fault crease to follow that distant, shimmering pool of light, he might have noticed, had he recalled anything from his high school geology, that the rock shroud was now paler and smoother: limestone! Thoroughly wet and chilled, his stash bag of crafts and as-saults soaked but salvageable, he became invigorated by the prospect of what lay beyond that pool of light. Poking his horns and head above the shallow pool of crystal water, he found himself in the deepest and most secret inner room of a three-chambered cave. The wet and slippery floor was strewn with the bones of dozens of different animals including catamounts and black bears, or maybe even mastodons; the skins of mummified rattlesnakes were preserved in this natural cold storage locker. The piercing, high pitched call of an army of little brown bats echoed off the rough walls and the thirty-foot high ceilings. Fittingly, this species was named for Lucifer (Myotis Lucifugus) and in a folk society was equated with the darkness of night and its foreboding possibilities. As his hot breath condensed to vapor in front of his hoary face, he strode through the chill air towards the entranceway. As he emerged from beneath a ledge of limestone not a hundred yards from the river, only an atmosphere of nothingness remained in the great cave. The devil incarnate, evil and earthy, thin and ugly, had arrived in Bucks County. And from that day forward this large and gloomy rockhouse in the Durham Hills would forevermore be known by the sobriquet "The Devil's Hole."

Hundreds of American Indian villages and campsites once dotted the creeksides and river shores in Bucks County. Had he arrived about a century earlier, the devil might have spied an American Indian encampment along the river's edge and not far from the cave. Here, people dried their nets and cooked fish, others dressed wild game and passed the hours fashioning jasper into arrowheads. The bone-strewn floor of the cave attested to the centuries-long presence of hunters who sheltered here and had, in fact, named a large "room" in the rear of the cave "Queen Ester's Drawing Room" to honor the notorious part Iroquois, British ally in the Revolutionary War.[11]

The devil well might have pitied these American Indians. Though treated kindly by some, they were dismissed by others as "the rude and untutored sons of the forest"[12]... poor devils who would soon succumb to smallpox and measles. Their disappearance would be left to the guilt of future generations to ponder. The devil could very much relate to their presence, especially the way they filled the world with spiritual energy – spirits both good and bad populated the cave and its environs.

---

[11] "Queen" Ester Montour was known as the "Butcher of Wyoming and was rumored to have put to death American civilian prisoners captured at Wyoming, Pennsylvania in 1778. Details of her life seem lost in legend and myth, but she's believed to have been killed by an American army at the battle of Newtown (Elmira, N.Y.) in 1779. (schuylerhistory.org,2013)
[12] William J. Buck, *History of Bucks County*,1855, p. 27.

In autumn, the county witnessed a grand American Indian jubilee when departed ancestors returned from the "spirit-land":[13]

> … The spirits came trooping over hill and dale in battalions of thousands … they again saw the grand old forest … (and after a while) they departed again into the misty great unknown.

Had he arrived just a half century earlier, he would have found that the cave had become a mine. The night skies above were lit with the fiery red glow of an iron furnace while brawny-armed artisans with faces beaded with sweat cast stovepipes and kettles. The surrounding hills were enveloped in smoke from charcoal burnings and the nearby forest was ravaged and pitted with mine shafts, and the landscape splattered with cinders, ash, and slag. That, he might actually have liked.

By the end of the nineteenth century the cave was all but destroyed by the spoliations of man. Although the cave had become something of a tourist attraction, the tourists saw only what remained after the quarrymen had had their way with sticks of dynamite. As in the Adirondacks and along the Hudson's palisaded shore, tourists could but shed tears for the scenes they'd been cheated of, conjuring up images of the grandeurs that had been. In the Durham Hills, the outer chambers of a once picturesque wonder had been reduced to rubble to lime the farm fields of the valley. Even the stalactites in the inner chamber were gone, replaced with dynamite drill marks.

Still they came to see and pose for the camera in front of the gaping hole in the ground. The devil himself did in fact return to the Durham Cave one Thursday morning in the spring of 1886; he was photographed with over 170 members and friends of the American Institute of Mining Engineers. His Lordship scrunched down in front for the group portrait, a portrait for posterity of very serious expressions on the faces of very serious people decked out in Victorian blacks and grays. The cave opening looks much the same today, but as the pale and ghostly faces in the

---

[13] *Bucks County Traveler*, November 1955.

photograph (*See below:* Fig. 1-2) remind us, the people are long dead. The devil, however … well, that's another matter.

Fig. 1-2. Durham Cave or "Devil's Hole," May 20th, 1886. Members of the American Institute of Mining Engineers pose with the devil (front row, circle). Papers of the Bucks County Historical Society, Vol. VI, 1932, p. 153.

  Today, if the devil were again to slither along that black earth fissure at the rear of the cave, he would find that "Chris was here," that "Tim Loves Lisa," and that "Chevy Trucks are #1" –or so the wall graffiti of latter day cave people would tell him. But when left to itself, the cave's ancient and timeless qualities still prevail. Inside, there is a profound and complete stillness; it's like the land lying still after the first snowfall. An unearthly silent world, a world deep in white. Not even the Om-like hum is heard. It's rather the sound of no sound inside a coffin six feet down. Maybe. But here, even the illusion of noiselessness is broken by the swish of traffic on the state highway, no great distance away.

If the devil strode across the cave's dim interior today, his smart black boots would be scuffed and scored by a carpet of litter. No mammalian bones now, but aluminum cans crushed by macho fists, bottle tops and pop-top rings, pieces of faded labels from any number of old Pennsylvania breweries, and a jagged and splintered rug of green and amber glass shards that would give pause to a Hindu nail-walker. Charred bits of wood float on this vitreous sea while fractured slabs of fallen limestone (used to smash the bottles) protrude above the carnage. The detritus of modern times. The cold vacuum of the great chamber echoes with the coo of pigeons and the high-pitched squeak of bats that inhabit the little alcoves in the damp, green discolored walls. As pigeon feathers and bat droppings accumulate on the glassy bed below, the fall of water droplets announces the birth of baby stalactites, slowly growing to replace those hammered away in the past. Climbing out of this violated and vandalized vault, the devil would today stumble onto the asphalt parking lot of a posh, country inn. If he had to use the bathroom, he'd first have to order either clams casino or stuffed mushrooms ... or be denied the use of the facilities. His rather dignified funereal attire would present no problem as to a dress code, once the dirt and dust of the cave were brushed away.

But all this lay in the future. When he arrived in the 1820s, when this fearful and yet pathetic form issued from the earth cave, there were few around to notice or to care, to scream or to snicker. The iron mining was gone with hardly any trace left behind. The stony hills were sprinkled lightly with a motley collection of log houses, general stores, and taverns. (Approximately one tavern for every eleven dwellings!). Fields were scratch farmed and cultivated to near the hilltops. People worked hard, died, or moved on ... and the fields reverted to oak woods. Charcoal-hungry miners would again return to rake the land over, but for now the "boldly carved hills (with) verdant slopes"[14] settled into a slow-paced existence not unlike dozens of other eastern "backwaters." A local historian did believe (correctly) that this secluded and deeply foliaged land might one day "engage the artist's pencil."[15] ....as seen for example in this book's cover illustration.

---

[14] J.H. Battle, ed. *History of Bucks County, Pennsylvania*, 1887, p.51.
[15] ibid.

The devil's arrival in the county went largely unheralded in this milieu. The few who did learn firsthand of his arrival beat a quick path to the new frontiers of Ohio and beyond; some did write back telling relatives and neighbors what one day had dragged its brimstone-smelling form out of the Durham Cave.

But, as always, he was on the move again. To ply his nefarious crafts, the devil looked to the more populous and pastoral region south of the Durham Hills, and across the Border Fault. As luck would have it, these great undulating farmlands of Indian red sandstone and shale had attracted pioneers of German and Scotch-Irish stock; they were people imbued with the teachings of Luther and Calvin ... and in bad, bad need of a folk devil. His wickedness burst upon the rolling and tumbled countryside like a demonic fire ball. The ridges and valleys of Bucks would be his exclusive domain. William Penn had said that "the country life is to be preferred: For there we see the works of God."[16] The devil begged to differ.

---

[16] As quoted by Jack Rosen in *The Face of Bucks*, 1981.

Fig. 1-3. The Durham Cave Today. Same view as 1886 photograph. Section of U.S.G.S. topographic map below.

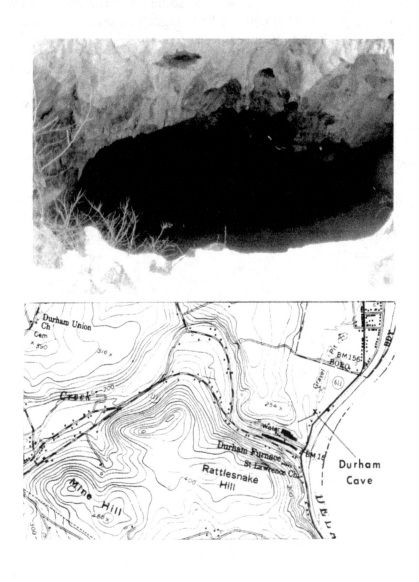

Down to the Bedrock

The dictionary says that to undulate is to have a wavelike, sinuous motion or form; to rise and fall in waves like a rippled potato chip or corrugated cardboard. The heartbeat creates a pattern of undulating blips across the cardiograph paper. Central Bucks County undulates in a sensuous way; its terrain surface and map contours are an exercise in hidden erotic art. The county's surface undulates according to the old historians and geologists who wrote their reports in the 1870s-80s. Venerable old gentlemen they, with gray beards and wrinkled brows, with stern expressions and vacant eyes, they have left the ghosts of themselves in the brittle, yellowed pages of their published works. Still dressed in Lincolnesque suits and high stiff collars, they lie buried now, their bodies turned to dust, they lie buried now in the silent, undulating earth they wrote about.

The great Triassic redbeds. Undulating Triassic ridges and lowlands. That's it! That's where the devil found his new home. Wedged against the firmer crystalline rocks of the Durham Hills and its limestone cave is a region of weaker and younger rocks that forms a series of disconnected basins from Nova Scotia and New England down through Bucks County, west to Gettysburg and down into Virginia and the Carolinas. Bucks is part of one such elongated basin that extends from the Tappan Zee on the Hudson River to northern Virginia. This basin, this ancient lake bed, is underlain with westward-dipping strata of weathered sandstone and soft red shale. These rock beds are thousands of feet thick and conceal beneath them even older limestone strata. Still further down, folded and faulted Paleozoic and Precambrian rocks lie buried. The visual effect is that of a rolling, open countryside with low horizons (shale) and subdued ridges (sandstone). The land is a lesson in curves; it undulates and it is Triassic.

The Triassic period of earth history began one morning about 250 million years ago and lasted perhaps 50 million years, give or take a few ice ages. It both began and ended with violent extinctions of many life forms. It was a time of transition when new forms of life (dinosaurs) would come to dominate the world. Very appropriately, the term "Triassic" originated in Germany, where so many of Bucks County's settlers came from. "Triassic" was coined in 1834 by Friedrich von Alberti, a minor official in the salt mine industry who first described a three-part rock sequence in central Germany. It was soon applied to rock strata of a similar age both in the western and eastern United States. The eastern Triassic strata were designated the Newark Supergroup in 1856 from their discovery and study near Newark, New Jersey. Strangely, when the Bucks County Soil Survey was conducted in 1936 it gave no recognition to "Triassic," describing everything between the upper end of the county and the coastal plain only as "the undulating to rolling Piedmont Plateau."[17] Strange, because eighty-five percent of the county's surface and bedrock is Triassic sandstone, mudstone, and shale that sits in downwarped basins and troughs.[18]

In the half light of morning when shadows begin to take shape, with only a hint of the yet unseen sun tinting the land pale pink, a stride before dawn when the air is still and scented with conifer on the western breeze, it's not too difficult to imagine the primordial earth in all its Triassic attire: a long lake-filled rift valley filling in with sediment carried by torrential streams spilling off the higher borderlands; the future African continent lying on the eastern horizon, beginning to break away, in the process fracturing and faulting the rocks in the Triassic Basin; the sediments pouring in and accumulating for millions of years. And in the muck and wash of a shallow Triassic sea that would in millennia be compressed into beds of sandstone and shale, small kangaroo-like dinosaurs hurried about in search of food and water, leaving their three-toed footprints in the red Triassic mud. These same dinosaurs left their fossilized bones in the Triassic redbeds of Germany and New Jersey; all they ever left in Bucks were traces in the mud. Marine reptiles splashed about the ferns and scouring rushes, and winged dragon-like dinosaurs soared through the skies. Horsetail ferns died and their fine filaments were cemented into a muddy red matrix of shale. Their slender, striated

---

[17] R.T.A. Burke et.al. *Soil Survey, Bucks County, Pa.*, Series 1936.
[18] Specifically, the Stockton, Lockatong, and Brunswick formations of the Newark Basin.

fossils are no wider than a pencil or a blade of grass. These delicate remnants from the Triassic age are found randomly scattered about the rocks today. Algae grew and died, died and disintegrated, and were also pressed into the ripple-marked mud. Generations of fresh-water fish lived and died, their scales and bony skeletons fossilized in the ground-mass along with the dinosaur tracks, the excrement, the teeth of carnivores, and the imprints of Triassic raindrops that pelted the mudflats that later dried, hardened, and cracked beneath a late Triassic sun. All this happened again and again as warm shallow waters alternately invaded the lowland, and then retreated.

It was the beginning of the age of both mammals and dinosaurs, a time when much of the earth was red, Martian-like in color, a time of iron oxides and redbeds. A red period of earth history suggestive of Coleridge's eerie opium-induced seascape in the *Rime of the Ancient Mariner* – lightning flashes illuminating a copper sky, a bloody sun above a silent sea, a slimy sea in which a thousand slimy things lived, a sea of water like witch's oil, a still and awful red. Such was the deep history of the gently undulating land the devil came to from out of the Durham Cave. And he loved the very thought of it.

The great red lowland held yet another fortuitous advantage for the supreme tempter. Like any good nineteenth-century tourist, he was under the spell of the then current Romantic doctrine that prescribed the viewing of great scenery – and truly great scenery Bucks was –from nicely-positioned elevations. Topographic eminences were the platforms from which local picnic parties, urban day trippers, and European aristocrats doing the "Grand Tour" could revel in the divine, God-inspired and God-inspiring tableau of the natural world. It was a mind-altering, religious revelation for some … while for the luckier, it was a shuddering, orgasmic, dizzying vision. Access to such a mountain prominence and its view were prerequisites for the cultured nineteenth-century traveler.

The devil was no stranger to the value of such places, a value which to him had nothing to do with the appreciation of heaven-reflected beauty. After all, this subordinate adversary of God had lured

Christ to the "Mount of Temptation" (Quarantania) on the road from Jerusalem to Jericho to entice him with all the kingdoms of the world at his feet. But here, amid the "ordinary tame-ness" of the Triassic lowlands, the devil again sought out and found a number of small mountains (mountainettes perhaps) from which to observe the movements of his quarry on the game board below. Perched atop these hills, he could plot his next mischievous attack, give pinpoint direction to the bubbling, diabolic lava that oozed from his fountain of wicked arts. And that's far more than a mere figure of speech, for in the same Triassic time when the redbeds were created, long upthrusted pipes of scalding lava poked their way to the surface, intruding up and into the soft rock layers and discharging into veins and sheets of dense, dark diabase rock. Lava might thus be defined as the "hot sperm of Hell" or as "demon semen." And diabase, diabase has the same Greek root as "diabolic."

Eons of time would go by, eons that even Carl Sagan would have found difficult to express in a meaningful way; eventually the surface redbeds would be planed away by erosive winds and rains, leaving exposed the little diabase hills with flat summits that today protrude upon the lowland. Here, atop the devil's own lava, the spirit of evil posted his own outlooks, atop Jericho, Solebury, Bowman, and Haycock Mountains. In time, these elevations would become the reputed haunts of runaway slaves, the hideout of outlaw bands, and the site of hermits' caves. None of this was at odds with Satan's plans.

River Roosts

So, where on this extensive lowland with its ridges and volcanic hills would the creator of darkness and chaos hang his hat, lay his ugly body down, and call home? Though be made frequent appearances on farms and in villages throughout the county, he adopted as his hearth, the fiery physical core of his world, the place called the "Devil's Half-Acre." First inhabited by Native Americans, the place is found in a hilly, almost New England-like area of Bucks called Solebury (originally, and most prophetically, called "Soul bury").

The devil chose to reside here for the following two reasons: When the Pennsylvania Canal was being built in the 1820s-30s as part of the national canal building frenzy, the old stone building that stands on this canal-side half-acre sold whiskey without a license, thus becoming the scene of much drunken revelry. Plodding mules drew their coal barges down from the upstate anthracite fields to tidewater. Foul-mouthed idioms and the smell of week-old bar rags fouled the air as immigrant laborers (paid a buck a day, part cash and part whiskey) and their wenches attempted to "raise the devil" each night. It was only natural that the devil, being at the root of all secret and uneasy pleasures, should be drawn to such a convivial place, obligingly giving the carousers their "fill of the devil." After the canal workers and their working girls drifted on to other canals on other frontiers, the devil stayed on. The site is reputed to be haunted to this day by nocturnal auras, ribald laughter, and the phonetics of fornication and fighting; devil-snatched souls are condemned to replay their sins of the flesh and of the bottle for an eternity. Some punishment!

Fig.1.4. Devil's Half-Acre Today. The Half-Acre, the old Tavern House, the Pennsylvania Canal, and the Delaware River's shore all converge here ... below the cliffs.

The devil furthermore chose this site for its seclusion and beauty. For the devil was of the earth, a creature of wild and impetuous nature, the kind that was swooned over by the period's Romantic travelers and transcendental thinkers. In his own way, he was an aesthete who was capable of cultivating an appreciation of the sublime scenery said to typify this part of the county and the valley. It was, after all, places with a dark and tempestuous nature that had the power to overwhelm the senses with cold terror that made the land sublime, at least according to the aesthetic theory of the day. This riverside half-acre had it all: sunless ravines cut into soft red sandstone, somber and fast-moving green-gray waters flowing below looming, tilting crags that hover ominously above the scene, above a half-acre of ground littered with fallen timbers. The sheer 400-foot cliff is made of dark chocolate-red rock strata like great slabs of a many-layered devil's food cake; it throws a shadow over the canal, a lengthening shadow that brings a premature twilight to the half-acre.

While he spent much of his free time at the half-acre by the river, for times of silent contemplation and repose he perched upon the brow of one of the nearby diabase hills, surveying the scene for opportunities to work his corruption. But his favorite "window atop the world" was the "Devil's Tea Table," a 400-foot stack of red rock that the U. S. Geological Survey kindly allows to retain its demonic toponym. This steep and quite dangerous cliff descends sharply to the river's edge from the New Jersey shore and affords a spectacular, unobstructed panorama of the valley and the precipitous bluffs above the gravelly Bucks shore that nineteenth century travelers called the "Pennsylvania Palisades." These palisades are actually the same Triassic redbeds that underlay much of Bucks, but they've been made harder and denser through partial meta-morphosis, and are therefore more resistant to erosion. Befitting the sublime connotations inherent in this part of the valley, there is a sense of deep mystery in the uncertain geologic events that gave shape to this titanic rock wall, and Victorian period travelers relished the cryptic pos-sibilities: powerful and ancient earth forces renting asunder the fabric of the land, perhaps.

Such upheavals of nature were of course beyond the puny facili-ties of mankind to grasp, so the best one could do was abandon logic to the rapturous siren call of sublimity. While for some, these deep earth forces called to mind the handiwork of God the Creator, for most – and most correctly so – the made-to-order sense of ruin seen in the down-faulted valley below the "tea table" and the shadowy reflection of the brooding heights cast upon the turbulent waters that churned about the flanks of island remnants, was associated with Satanical powers. The devil was pleased. His black form, in the form of a raven, would be seen soaring over the rolling lowlands and cliffs of Bucks, coming to rest atop the "tea table,"[19] that hoodoo rock where his lordship would sometimes be overcome by a sense of melancholy and loneliness – a fallen angel adrift in cosmic space with the world far below, the silent, detached world of the balloonist with the faint bark of dogs the only connection to the land. A poor devil adrift in cosmic time, chased and chastened around the world till he came here. This land of red rocks and yeoman farmers, the infamous half-acre and the "tea table," were his, for a while.

Thus it would be here among the dark red soils and red rocks of the Triassic lowland, and here among the darker diabase hills, that the travel-weary prince of apostate angels would call home. His shadow would attend the moan of the wind as it swept above the orchards and wheat fields, the bone orchards and the village churches and meeting-houses. His hunched and hurried form would be seen flitting across fields as neat as a Napoleonic battleground, a trim patchwork of greens, browns, and yellows interrupted only by copses of trees. A countryside as precise and measured as a gameboard. A toy-like terrain with the meticulous, sharp-edged precision of a Grant Wood painting, a land-scape with heaving furlongs of wave-swelled earth combed and fur-rowed by generations of farmers. A Lionel train board with thoughtfully placed lichen shrubs and store-bought miniature trees, Plasticville houses and barns, lovingly positioned on a grainy paperboard mat. This was Bucks at its best.

He shook off his boots and called this "kindly and productive land" his, with all its "richness of soil, sweetness of situation and wholesomeness

---

[19] Devilish place names like "tea table" and "half-acre" were quite common on American maps in the 1700s-1800s. The broiling waters of Hell Gate in New York's East River were called the "Devil's Frying Pan" or the "Devil's Gridiron" by sailors attempting to navigate the area. As a toponomic designation, "Devil's Half-Acre" is found all across the U.S., including a slave jail in Richmond, Va., a campground in Oregon, and a bar in Glendale, Arizona. The term was frequently used in slang to refer to a city's slum district. It was used interchangeably with Hell's Kitchen, Poverty Row, the Gas House District, and "Down by the Vinegar Woiks." Alternately, "Hell's Half-Acre."

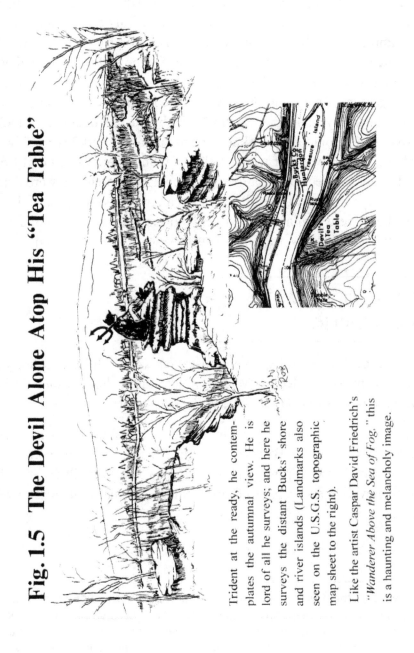

Fig. 1.5 The Devil Alone Atop His "Tea Table"

Trident at the ready, he contemplates the autumnal view. He is lord of all he surveys; and here he surveys the distant Bucks' shore and river islands (Landmarks also seen on the U.S.G.S. topographic map sheet to the right).

Like the artist Caspar David Friedrich's *Wanderer Above the Sea of Fog*," this is a haunting and melancholy image.

of air." As with the origin of the fossilized dinosaur tracks embedded in their layered stone crypts far below, fossils which were then considered "artifacts of the devil," the trace marks of his cloven hooves became imprinted in the richly-tinted soil. The iron-tipped plows would eradicate the marks during spring planting as the soil was churned and crumbled to a chocolate-rich, cocoa-like powder. But the plowmen knew, knew by the darting shadow on the edge of the woods and at the corner of their eye, and knew instinctively by the feel of someone looking over their shoulder. They knew the nature of the dark visage silhouetted against the white of winter fields. Upon his arrival, an evil frost killed countless vegetable gardens, and dozens of orchards were damaged throughout the county. Shortly thereafter, barns collapsed and carriage sheds were torn apart by violent storms. A farmer was attacked by his bull. They knew then that their folk devil was in the land.[20]

A Closer Look: Which is it? Is it or isn't it?

Speaking of diabase hills, river roosts, palisaded cliffs, and hoodoo rocks, the historian George MacReynolds raised this question in his 1942 *Place Names in Bucks County, Pennsylvania:*

It (Haycock Mountain at 960 feet in elevation) has always been assumed to be the highest hill in Bucks County, but this is not strictly correct … northwest of Passer, Springfield Township, is another hill (Flint Hill) with an elevation according to Geological Survey maps, of close to 980 feet …

---

[20] There were other places in Bucks County that were also named for the devil. For example, the ten-foot deep seven acre diabase boulder field (Ringing Rocks Park) in Bridgeton Township was sometimes called the "devil's potato patch." This is an unusual site that some claim has mystical or supernatural properties. Parenthetically, the much larger Triassic diabase boulder field on the Gettysburg battlefield is called the "Devil's Den."

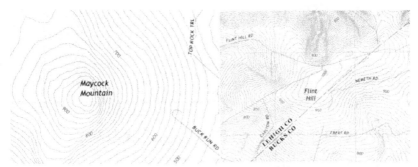

U.S.G.S. Topographic Map Sheet details (1:24,000 series) 2013. (Left) Haycock Mountain, Bedminster Sheet (incorrectly identified as "Maycock" Mountain); (Right) Flint Hill on the Hellertown Sheet.

Flint Hill is located on the border between Springfield Township, Bucks County and Lehigh County. It rises to 1,000 feet just across the Lehigh County line, but it achieves an elevation of between 970-980 feet on its lower slopes in Bucks. The hill is not as visually distinct as Haycock; nor is it as easily accessible (surrounded by houses and farms, it is topped by an FAA radio tower).

Haycock Mountain (in a township with the same name) overlooks the waters of man-made Lake Nockamixon. Its long, low distinctive profile is said to resemble the conical heaps of hay raked up by the old farmers. It rises to 960-plus feet and is visible across much of the central and upper county. A U.S.G.S. copper benchmark is attached to a diabase boulder at the top, but the way up is extremely rugged (pathless slopes with rocks and fallen trees). The mountain is designated State "Game-lands." Once (1740s) a small community of Irish Catholics settled at the mountain's eastern base (St. John's Church).

Thus, while Flint Hill is technically the highest point of land in the county, Haycock Mountain is the highest and most prominent peak entirely within the county.

CHAPTER 2

FROM OUT OF THE CAVE:
THE WORM THAT EATS THE GARDEN

The Devil in folklore is entitled to our un-grudging admiration for his indefatigable energy ... He has had his finger in the pie everywhere and appears to be all but omnipresent and omniscient ... without him there would be no plot, and the story of the world would lose its interest.

– Paul Carus, *The History of the Devil and the Idea of Evil, 1900*

Indeed, it was hard to believe in the Devil's existence ... Yet the Devil was real enough, he knew, somewhere far away – or maybe not so far away. He thought of ... the shadow of movement that might or might not have been a deer.

– John Gardner, *Freddy's Book, 1980*

Without Disguise,
His Guise and Temperament

Satan can take any form or use a multitude of snares or blandishments to get his way. The great deceiver is especially adept in the makeup and wardrobe departments. "Protean" is probably the best way to describe him: a multiform, highly changeable, constantly varied appearance. In other words, a silly putty quality. But, assuming his unaffected "Old Scratch" form, the "old boy" of folklore, the one he relaxed in when lying on his brimstone bed, what was his guise? All pretense and camouflage aside, how did he appear in his day-to-day encounters with Bucks' country yeomen? And what does this tell us about the county and those who came to settle here?

Did he look like the poet's devil of old who stalked the earth when forests walked and the moon was blood, a creature with monstrous head and sickening cry, and ears like errant wings? Was he a club-footed devil with coat of red and britches of blue, with a hole where his tail came through? Was he the pug-nosed, overweight devil in monk's clothes often depicted in seventeenth-century wood carvings? Did he resemble the Underwood Deviled Ham devil, in a red union suit, with trident, pointy tail, and a smile and hello? A happy devil!

Did he retain more of the image of the horned and hoofed devil born with Paleolithic man more than 40,000 years ago? Was he like the Tarot card devil, a medieval image with leathery wings and horns, a powerful primordial figure drawn from the dawn of existence, squatting on a stone plinth lording over the creatures of the underworld enchained below by his dark forces? Was he like the hulking, ragged winged demon Pazuzu with talon feet, bulbous jutting penis, and mouth stretched taut in feral grin? Was he a hot-shot ladies' man like the "Silver-Tongued Devil" of song who slipped from the shadows, "hiding intentions of evil under the smile of a saint," to lie and lay his way into the hearts and beds of shy young maidens? Was there a family resemblance to his nearest kin, the Jersey Devil, an impish nattily-dressed lothario with swarthy complexion and a mischievous Jack Nicholson grin who lived and worked just across the river?

Rather than face the devil head-on, people in early Bucks County no doubt declined a chance for a really good look at him by simply burying their heads under the quilts at night when they knew he was on the prowl in the hideous wild wood. On other nights, he may have been unavoidably encountered on covered bridges. The concept of these bridges was brought from New England around the same time as the devil. And, while not by design, these "timber tunnels" did provide shelter on stormy nights for weary travelers too distant from the nearest "ordinaries," or coach houses. They must have spied him clomping across the planking, his footfalls and heavy breathing echoing from the trussed wooden walls and beamed roofs. Unnerved and unlettered, these night travelers either chose not to, or could not, commit what they had seen to writing. Pity the poor highwayman, springing from his hiding place among the rafters, pouncing down upon his intended victim to relieve him of a few coins, only to come face to face with the devil himself.

The county's alternately dusty and then slushy farm roads were crowded with itinerants of every sort in the 1800s. Walking to and fro along the red-rutted roads were vagabond loners, true and early exemplars of the mobile, dream-chasing foot-loose society that America had already become. Peddlers, tinkers, rag and bone collectors, outlaws, tramps, gypsies, and assorted others also populated the byways. The devil was partial to gypsies, for in their language his name meant "god." Every spring gypsy bands camped in the fields and caves around Buckingham Mountain, a two-and-one-half mile long ridge of fine-grained glassy white quartzite flanked by limestone beds – all of it older than the rocks of the surrounding lowland. Locally, this low ridge was called the "Great Mountain." It was a lonely and secluded place that sheltered fugitive slaves and elusive hermits in its caves and dense chestnut forest. At its base, the colorfully-decorated gypsy wagons congregated in the trees, bright shirts and sparkling jewelry giving color to the still drab wood. The gypsies lived in tents and slept on piles of rags and were alleged to steal chickens and even children. Here, when the world was

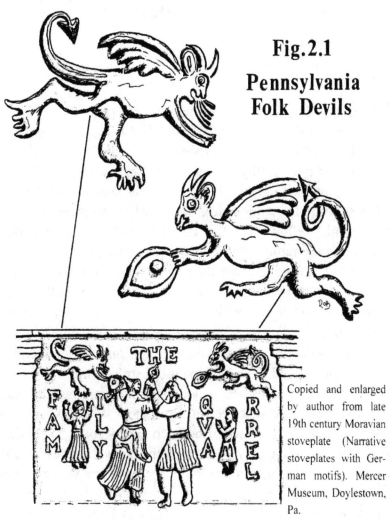

Fig.2.1
Pennsylvania Folk Devils

Copied and enlarged by author from late 19th century Moravian stoveplate (Narrative stoveplates with German motifs). Mercer Museum, Doylestown, Pa.

Glazed Clay Tile Showing Devils Fanning "Family Quarrel"

born again in early April, they gave birth to "hordes" of babies, usually born on terribly rainy nights when thunder rolled off the mountain's hardrock walls. The devil liked all this – the violins, tambourines, and red pleated dresses; he shared their campfires. Local gypsy lore has, however, left no written account of how he looked.

The Road

The roads that bend to avoid the sides of Buckingham Mountain, roads that serve to tie together the farms and hamlets of the lowland, were well traveled by the devil. These were, and still are, high-banked roads worn into the land by the daily grind of wagon wheels, horses' hooves, and plowmen's boots. These are roads along which the traveler must look skyward to see the field crops growing, to see the dense crowd of white, purple, yellow, and other colored weeds springing toward the firmament like the multi-colored blur of hats and jackets in a baseball stadium crowd springing from their seats after some great slugger's homerun. These are roads where the world is seen at eyeball level; level with seed pods and barbs, with weeds and barbed wire, with weeds wrapped around the old barbed wire. One who knew such roads could not help but feel deeply meshed with the land, sunk into the terra firma beneath the shoulder-high embankments, absorbed into nature and enveloped as part of it. This was a landscape in which the land was important, where one's perspective was from the inside of what one saw, and not from above. One who trod such earthy roads, one who had oozed up from out of the bowels of the earth, one who more than anyone else could claim a kinship with natural forces, and one who could therefore appreciate roads that had the reek of animal odors and a medley of animal sounds, was the devil himself. He was born of the feral earth and for roads such as these. And it is along one of these well-grooved roads, cut deep into the redbeds, that evidence of his appearance may be found.

The House

Along one such ribbon of country road that dips and climbs across the washboard surface of the red rocks and redder soil, a long but infrequently-traveled road that traverses the very heart of Bucks, stands a house cradled by the Triassic ridges. This house discloses all:

Its shape and history typify that of most farmhouses in this region, i.e. a generously proportioned rectangular box of fieldstone construction. It's a two-story house with a one-room deep floor plan; the upstairs bedrooms and the downstairs family room and parlor are all connected by a central staircase. It has interior gable end chimneys and massive fireplaces. It's a two-wing house as well, with a small side

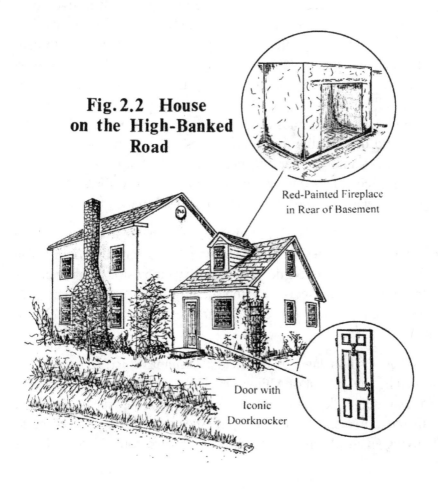

Fig. 2.2 House on the High-Banked Road

Red-Painted Fireplace in Rear of Basement

Door with Iconic Doorknocker

kitchen being the original dwelling. It was built in the 1740s to replace a log cabin that housed the settlers when they first arrived. Actually, this colonial kitchen wing is built atop a German-style log cabin, even incorporating some of the original logs. The larger two-story "main" house was built in 1814-15, a time when the food needs of a war-troubled Europe buoyed the price of wheat to an all-time high, thus bringing prosperity to rural Bucks and permitting local farmers to indulge their growing families with larger houses. Like many houses from this era, this one too has an almost perfect compass alignment. Its length runs north and south, and it faces east. The east face, which includes the bedroom windows, catches the rising sun as it pops above a Triassic ridgeline across the fields. Many are the farm people who lived here whose mornings began with a red and ready sun presenting its face through the dusty panes of the window glass and, like a nineteenth-century alarm clock, signaled them to a new day's labor. The rear or west wall faces the late afternoon sun, bathing the kitchen and work areas with pale yellow evening light. The north gable end is blank, blank and unyielding to the north winds of winter. Protectively and familiarly, the house is held beneath the limbs and leaves of towering, ancient trees. Two and three-hundred year old specimens of hickory and maple keep the dwelling cool in summer and, defoliated, allow for a relative – though only relative – degree of warmth beneath the winter sun.

The house is built with red-brown sandstone quarried and hauled from the banks of the nearby creek and from the surrounding fields. The foot-thick stone walls make deep and handy windowsills and havens for assorted animals and insects. An iron shell from the Revolutionary War lies forgotten, embedded in the wall near where a family of wrens keep house.

When fashion later dictated, this farmhouse had its stonework concealed beneath a coat of whitewash. The wash was a mix of crushed lime and animal milk reinforced with straw, cow dung, and the hairs of slaughtered animals; it would eventually become crumbly and begin to peel, giving an air of time-worn dignity to the structure. Nothing better characterizes the landscape of the Triassic lowland from New Jersey to Virginia than these old stone and plaster houses. Floodlit in the white moonlight, their blank gable walls reflect pallid and ghostly in a car's headlights. They stand as a silent testament to the craft and ingenuity of a folk society. This house, then, is simply an old Bucks County farmhouse and nothing more need be said about it, except …

In the low-ceilinged basement, inset into the rear wall of this otherwise rather typical farmhouse, is a great fireplace, a vast cavity of a fireplace painted red. A colony of spiders have hung their webs like mobiles, dangling them from the red oaken support beam that substitutes for a formal mantel. Why this gargantuan fireplace should be lodged within the rear of the house, rather than at the gable end, is part of a convoluted and complex history that only an architectural historian could understand. And why it is painted red – devil red (if such a color exists) or the red of a store-bought Halloween mask – is a question no longer answerable by any living person. Does one dare prod the house to reveal its secrets? Does one dare suggest or presume what any of this means? "The doorway of Satan?" "The entranceway to hell?" The only certainty is that at some point in the past someone saw fit to block the fireplace flue with rubble and seal off the fireplace room from contact with the rest of the house. The only living things in and around the hearth are the spiders and mice.

The Iconic Doorknocker

What tells us more about the devil himself is on the outside of the house. It's a very old brass doorknocker attached to the front door. It's a likeness of the devil cast in a long-vanished foundry and screwed to the door by hands long cold. Mutely, it stares out onto the high-banked road.[21] This Bucks devil is naked and shameless, a nakedness that makes us feel moral and good. He is nature personified. A caricature of an animal or parts and pieces of animals. But it has nothing of an animal's

---

[21] The same or very similar likenesses appear on candlesticks as well as doorknockers.

innocence. He appears to have an inherited similarity with devil icons seen on the facades of great cathedrals; turned to stone by an angel, these devils perch above townscape and countryside "with a sour and malicious countenance" as if to say that "all this is mine."[22] He, and this is how we know it's a he, sports oversize organs; the most noticeable is a large penis made of bone or horn. It's iron-hard and has long since come through his underwear (if he ever had any to begin with). His breasts are hairy and much overdeveloped, an indication that the devil – like the toad –has a hidden transsexual potential. He can be equally male or female as the situation dictates. Situations usually dictated a male presence. An exposed, rather chubby behind serves as the part of him that raps the strike plate on the knocker.

His head is rounded and perhaps a bit too big for the rest of his body. It is topped by curving horns and dominated by large, protruding eyes. His eyes, eyes that glowed red with the earth's first sunrise, bulge omnivorously and their swampy blackness is the repository of a million years of evil images. His nose is big, far too big. It's a W.C. Fields' nose. A lecherous tongue no doubt hides behind the toothy, sneering grin. This is the face Poe had in mind when he described a ludicrous "finicky little person" grinning from ear to ear. He is said to have been handsome when he was young, but his features are now wrinkled with age (the ages). His head is bald; like hell itself, no parting there! He has lost much of the visual awe which he possessed during the Middle Ages. An appetite for sacrifice and torture is gone. Only a trace of that legendary and menacing glint remains in his eyes; in general, times and miles beyond human reckoning appear to have taken a heavy toll. His is the face of a tired devil, tired and drawn like the faces of the 3 a.m. shoppers at the big box store. In fact, without the horns, he has the face of a rather weary senior citizen who, after a lifetime of toil, has earned the right to

---

[22] Foss-Dyke, "Lincoln Minster and the Devil," in *Folklore*, Vol. 9, #3 (September 1898), p.275. A variation on the Bucks' devil is the devil with one leg (the "Lincoln Imp"). This may be the devil of Lincolnshire legend, affixed to the shire's Gothic Cathedral when built. The cathedral was built atop land previously occupied by "a heathen godhouse."

doze the afternoon away on a park bench beneath a tree in some Sunbelt city park.

Temperamentally, he liked his privacy (as has been seen); he sought out secluded places to board and brood. He was described as a Puck-like trickster, generally good natured and good humored. In fact, this eternal mischief-maker was never blatantly hostile to man, except in that man was often more a friend to God than to him.

Fig. 2.3

The Iconic Doorknocker

Eyes That
Glowed Red
With the Earth's
First Sunrise

He exhibits none of the noble or tragically heroic qualities of Milton or Goethe's devils – Satan, the great dissenter; Mephistopheles, the sage and scholar. He is but a feeble shadow of these. He could be outwitted by simple rustics. It was humiliating. Like St. Dunstan of Glastonbury, they would tweak his nose with pincers. It hurt! His hat would blow away and his clothes would rip. He would slip in the mud. His fly would be open (this, perhaps intentionally). He had more bad days than good. In short, he seemed beset with all the frailties of mankind. He radiated a homey warmth, a warm empathy for fellow travelers in this earthly vale of tears. A divinity with foibles and debilities like those of fallible mortals. This American devil had been reduced to a comic figure, "as little dignified as the worm that eats the garden."[23]

Or so it seemed. But caution: this "King of Deception" was still a dangerous nuisance, his face still "the map of malice," his mouth the font of "black sermons of death." He was as deceptive as the January thaw. He was the "Siberian Express" taking a pit stop, recharging himself before blasting unsuspecting window shoppers eying summer beachwear. To all the world, this "Prince of the World" may have looked like a plain country cousin – until his combative instincts were aroused. Then, like the pro who toys with the amateur … like the cat that paws the mouse before the kill, his chaotic and tempestuous nature is revealed and he rises on his hind legs to remind everyone who he really is: a demonic and threatening natural force, as pure, destructive, and as ancient as time itself. He was a crude and lustful obscenity ("Lord Carnal Knowledge" in *Pilgrim's Progress*) who played heavily on sex in his relations with people. He was an unmitigated evil always and forever lurking in the shadows, constantly at the ready to do battle for the highest stakes of all, the immortal soul. That contest was about to be played out on the Triassic lowlands. Like a weevil, he would creep into the uncorrupted wheat. He was the original Pac-man, insatiably gobbling up souls on his play board, this rolling red earth.[24]

---

[23] Louis C. Jones, "The Devil in New York State," *New York Folklore Quarterly,* Vol. VIII, #1, Spring, 1952.

[24] The devil's appearance and how it's changed over time remains a popular topic. In the summer of 2014 the Cantor Arts Center at Stanford University in California held an exhibition *("Sympathy for the Devil: Satan, Sin and the Underworld")* that explored the visual history of the devil in artwork. Representations spanning over 500 years show his evolution from a bestial horned creature to the shrewd villain (the trickster, the wicked dandy) to the romantic hero and finally to the abstract force of the past century … much as the reader will soon see.

CHAPTER 3

LONG AGO
ON THE SETTLING GROUND:
DIABOLICAL PREOCCUPATIONS

Having a desire to go Beyond the Sea ...

–Ambrose Barcroft, 1722-23,
(Future settler of Solebury, Bucks County)

*Tis blooming as Eden, when Eden was blest, As
the sun lights its charms with the evening glow.*

– Bucks County described by Wm. H. Davis,
History of Bucks County, 1884

*... They looked around and the nicest gen-
tleman stood there but had one horse foot
and was digging in the ground ...*

–Aunt Sophie Bailer talking about devils
and witches in *The Pennsylvania Dutchman*,
(No date)

Who Were They?

Who were they? These God-fearing, devil-believing settlers who cleared off the Triassic red earth where "the soyle was good" and "the aire sareen" ... and who did their field chores, barnwork, and fence-mending from sunrise to sunset? Who were they?

Who were these people who shared in the devil's domain, anxiously subjecting themselves to the demon's varied ingenuities? They were a stout people who had conquered the land, but not their fear of all its darker places and hidden recesses. Terrible superstitions and a belief in an incarnate evil were old world folkways that, along with their Teutonic and Celtic traditions of Walpurgis Night[25] and Halloween, quickly took root and flowered in the undulating farmscape of Bucks.

This pluralistic polyglot Pennsylvania society of the eighteenth and nineteenth centuries was composed primarily of working class Protestants, refugees from religious repression, persecution and economic impoverishment. They all brought with them what the psychohistorian Erik Erikson called "Protestantism's diabolical preoccupation." This ethnic mosaic was largely in place when the devil arrived. His arrival provided the reality to match their expectations. From all available maps and histories, the folk occupation of this large 610-square mile block of the American landscape (an area one-half the size of Rhode Island) came about as shown in Fig.3.1.

The most numerous folk-religious group was described by English-speaking historians as "persons of Teutonic descent," i.e., hard-working, frugal farmers and craftsmen from Wurttemberg and Saxony, from Baden and the Alsace, from the Swiss Jura and the Alps, and from the Saarland and Rhineland. In Philadelphia, they were welcomed by William Penn; from "German Towne," they pushed up the Perkiomen and

---

[25] "Walpurgis" is the antipodal calendar date of Halloween (the evening of April 30th) when witches and devils reveled on the Brocken, the highest peak in the Hartz Mountain in Germany. It is (was) a night of wild and unrestrained goings-on ("People filled with a sort of madness . . . "). Ironically, the night of pagan debauchery is named after a pious missionary nun who founded holy houses.

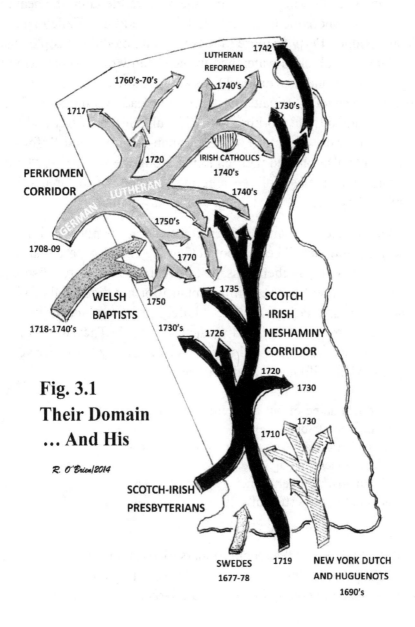

LUTHERAN
REFORMED
1742
1760's-70's
1740's
1730's
1717
1720
IRISH CATHOLICS
1740's
PERKIOMEN
CORRIDOR
GERMAN LUTHERAN
1740's
1750's
1708-09
1770
1750
1735
SCOTCH
WELSH
BAPTISTS
-IRISH
1718-1740's
1730's
1726
NESHAMINY
CORRIDOR
1720
1730

Fig. 3.1
Their Domain
... And His
1710
1730

R. O'Brien/2014

SCOTCH-IRISH
PRESBYTERIANS

SWEDES   1719   NEW YORK DUTCH
1677-78   AND HUGUENOTS
                 1690's

Unami Creeks in the 1730's in search of an agrarian Arcadia. With their good instincts for farming, they chose the most fertile land (the heavily timbered lands where the trees grow tall)[26] in the Indian Valley and up on Penn's Ridge. Forty or more of these, "plain, plodding people" had moved into the Tohickon watershed in the shadow of Haycock Mountain by the 1740s, and then drained the swamps around Quakertown (the *"Grooten Schwamb"*), irrigated pastures and meadows, removed fields of boulders, and despite working with difficult soils grew hay and fodder that were sweet and clean. The German Lutheran and Reformed Church people also planted their churches along the way; these "hardy and culturally tenacious" folk became the backbone of the area's farm economy. They planned on staying --- and stayed put.

Many of the Germans (and Irish) arrived at the port of Philadelphia as "redemptioners," being "bought" at the docks as potential field laborers. Unable to pay their passage to America, they were "disposed of at £10 each" (paid to the ship's captain) for a period of five years servitude. Newspapers advertised: "Lately imported, and to be sold cheap, a parcel of likely men and women servants." They were driven up into the county and they and their services sold by "Soul-Drivers." County historian William Buck described it thus:[27]

> No doubt some of our aged citizens can yet remember the "Soul-drivers" … This was a name given to a certain set of men who used to drive redemptioners through the country, and dispose of them to the farmers. They generally purchased them in lots consisting of fifty or more.

Once in Bucks, some of the redemptioners tried running away from their masters, disappearing into the woods and caves. Eventually, this "ignominious" episode in county history would largely be forgotten.

---

[26] Charlotte Stryker Pervy, *The Bucks County Scrapbook of Old Roads and Towns*, 1948, p.50.
[27] William J. Buck, *History of Bucks County*, 1855, p.48.

Mid-county, this wave of German settlement encountered an English-speaking wave of Scotch-Irish Presbyterians. Some had also come as redemptioners, working off a period of three years servitude. These were the lowland Scots from the Ulster plantations who later rebelled against the domination of the English and the Anglican Church. After leaving Derry, Belfast, and Antrim, they sailed for New England where their ships were turned away by the Calvinists who regarded the Scots as heirs of "Satan and his sons." Forced to detour to more tolerant and brotherly environs, they disembarked at the port of Philadelphia. By the 1720s these "adventurous, determined, independent-spirited" pioneers advanced into the wooded country to the northeast of Philadelphia. They "pushed their way thither" up the Neshaminy and Little Neshaminy Creeks (a Presbyterian "stream.") to the Tohickon Creek, establishing log meetinghouses first at Warwick (1726) and then as far up as Deep Run in Bedminster by 1732. They were said to have badly treated what remained of the American Indians, and were contemptuous of their neighbors. Neighboring Germans regarded them as "hot-tempered and ill-mannered troublemakers." Local church records describe them as "audacious" and "boisterous" folks among whom Sabbath-breaking and witchcraft were common past times. But it was the more numerous "German Race" which would eventually displace the Scots and take their lands while the latter would drift away through the mountain valleys of Appalachia to Virginia and the Carolinas.

Here on these Triassic lands, these foot-loose Scotch-Irish feared no man, but – coming from a Celtic world where Christianity was still only a thin veneer overlying pagan ritual – the devil was an entirely different matter. "The deil" it was said had worn a tartan with the best of them. "Auld Hoofs" even played the pipes in the "Tale of Tam O'Shanter."As indispensable to life as smooth highland whiskey, "the fient" in beastly form was at home among the clans. Indeed, he received a piece of the best land in every community; it was walled in and posted as "the Devil's Croft." This propitiation was supposed to keep him from mucking about in peoples' farm yards. And as Robert Burns expressed it, "tho' yon flaming hollow's thy home, thou travels far ..." The Scottish-Irish who arrived in Bucks would surely have felt neglected had not the devil traveled as far as them to reach these same Triassic lands.

From the depressed and crowded towns of Wales came another, though smaller, wave of refugees. The Jones', Lewis', Lloyds', Thomas', and Davis' came into the county (1718-1740s) from the heavily populated Welsh area immediately to the west of Bucks. The "Welsh Tract" in neighboring Montgomery County perpetuates the Welsh presence in tongue-twisting place names like Bala Cynwd, Bryn Athen, Bryn Mawr, and Gwynedd; and in not so tongue-distorting ones like Radnor, North Wales, and Montgomery itself. But in Bucks County, the Welsh presence was light, and little was left to preserve the memory of these Welsh farm families whether in the form of place names ("Aberyswyth" became "Hilltown"), surnames in the Baptist cemeteries, building styles, or local folklore. Some eventually drifted northward to the state's hard coal fields; but, all in all, it was good they should be here. For as one of Shakespeare's characters said in "Henry IV", the devil understands Welsh very well!

Dutch and Swedish settlers appeared early (1670s-90s) in the lower county, preparing the way for William Penn. The Dutch did not arrive directly from Holland, but were third-generation Americans migrating down from the New York City and north New Jersey areas. Seeking better farmland than was available in the lower Hudson Valley and on Staten Island, they moved into Bucks; they settled in and built their churches, and then – through intermarriage – faded away as an identifiable culture. It should, however, be noted that they were considered to be a superstitious people who believed in and feared the "*duyvel*" and populated the vast and hauntingly empty places they came to settle with an army of fantasy figures. The Swedes were said to be rather quiet and industrious ... but had no trade goods to sell the Indians. The Indians didn't quite know what to make of them; they thought perhaps to kill them all.

In addition to those who came to call the Triassic lowland their home, there were of course others (much smaller in numbers) who created tiny settlement pockets based on ethnicity and/or religion: Irish Catholic farmers ("a little colony ... settled in the woods" near Haycock Mountain); French Huguenots who came here to avoid being massacred by King Louis XIV. These populations also shared in a powerful Old World demonology.

Medievalisms on Triassic Soil

These European arrivals had come from a world where the practices and attitudes of a medieval society had barely begun to ebb. For example, they still farmed their land in narrow strips with the tools of the sixteenth century. Moreover, they brought with them a belief in the devil that governed all expressions of thought as well as the imagination. The lingering legacy of medieval Christianity informed them of the literal existence of demons, grotesque figures, and satanic monsters they saw carved on their oversized cathedrals. It was Christianity that had saved mankind from the "Evil One," so people at least had better believe in devils, even if only as an exercise in spreading Christianity. To convince the common folk of the devil's reality, his demonic image was cast in cold stone in the form of huge, grim, gray gargoyles with snarling grins and clutching talons. One's only protection was the sanctuary of the church.

The farmlands of Pennsylvania were of course far removed in memory and miles from Europe's great religious architecture. And twelve-foot tall stone gargoyles really don't travel well. What was more easily transported to the colonies, as a perfectly agreeable companion to cathedral art and church doctrine, was a parallel folk world in which spirits and demons had the power to interfere with, and perhaps even influence, human affairs. An obsession with spirits and demons was a means of mastering the unknown. Again, in the words of Erik Erikson, "In a world full of dangers (a farm frontier pressed up against a hideous wilderness) they may even have served as a source of security, for they make the unfamiliar familiar, and permit the individual to say to his fears and conflicts, 'I see you! I recognize you!'"[28]

If what is out there in the dark can be visualized, even fancifully, a comforting familiarity is gained; and whatever it is that's abroad in the night, in the dimly-lit corners of the cellar and attic, need not be feared so much. "Around (their) fire-places ... would our forefathers on the long evenings of winter be assembled ... when astonishing stories would be told, perhaps of witches and ghosts ... and devils."[29] An imagined folk devil, whether wondrous or awful, adroit or clumsy, was a welcome release from all the mundane drudgery, from all the years of a plowman's life spent tending the land.

A crate full of magic and devil lore was gathered together over the centuries in the pine dark and Dark Age forests of Teutonic and Celtic Europe. Hauled out onto the farmlands of southeastern Pennsylvania, the crate spilled open and out came witchcraft and sorcery. Among the rich cache of legends and myths that also spilled out were gremlins, ghosts, goblins ("hobo" demons who camped out in abandoned farmhouses and quarries), and "wee" folk or fairies. The German settlers of Nockamixon believed that fairies could be caught if on a cold and windy night a blanket or open sack was spread out on a hillside ... once caught, they would bring much money when sold.[30] Nurtured by fear and faith, belief in such presences thrived – just like everything else planted in the fertile red soil.

There was also a general understanding that the devil too would come to dwell among them and become part of their work world and home life. "His Satanic Majesty" could be thwarted by prevention though, or so it was hoped. Thus, carefully packed and wrapped with the colorful impedimenta of a folk people were bottles of holy water, books of exorcism, boxes of candles, and packages of incense. All of

---

[28] Erik Erikson, *Young Martin Luther, A Study in Psychoanalysis and History,* 1958.
[29] William J. Buck, *History of Bucks County,* 1855, p. 55.
[30] ibid., p.60-61.

which might keep the devil at bay. In the immigrants' gardens, religion thrived … as did its weed: superstition.

Although they were well-prepared for their encounters with him, all this would not be enough. Magic is the devil's game. But the Bucks folk devil had no polished act to offer. Locally, the powers and acts attributed to this hell-fired cuss were merely humorous and sad, and so hum-drum as to be almost pathetic. He got his kicks by jumping from shadowy woods and dark places. Just scaring people; no cosmic message here. He enjoyed walking country lanes at night, in disguise, to see if anyone could guess who this stranger was. He got quite good at this. Sometimes life seemed like an endless masquerade. An endless round of horseplay, antics, and shenanigans. "Old Nick" and old St. Nick shared chimney duties as well. The devil would "haunt" chimneys by howling down the flue in the dead of a windless night, on any night of the year but Christmas Eve. Sometimes he would fall in. Such was the nature of a clumsy folk devil. He was the wind that shook the shutters. Strange noises made by the wind and strange sights seen in the "traitorous twilight" were further hints at the devil's presence. When restless leaves began to move, swirling across roads like so many little brown animals – on perfectly calm days yet! – this was also said to be the devil's work. On this last charge, he pleaded innocent, wondering himself what other force might be at work.

In this gently rolling, washboard world of "beauty, fertility, and salubrity," his influence was said to be present when the marriage match of the family's favorite daughter turned sour. Good housewives knew that their spouses were out cavorting with the devil if they wandered home late under the influence of bad whiskey. Sometimes the husband would disappear for a week or longer; wives knew they were "Devil dealing" with "the Devil's Picture-Book," impiously absorbed in an ungodly marathon card game at one of the local stagecoach inns or keg houses. In a more serious vein, murderous and avaricious inclinations and sudden mood swings from melancholy to frisky were charged to his account. Lust and adulterous temptations were also part of his game: he caused all too vivid dreams, "night fevers" that led people to sin. He achieved this by sneaking into the lonely bedrooms of isolated farm-houses and lying beneath sleeping men and atop sleeping women *("unter oder oblegen"* in Luther's words; *"Succubus et incubus"* in the parlance of theologians; and just "wet dreams" in later day slang). That tired feeling on waking up in the morning was probably caused by having been ridden by devils (or witches) during the night.[31]

Despite his frequently heavy antics, this devil engaged in no cosmic dialogue with man, no Faustian conflict with great and holy men. Ever since leaving England he had lost his appetite for soul stealing. Now, he was the old trickster content to purvey his ruses on the locals, taking the blame for the assorted common ills that befell rural households. It was his doing if the farmers' cows gave vinegary milk. He, not God, was the culprit if a sudden hailstorm flattened the crops. And if a barn burnt... and so it went. Everything from miscarriages to broken carriage wheels occupied his days and years here in Bucks.

Infrequently, something good might come about through his influence. Both the German and Scotch-Irish farmers practiced water dowsing, seeking underground streams and aquifers by using the traditional forked divining rod of witch hazel. Drawing as it does upon occult forces within the earth, it was admitted to be "the work of Satan;" although condemned by churchmen and geologists alike, the farmers felt confident enough in its use – as long as the rod itself was "Christianized" by placing it in the bed of a newly-born and baptized child and by giving it a saint's name. Satan, when handled with respect, could be made beneficent.

A Great Arc of Superstition

Southeastern Pennsylvania is "Dutch Country," an arc of ethnically and historically German *("Deutsche")* speaking counties surrounding Philadelphia. In the 1700s over one hundred thousand Palatine Germans arrived to claim land in this area. Though exurbanized

---

[31] "Folk-lore of the Pennsylvania Germans," *Journal of American Folk-lore,* (1889), Part II, p. 31.

and suburbanized, the region draws much tourism because of the remaining pockets of rural life. Part of the appeal is the palate-pleasing German dishes like sauerkraut cake, *schnitz un knepp* (apples, dumplings, and ham), *fastnachts* (fried potato mash), and wet bottom shoe fly pie with molasses. Wacky (funny) cake and potato and onion kugels are sold at area food stores, and funnel cake at the county fairs. Food itself can be preoccupation here, a testament to the bounteous Triassic soils. Perhaps more incredibly, other folkways survive on the very fringes of the Megalopolis: eccentricities like houses without telephones and electricity --- and bearded, camera-shy men in black attire parking their horse-drawn gray buggies in Wal-Mart lots. Interestingly but incorrectly, "Amish country charm" complete with horses and buggies was claimed to be a positive quality of Newtown Borough, Bucks County by a travel blog.[32]

What is true of Bucks County is this: superstition and a practical knowledge of the supernatural have clung as tightly as bark on a tree to this once heavily German country draped like a great shroud over and around Bucks County. In the Bethlehem and Reading areas just north and west (the Lehigh and Lebanon Valleys) and on the Amish farmlands of Lancaster and York Counties, daily life and the yearly calendar traditionally included not only herbal remedies and homespun recipes, but a powerful dose of the occult: witchcraft, omenology, divination, astrology, and spirit rapping. How much of this trickled in from the "Dutch Country" to Bucks County is for the folklorist to ponder. However, the one undeniable and ubiquitous belief that did penetrate deeply into the hearts and psyches of the county's German settlers was a singular obsession with the devil.

For all their practical values and common sense, for all the judiciousness and industry they brought to the pursuit of farming, they retained a perhaps medieval conception of what was evil. And this was far from empty superstition: the devil himself actually walked the world and stalked the Triassic lands of Bucks. The folk Germans had many

---

[32] "Coolest Small Towns in America," *Budget Travel* at http://travel.yahoo.com

devils: "Friar Rush," the drunken bartender who seduced through alcohol, and who would have been very much at home on the Devil's Half-Acre; the *"Kabotermannekens"* or fat little demons who played tricks on women as they tilled the fields; and of course, the somewhat tired and traveled old devil who visited the gypsy camps and surveyed the great lowland from atop the diabase hills. [33]

The German settlers were spiritual heirs of Martin Luther and Lutheran was their denomination. Many had in fact come from the city of Worms – Luther's Worms. Though more than two centuries had passed since Luther's death, they likely shared his firm belief in the universal presence of spirits; he furthermore believed in a literal devil, a concrete personage who toyed with and tormented mankind. There "must be a devil," said Luther, "so that virtue will not languish without an enemy." "Many regions are inhabited by devils," he said; Prussia, like any agrarian region, was full of devils. Luther's "reality" became that of the Bucks farmers, frontier agriculturalists daily immersed in things close to the devil – mud, manure, horned animals, red soil, and fertility. The German farmers were buoyed in their convictions about the flesh and blood genuineness of the devil with pronouncements in the *Lutheran Quarterly*: "No literary critic dare call it allegory. (He) is real … as reality."

They spread their Lutheran faith across the upper Bucks farmlands and assembled one congregation after another until their church was by far the predominant sect throughout the area. These German yeomen remembered afresh the mesh of folklore and dogma in their mentor's highly personalized personification of "the Emperor of Hell" – Luther's arguments and conferences with the devil: the dirty splash mark on the wall in Luther's room (made when he hurled an inkpot at Satan who annoyingly stood grinning while Luther worked at translating the

---

[33] Superstitions and supernatural beliefs traveled into Bucks with Old World German farm folk from the Upper Palatinate (Franconia and Bavaria). An excellent and entertaining source of information on Palatinate Folklore in the 1660s is Oliver Potzsch's historical novels *(The Hangman's Daughter* series).

Bible into German); his screaming at the devil to stay out of the cere-mony when a ring was accidentally dropped during a wedding; and, only days before his death, Luther being mooned by a teasing devil who was sitting on a drainpipe outside his window. Luther believed that no church ritual or saint's intercession could protect man from the devil; everybody went one-on-one with Satan. A sure enough personal defense against the devil was flatulence; but an even surer defense, and the thing he feared most and fled from, was the all-out anal affront. Luther said to the devil: "I have shit in the pants, and you can hang them around your neck and wipe your mouth with it."[34] This was part of the very real religious and folk legacy transplanted onto the Triassic lowlands. How much actual "pants' shitting" occurred in Bucks was not recorded, but that they took Luther's incarnate devil seriously is found in other more visible and less banal ways.

Question: Why Were Porch Ceilings Painted Blue? Answer: For the Same Reason Schoolhouses Were Eight-Sided!

One could cope with the devil by means of caution and supersti-tion. Better still, he might be warned away by a variety of visual devices, symbols, and talismans. For example, the Pennsylvania Germans drew upon medieval church legend in their use of the pelican bird. Along with flower pots, tulips, and duck tracks, the pelican was a favorite symbol sewn into country quilts. Its most frequent use, however, was reserved for *"fraktur,"* a blend of Old World-style calligraphy with folk motifs. Birth and baptismal certificates were artfully turned into highly stylized "illuminated" documents. In some of these, the adult pelican is shown feeding its blood to its young, suggesting (perhaps) the redemption of Christ. In German lore, the pelican is the bird that SERPENTS avoid!

---

[34] These and previous quotes from Luther as quoted by Erik Erikson, op.cit.

Fig. 3.2 Devil Defenses

Pelican Feeding
its Young

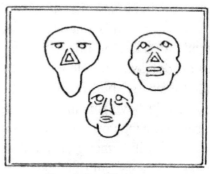

Crudely-Drawn
Defense Heads

While witches may have preferred springhouses and bake ovens, *"der feint"* went straight for the barns and houses. These structures could however be protected in a number of ways. The ancient swastika was painted on walls and doors "to ward off evil." And "defense heads," primitive-looking face masks were used to repel "the forces of evil and darkness." The huge, well-kept German-Swiss barns that reflected the bounty of the richly   productive fields were unmistakable exercises in ways to keep malevolence at arm's length. While the ranks of glass-ball lightning arresters on the roof ridge would protect against a known physical danger, more was needed to protect against the unknown and unseen. Horseshoes were nailed with prongs up to catch the good luck and deter the bad. Crosses made of elder were nailed to the barn walls to serve the same purpose. The doors themselves became "devil doors" when trimmed with white paint to prevent him from entering and messing around with the livestock. Stories were told of farmers who smeared their barn doors with the blood of butchered cattle and hogs to deter evil. Holy bells were hung on cows to scare away the demons. And on Walpurgis Night (April 30th), when even greater evil was abroad, the barn doors were locked and sealed with crosses made of ash, hawthorn, and juniper.[35]

Hex signs ("hexerei" or "hexefuss") began to appear in southeastern Pennsylvania shortly after the devil's arrival. In upper Bucks County (Springfield, Milford, and Richland Townships) these curious abstractions introduced by the German farmers may still be seen (though barely) on the cracked wooden boards long given over to time and weather. There is still dispute among the experts concerning the true and original meaning of the once brightly-colored, round abstractions that were either carved or painted onto the gable ends of the barn. Some will argue that they're not talismatic at all, but done "just for fun." Any other interpretation is said to be a falsehood and a "slander" against Germans by "outsiders." Others claim that hexes were preventives against random acts of God like lightning and fire. Still others know for certain that the oldest twelve-pointed stars (the twelve apostles?) were derived from Christian symbols and clearly possessed the power to ward off evil and discourage demons that prowled near the barnyard. Hexes would thus ensure healthy animals and bountiful harvests.[36]

The more decorative and fanciful hex designs (sunbursts, tulips, and hearts) came much later, finding favor only after the devil's departure and the arrival of the tourists. In the end, the true nature and meaning of these colorfully-patterned designs created by the hands and minds of a folk culture may only be surmised. One authority says that "hex signs are not for decoration ... Their connection with ... spells and hexing cannot be doubted." But replies another: "Balderdash, fiddlesticks, and nonsense." And so, the scholarly debate continues.

Household items and houses too reflected a concern with keeping evil at a distance. There were many "devil devices" that were used. At

---

[35] "Walpurgis Night" Chapter XIII at www.sacred-texts.com.

[36] The writer Wallace Nutting described hex signs as "a kind of spiritual and demoniac lightning-rod!" in *Pennsylvania Beautiful* (1924), p. 28. It is believed that Nutting most likely confused the Pennsylvania German word for six-pointed ("sechsafoos") with the word for witch's foot ("hexefuss"). Ian Urbana, "The Pennsylvania Dutch, A Long Tradition Fades," The *New York Times*, July 15, 2006.

the Durham iron furnace biblical designs and illustrations were molded onto stove surfaces, flashbacks, and fireplace screens; the "Bible in Iron" might discomfort the devil (along with religiously decorated cake pans and cookie molds). Though only a small architectural detail, many of the older fieldstone farmhouses had the undersides of their roofs painted blue. And it's a cerulean blue, the blue of a heavenly sky on a bright, sunny day.[37] Few yellows, whites, greens, or reds were used – just sky blue. Today, few know why this was even done ("I don't know; aren't they all blue?"). Suppositions range from keeping insects away to keeping temperatures cooler in summer. "It keeps the flies away; they don't like that color no how." [38] The truth may be this: the devil will not darken a doorstep at night if he thinks it might be day. He'll be so put off and disoriented by the cerulean blue, he'll slink away mumbling and all confused. It's a wonder why itinerant folk artists weren't employed to add angels on heavenly clouds to these ceilings, thus creating an even more powerful illusion and admonition. All was not lost even if someone had neglected to paint the ceiling blue and the devil did darken the doorstep. The ashes of a burnt snake, if strewn in a circle around the house, would prevent any other snake from crossing. Sprinkling salt on the doorsteps and windowsills was also a strong deterrent. But, the final line of defense was the door itself. As shown in Fig. 3.3, farmhouse doors had a warning, a message molded into the wood. The upper panels are a representation of the crucifix. And the lower panels show a motif also found on many an old gravestone – i.e., both halves of an open book. That, of course, being the Bible. What respectable devil would dare challenge such strong Christian symbolism? God only knew what was on the other side of the door. Possibly God himself! It was the folk architectural equivalent of Luther's anal affront, without the messy drawers to clean.

---

[37] Upcounty, the same sky blue color was used in the stained glass windows of German country churches. In some, the altar crucifix may have featured sky blue colored glass.

[38] It may only be a roadside census, but driving through the central and upper county today shows very, very few remaining blue porch ceilings.

Fig. 3.3 Abandoned Farmhouse in Buckingham Township
The Warnings: Blue Porch Ceiling and Door

Farmhouse now demolished
(Photos and sketch by author)

Foul and disruptive devils had to be kept away from the young people, especially when going about their schooling. During the first half of the nineteenth century a quite unique way of constructing one-room schoolhouses developed in the Delaware Valley; over one hundred octagonal-shaped structures were built in southeastern Pennsylvania, New Jersey, and Delaware. Nine of these small "eight squares" were located on the farmlands of Bucks County (the earliest being built at Oxford Valley in 1773; others were located at Lumberville and Perkasie). Why and by whom they were built still seems to be a matter of some conjecture. The Dutch had built octagonal windmills, trading posts, churches, and houses both in Holland and in the New York area. Perhaps this building concept was carried south into Bucks by the Dutch. Perhaps. Most of the approximately one hundred "octagonal athenaeums" were however constructed in German-settled areas.

Fig. 3.4 Wrightstown Township Octagonal Schoolhouse

This last-surviving "eight-square" is located at the intersection of Swamp Road and Second Street Pike. It was used as a school from 1802 to 1850. (Photo by author)

As to why they were built in this particular shape – well, to facilitate control over the young students is a believable enough reason. Economy of space (sixty pupils in a room not ten yards wide) and economy in heating were no doubt pragmatic considerations that also benefited from the eight square arrangement of thick stone walls. These small buildings were very practical affairs: made of multi-colored stone gathered from the nearby fields, with no attempt at uniformity or size as in a house. Plain, undecorated stone outside and whitewashed walls within, "void of any decorations except a tapestry of delicately spun spider webs and weather-stains." A "ten-plate stove" for burning wood, and later a cylinder stove for burning coal, was positioned at the center of the room, thus allowing for equal heat distribution throughout. Indeed, this arrangement "nearly roasted the little fellows (and gals) who occupied the seats near it." That these "ink bottle" shaped schoolhouses were built with energy efficiency in mind is quite probable in that this eight- square design further allowed the maximum amount of light to enter at all hours of the school day.[39] The door was, moreover, set to face the south-south-east, allowing for the maximum sun's warmth and the least winter energy loss. The eight-squares then mirrored the same southerly alignment of bays and livestock pens found in the German barns. A very commendable example of nineteenth century energy conservation.

While this may explain why the eight-square design was originally used, there's more to consider here in this world of McGuffey Readers and Appleton Elementary Geographies. Folk belief attached itself to the little schoolhouses long after their construction. Local lore suggests that the octagonal buildings were so designed to give the devil no quarter to hide in, no shadowy, dirt-collecting corner to lurk in. He was thus denied the opportunity to sully young minds. Fastidiously sweeping the corners (or more precisely, the obtuse angles between the walls) clean of dirt was a required daily chore. Sometimes though, somehow the devil might work his way into some small malleable mind and body, an event reflected in an unprepared grammar lesson or the mischief of plugging the terra cotta chimney with sticks and leaves, thus enveloping the room in smoke.

---

[39] Robert W. Craig, "Temples of Learning: Octagon Schoolhouses in the Delaware Valley," Ms. in Historic Preservation, Columbia University, 1988. See also the website for: "Inventory of Older Octagon, Hexagon, and Round Houses" by Robert Kline and Ellen Puerzer.

The "appliances" used to correct such devilish acts were the hickory switch, the dunce's cap, and a grotesque medievalism (so grotesque as to be almost comical) employed by teachers in the German schools – the dreaded "Leather Spectacles." This was a black Lone Ranger-type mask with horns. Suitable and symbolic punishment then! One "little devil" is shown below wearing the mask in a vintage photograph.

Fig. 3.6 Leather Spectacles/Horns

This device was used as a means of punishment (From: Henry Mercer, *Photo Collection*, Vol. I, 1897, p.42, Spruance Library, Doylestown.

A Closer Look:
Metes and Bounds …
and Devilish Doings

The "Great Law" of 1682 required county farmers to enclose their properties with fencing at least five-feet high. But property lines were poorly indicated, having incorporated not a few temporary and changeable landmarks. County farmlands evolved as "a patchwork of odd-shaped, various-sized parcels … with boundaries oriented in any and all directions." [40] This had been the method of land division used in England for centuries; it was brought to America and applied to lands in the original colonies. It was most commonly referred to as "metes and bounds" (or "Meets and Boundaries" in some old deeds) with metes being the measurement of straight run distances between the terminal points and "bounds" being a word description of boundary markers such as watercourses, stone walls and "line stones," public road ways, and even large, old trees.

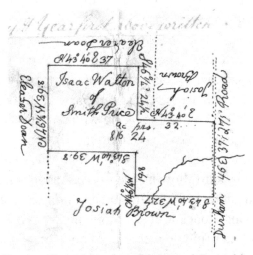

Property Deed Map from Plumstead Township, Bucks County (1798) showing "metes and bounds" measurements and directions. (Author's collection)

---

[40] Norman Thrower, *Original Survey and Land Subdivision,* 1966, p. 120.

Shown above is a "metes and bounds" map from a deed (property "conveyance" or "indenture") in Plumstead Township, Bucks County dated March 31st, 1798. Sixteen acres ("more or less") along Durham Road (today's Rte. 413) were conveyed from Smith Price and his wife to Isaac Walton for the sum of £218 "current money of Pennsylvania." The language of the deed is classic "metes and bounds," i.e. exacting but confounding to modern ears. A small sample:

> Beginning at a stone in Durham Road … south 43 degrees
> and 40 minutes west thirty-two perches and seven tenths
> of a stone, and then 46 degrees and a quarter west …

The geographer Norman Thrower (*Original Survey and Land Subdivision*) described the arbitrary, sometimes disorienting, and unsystematic use of "metes and bounds" as "as one of felicitous adjustment between nature and man." It speaks of a time when the natural world, with all its irregularities, was worked with and not so much imposed upon. And, of course, the devil was very much an omnipresent part of that natural world. What might happen was this: On a dark and moonless night and with the devil's encouragement, a less than honest neighbor might reposition the "line stones" and corner posts marking the boundary between your land and his … thus encroaching more upon yours. This was the devil's influence at work; that neighbor's afterlife was guaranteed to be not very restful. Tampering in life with "metes and bounds" markers could cause many a ghostly visitation: "In some of these the luminous outline of human forms will be seen (and) fiery balls observed flying through the air and following the true boundary lines."[41] After sunset, locals would gather to watch the ghostly farmer flit around the farm-lot borders carrying stones to make atonement. "Where shall I put this stone" he would utter (in Old German, of course).

---

[41] W.J.Hoffman, "Folk-lore of the Pennsylvania Germans," Part II, *Journal of American Folk-lore*, 1888-89, p.33.

CHAPTER 4

THEIR DOMAIN ... BUT NOT HIS; DEHORNED AND ADRIFT IN THE PEACEABLE KINGDOM

Speak of the Devil and he appears, speak not of him and ...

– Old Proverb

The suckling child shall innocently play on the dark hole where poisonous reptiles lay; the crested worm with all its venom then the weaned child shall fasten in his den.

- Edward Hicks, Bucks County Quaker Preacher as quoted in J.W. Brey, *A Quaker Saga* (1967)

The southern end of Bucks County is occupied by a belt, five miles wide, of ... gneisses, and mica schists of unknown age ... and covered with gravel of recent but various ages ...

- J.H. Battle, ed. *History of Bucks County* (1887)

E. Digby Baltzell (1915–1996) was an eminent professor of sociology and history and a social commentator who dealt with themes of politics and class in eighteenth and nineteenth-century America. He is credited with having introduced the term "WASP" to the language. He was also an authority on Philadelphia and its Quaker traditions of "drabness and middle-class complacency." In his voluminous and finely detailed 1979 work, *Puritan Boston and Quaker Philadelphia*, Baltzell advanced the thesis that the religious doctrines and social attitudes of the founding Puritan and Quaker communities endured through time and moreover came to influence social practices and patterns of political leadership in the two respective cities and their hinterlands. It's quite an interesting thesis in that the good citizens of today's Philadelphia area (whether they be Catholics, agnostics, or Phillies Phanatics) are still said to be marked by the original ethics of Quakerism. In other words, the values of the 'host' culture, Quaker values, were absorbed into the mind sets and lifestyles of later-day arrivals. Philadelphia and its hinterland march through time not as a Quaker city and region, but as one of Quaker influence. This means that even though the Quakers quickly became a minority on their own turf (as early as the 1720's in fact!), their ways and mores were osmotically assimilated by all those whom the Quakers tolerated to live among them. And that was nearly everybody. Apart from a universal tolerance as wide and accepting as the whole human rainbow, other abiding Quaker values included egalitarianism, anti-authoritarianism, and a deeply human individualism. Add to these a highly prized sense of personal resignation and submission to the mysterious ways of God.

So what does all of this have to do with the price of milk at the convenience store? What does it have to do with the folk devil and with Bucks County? Everything! Bucks was Quaker before it was anything else. And Quakers did not then and do not now believe in an actual devil! While New Englanders dealt with Old Scratch by assertively booted him out, while the German church people, Scotch-Irish and others adopted him, fought with and dallied with him, and came to regard him as a necessary appendage of the farm ecology, the Quakers simply denied his very existence. He was treated by them as a medieval remnant best thrown onto the trash heap along with witchcraft and superstition. So, no need for blue porch ceilings, hex signs, or shitty pants.

All this hurt more than the thought of Luther's inkpot hurtling towards his face; it smarted more than the tip of Daniel Webster's boot. His credibility was shattered by a good and gentle people whose religious creed negated the very idea of anything evil. Poor devil, he didn't know that he didn't even exist, that he was no longer relevant. At least, that is, on the outwash plain of the Delaware River. Who were these gentle Quakers and what was the consequence of their so presumptuous denial of the devil? And what is this "outwash plain" the author so presumptuously assumes the reader knows about?

The Light Within Touches the Outwash Plain

At first, this close-knit religious culture was known variously as Friends of the Truth, Children of the Truth, or Church of the Light. This was in the 1650s when the "Religious Society of Friends" or Quakers was founded by George Fox. He gathered around him like-minded preachers who agreed with his determination to make life a "walking in the light." From out of the lonely dales and fens of the English north country, and especially from along the Welsh borderlands, the word spread – live life simply and spiritually; reject the external manifestations of Christianity such as baptism and the Eucharist. An "Inward Light," the light of an imminent Christ dwelling in each human soul, meant that all men (and even women!) were equal and basically good. Peace among all mankind would therefore follow. For subscribing to these beliefs, and because they felt no need for a Church of England ministry (for no ordained ministry at all), and because they didn't feel obliged to pay tithes or even attend any established church, the Quakers were ridiculed and cruelly persecuted. The time had come to seek their peaceful haven elsewhere.

In England and on the Continent the Quaker aristocrat William Penn had used his excellent publicity skills to recruit colonists for a journey to a place across the ocean where testimonies of peace and brotherhood could be experimented with in a spirit of utopian peace and brotherhood. The stage was set for the "colony of heaven." Fox had scouted out the Delaware Valley in 1672, traveling along the river with "Friends" and friendly Indian guides. Guided by the "Inward Light," small boatloads of Quakers began arriving on the Delaware's shores in 1679-80. They were largely poor and poorly-educated yeomen from the poorest parts of England and Wales. They were farmers, shopkeepers, and hired servants stepping out of a feudal tableau, aroused by the Quaker appeal to the heart rather than the mind. To people who had for generations scraped out a barebones existence on worn and poverty-ridden hillsides, the endless, rolling waves of virgin wood must have seemed like heaven. The countryside was well-provisioned with fish and fowl and venison better than that of England. Bucks County was surely the searched for and hoped for peaceful haven on the sylvan shore,that looked for bountiful and boundless "contiguity of shade" amid a vast wilderness. This "second colony of Puritans" (just less aggressive and a whole lot more tolerant) arrived on and began occupying the outwash plain, making Bristol the hub of activity. Quaker Bristol, along the "King's Path" between Philadelphia and Trenton, thus became the oldest established borough in the county (indeed, in the state). It served well as a market town (Thursdays) and site for semi-annual fairs. Later, when the canal arrived (1830s) and Bristol became a coal port, and when waves of famished Irish immigrants arrived (1840s), the town became a far more boisterous haven for gambling, horse racing, and drinking. Very un-Quaker-like … but also very much later.

There is really no conceivable way in which this outwash plain can be thought of aesthetically or described poetically. It's as dull a piece of terrain as anyone can imagine. But this was, of course, just fine with the Quakers. The anti-aesthetic outwash plain suited their disposition perfectly. A plain plain for a plain people.

What the outwash plain was, was fertile, easily-worked farmland; and that's what was ultimately important to the Quakers. That it was disparaged by early travelers for its lack of picturesqueness ("this part of the route is not interesting … monotony … rule(s) over this region."), bothered the Quakers not at all. To them, this wide and sandy *"allée"* was "fruitful and abundant" land, relatively level and unobstructed by either hills or large fieldstone boulders.

This plain was the creation of the last great glacial meltoff of the Pleistocene period. When the glacier's front began to melt and recede some sixty miles further up the valley, meltwater began to rapidly pour off the 1,000-foot high wall of dirty ice. This happened perhaps 12,000 or more years ago. (The devil did have some vague recollection of reading about this while in the Middle East). The Delaware River served as a funnel, a gutter along which the billions of tons of pulverized debris was carried south. This icy sewer of seaward-moving detritus backed up and slowed to a crawl at a point where the great river took a sharp, right angled change of direction below Trenton and Morrisville. To the north of here, huge erratic boulders had come to rest on the Durham shore while coarse gravels built up a river terrace where New Hope would one day be. Lower Bucks was blanketed with all the crushed and crumbly ice slush. Across the lower end of the county ancient Triassic sediments lay buried like a secret, unseen heart beneath stratified layers of sands and gravels. To the geologist, this layered and porous rubble from a distant age is just unconsolidated Pleistocene material. But to the Quakers it was God's gift of fertile, well-drained farmland. William Penn, in a letter to the Free Society of Traders in London (1683) described it as "a fast fat earth … God in his wisdom having ordered it so."[42]

From everywhere across the Quaker-settled outwash plain there is a hazy ridge visible on the northern horizon; it rises several hundred feet and is actually the northernmost part of Appalachia's foothills. It terminates near Princeton Junction, across the river and east of Trenton.

---

[42] As quoted in Jack Rosen, *The Face of Bucks,* 1981.

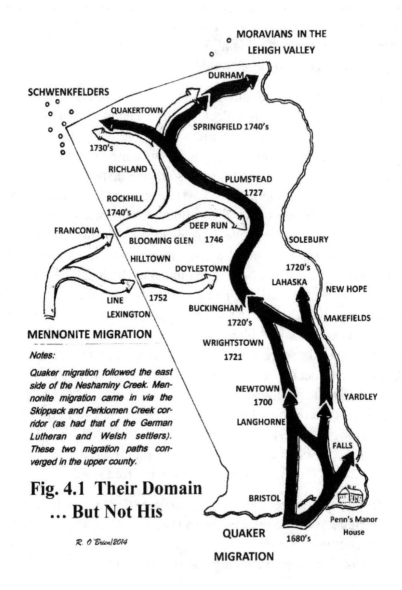

MORAVIANS IN THE
LEHIGH VALLEY

SCHWENKFELDERS

DURHAM

QUAKERTOWN

SPRINGFIELD 1740's

1730's

RICHLAND

ROCKHILL
1740's

PLUMSTEAD
1727

FRANCONIA

DEEP RUN

BLOOMING GLEN   1746

SOLEBURY

HILLTOWN

DOYLESTOWN

1720's

LAHASKA

NEW HOPE

LINE   1752

LEXINGTON

BUCKINGHAM

1720's

MAKEFIELDS

MENNONITE MIGRATION

WRIGHTSTOWN
1721

Notes:

*Quaker migration followed the east
side of the Neshaminy Creek. Mennonite migration came in via the
Skippack and Perkiomen Creek corridor (as had that of the German
Lutheran and Welsh settlers).
These two migration paths con-
verged in the upper county.*

NEWTOWN
1700

YARDLEY

LANGHORNE

FALLS

Fig. 4.1 Their Domain
... But Not His

R. O'Brien 2014

BRISTOL

Penn's Manor
House

QUAKER   1680's

MIGRATION

It's a stake hammered through the entire width of the county. It's a broad, flat-topped wedge of hard Precambrian rock 500 million years in age that separates the red-brown Triassic lowlands on its northern side from the pale-colored gravelly and sandy soils of the outwash plain. It's tempting to say that this rise, variably called the Langhorne Ridge or Trenton Prong, separated the devil-believing cultures (his domain!) from that of the Quakers (their domain, not his!).Temptingly neat, but incorrect. While the devil more or less conceded the outwash plain to the good Quakers, they in turn trespassed deeply into his territory. Very quickly, the Quakers gathered wealth, moved up in society, and began moving up across the ridge and through the county.

The Neshaminy Creek is the county's principal stream. It originates from hillside springs in Hilltown Township at around 500 feet above sea level. Its narrow and muddy channel winds 50 miles through eleven townships before entering the Delaware River at eighteen feet above sea level on a line between Bensalem and Bristol Townships. North from Bristol this was the corridor along which early settlers "reached the unknown central and central northern parts of the county."[43] Coming up the Neshaminy from Fallsington and Pennsbury in the late 1600s, the Quakers brought their "inward-dwelling light" to these new lands, planting their optimistic faith and their great boxlike meeting houses at Langhorne and Newtown. They crossed over the Triassic ridges and valleys, building meetinghouses at Wrightstown and Buckingham by the 1720s. Eventually (by the 1730s-40s) they spread north to Quakertown, becoming in-town "squires" and merchants. Then, they finally arrived in Springfield and Durham Townships. Seeing themselves perhaps as pilgrims in a transient world, they came to use the land's riches with a sense of restraint; they tended the land more gently than others so that something of worth might be passed along to future generations. Furthermore, their compassion for their fellow man was extended to the creatures of fields and woods, to the very fields and

---

[43] George MacReynolds, *Place Names in Bucks County*, p. 256. The Quakers generally stayed east of the creek, leaving the western side to the "Hollanders," English and Welsh Baptists, and Scotch-Irish Presbyterians.

woods themselves. A world of so much restraint, gentleness, and compassion could not harbor evil; it had no evil places or presences. Like any threatened species denied habitat, the earthly devil found it difficult to even exist in the Quaker world. This was a challenge brought to his own backyard. Things were serious.

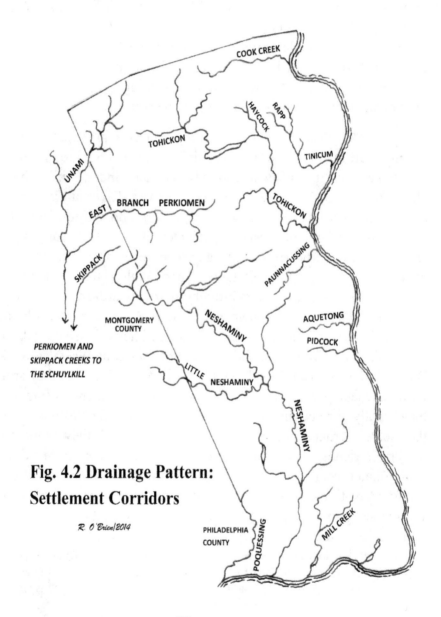

Fig. 4.2 Drainage Pattern: Settlement Corridors

R. O'Brien/2014

No Earthly Evil Here

Between the devil and the Delaware's deep blue waters there emerged a distinctive Quaker culture. In the words of an old Quaker sermon, it was a way of life illuminated by "the light from heaven descend(ing) to overcome oceans of darkness." It was a sober, quiet, and orderly life guided not by scripture but by a code of discipline decided upon by the London yearly meetings. Daily affairs centered on the local meetinghouse and, in rural areas such as Bucks on the family farm. "Quaker curfew" meant 9 p.m. Lives were balanced between moderation and asceticism, often tilting more toward the latter. Described as a "cult of caution," they were reserved in their business and social dealings, not taking risks and not hustling anyone. This is not to say that they weren't good at making money; there was no prohibition against acquiring wealth. Their dignified shad belly coats, curled periwigs, and superfluous buttons (the Quaker Oats box Quaker) gave some a reputation as not just good, god-fearing people, but as a money-making people "with one foot in the meetinghouse and one in the counting house." However, as Digby Baltzell said, the snobbery that came with having made lots of money attaches itself more to the urban, Philadelphia Quakers. In the rural meetings like Bucks, success in life was measured not in greenbacks but in the green fields of a well-managed and prosperous farm.

Across the Triassic lands and down on the outwash plain, to be too successful in fact necessitated rebuke. The hard work that produced success was to be followed only by more hard work … and continued modesty in dress. Too much happiness too, the reward of all that hard work, was not to be sought after. True and lasting happiness came only through self-denial. One was not to take too much pleasure, and perhaps none at all, in the things of this world. This was especially so with earthy and earthly physical pleasures. The Quakers conceded that bad things, not evil things, things of a licentious nature, did indeed exist. Heading that list was gambling, followed by drinking, partying, cockfighting, and dancing. These things could be rooted out by education and good example. In other words, there was no other devil to exorcise. Yet, by the early 1800s an "ocean of darkness" was threatening to extinguish the Quaker beacon of light. More than ever before, human perversity and unfriendly ways were, in the Quaker view, circling around like vultures as "calico and silk and sin, by slow degrees, kept coming in." What were the Quakers to do?

Peaceable Kingdom

Consider Edward Hicks' reaction. Hicks (1780-1849) was said to be the best Quaker preacher in Bucks County and a man who was much bothered by the incompatible things beginning to surround Quaker life in the county: he said of his native Newtown that "every tenth house was a tavern and every twentieth was of bad repute." Hicks was one of the very few Quakers to create anything of artistic merit since the human appetite for beauty was to be strictly curbed. At first, he employed his paint brushes in the service of fire buckets, carriage exteriors, lettered blocks for children, sleighs that sped across the snow and – ironically – tavern signs. His "ministry through painting" eventually turned itself to the artist's canvas.

Fig. 4.3 Edward Hicks' Peaceable Kingdom

(Left) Portrait of Edward Hicks by Thomas Hicks, circa 1838. As reproduced in *Bucks County Historical Society Papers*, Vol. 6, 1932, p.1. (Right) "A Peaceable Kingdom," oil on canvas, circa 1833. Brooklyn Museum, N.Y., Creative Commons Attribution ShareAlike 2.0 (Generic).

Hicks had joined the Friends after blundering into a meetinghouse when he was twenty-three years old and painfully hungover. Or so the story goes. He apparently decided then and there that the only important reality in the world was the mercy and forgiveness of God; that life's only correct path was one of abstinence, a slamming of the brakes on self-gratification: "may self be denied and the cross of Christ worn as a daily garment, may his peaceable kingdom forever be established in the rational, immortal soul."

Hicks supported himself and his family partly through commissions to put on canvas his wealthy Quaker neighbors' farms; but his artistic reputation, as perhaps the best of the nation's folk or "primitive" painters, rests on the output of his iconic *Peaceable Kingdoms*. One day he painted a *Peaceable Kingdom* inhabited by crudely drawn, stiff two-dimensional figures of wild beasts such as the lion, leopard, wolf, and bear. He painted them lying down and cuddling up with domesticated farm animals and baby animals such as the lamb and kid. However poorly drawn (as art critic Robert Hughes says, "Hicks is not a great painter, not even a very good one"), it was the message that mattered: this world, this New World wilderness in Penn's woods, could be one of peace and tranquility, an earthly paradise of jungle and barnyard harmony where warring animals were spiritually reborn into a world of light and tranquility. All animals could claim room in this kingdom, all the innocent-looking and wide-eyed stuffed toy animals on the Quaker canvas, except for one – the serpent! Hicks' vision of the "Friendly Arcadia," this garden of agrarian innocence, was one in which the dark shadows of evil did not exist. A tiny, disproportionately small horned goat does appear in many versions of the *Peaceable Kingdom* --- could this be a semi-hidden commentary on the "beast's" diminished status? Again, the very idea of the devil and all that he implied in terms of Darwinian carnivores tearing great chunks of red meat out of each other's hides amid a ruthless ecology of competition and survival was simply denied. "The Angel of the Bottomless Pit" had vanished far below the bottom of the pit. Hicks liked what he had painted so much that he painted a second version. Then a third. And then a fourth. He made gifts of the canvases to Friends. Though he forever agonized over what he considered his unfortunate weakness for creative expression in art, though his anti-aesthetic Quaker guilt may have gotten in the way, he kept painting more and more *Peaceable Kingdoms*. He spent the next thirty years of his life doing quite possibly over one hundred such scenes, showing his amicable animals aging and graying, along with their painter.

Quakerism had already past its prime when Hicks died in 1849 with yet another (unfinished) *Peaceable Kingdom* on his easel. By then the Society of Friends had been badly split into rivaling sects by a complex philosophical argument that weakened their zeal and kept the faith divided well into the twentieth century. By the mid-nineteenth century Quakerism in America had greatly receded in importance, impaired by the energies of a powerful nationalism. The sect had little assimilating power. To some historians, the Quakers were robbed of "a certain vitality" and seemed preordained to a diminished role in national and local affairs. The German Lutherans and Scotch Presbyterians did not convert to Quakerism, nor did the Catholics (who were arriving in large numbers at Bristol, Philadelphia and New York on board the "coffin ships" from hunger-ravished Ireland). Yet, as Digby Baltzell theorized, all across the undulating lowlands of southeastern Pennsylvania, some Quaker values were likely absorbed by other groups. The religious views held by Hicks and his Friends that placed an innocent faith in the goodness of human nature, and a faith in a virtuous peaceable land, were dead as the hard rocks of the Langhorne Ridge. Yet there somehow remained as some small part of the national vision, a hidden aspiration that coolly refused to give up on the splendid idealism of the Quaker garden of innocence.

Embarrassment in the Pale Moonlight

By subtle and friendly persuasion then, the taut sinews and tensions of Christianity were taught to relax. No need for the paranoia and mental stress produced by battling devils in some cosmic contest of good and evil. All things, either inherently or potentially, had the comforting light of a loving God dwelling within them. Germanic and Celtic devils were not to be feared. How could something be feared if it didn't exist? For the Quakers, myth and superstition led only to unhappiness and anxiety. Injudicious exposure to witches and devils, apparitions and "marvelous things" caused psychological injury; parents were to unremittingly safeguard their children's susceptible minds from the imaginary fears generated by exposure to such bunk.

Thus, the Quakers did not have a rich folklore. They avoided the vulgar and rural Old World-derived supernatural beliefs and tall tales. The blame for life's misfortunes, such as the occasional poor harvest or sick animal, was not attributed to a malicious devil, but was rather a lesson in the vanity of all earthly delights. Be thankful for misfortune because it served as a reminder that true good fortune and happiness were found in spiritual, everlasting values. There was plainly no place in such a scheme for Satan.

And because the Quakers subscribed to no personification or symbolization of evil, the local folk devil was denied an abode on lands settled and farmed by the Society of Friends. In such circumstances, it was no doubt difficult for members of other cultures to persist in what had obviously become a childish fantasy – a horned, hoofed, and winged nightmare AWOL from the realm of the Brothers Grimm. How could anyone face their Quaker neighbors the morning after, when one's whole family was seen in the pale moonlight chasing what was thought to be the devil with rakes, brooms, and dogs across the rolling red earth? How embarrassing! Belief in a tangible and touchable creature of evil looked as if it had withered away … at least in some areas and among some people.

Separation from the World

Something similar occurred on the northern side of the county, an area drained not by the Neshaminy but by the Perkiomen Creek. The muddy waters of the Perkiomen flow toward the Schuylkill, and then into the Delaware. But here, in its uppermost reaches, the Perkiomen and its tributaries (Stony Run, the Unami and Indian Creeks) drain the surplus waters of one quarter of Bucks County. The East Branch of the Perkiomen actually has a source less than half a mile from the headwaters of the Neshaminy Creek. And like the Neshaminy, the Perkiomen became the avenue of in-migration for another "plain people" – not English Quakers, but "plain people" of German origin: Schwenkfelders, Dunkards (Church of the Brethren),[44] and most especially Mennonites. Today, the Perkiomen Creek – Indian Valley (in Milford, West Rockhill, and Hilltown Townships) is still referred to as part of the "Mennonite Corridor."

The Mennonites were part of the European Anabaptist movement during the 16th century. Because they rejected infant baptism and because of beliefs in pacifism and nonviolent resistance, they were relentlessly persecuted and executed ... by drowning, burning at the stake, and other means. They were discriminated against in the South German Palatinate and banished from Switzerland for heresy and treason. Naturally, they eagerly responded to William Penn's solicitation of settlers for his new and religiously-tolerant colony in the New World. Eventually, most of the European Mennonite congregation immigrated to the Philadelphia area. Beginning in 1683 Dutch Mennonites arrived in Germantown along the banks of the Schuylkill River's Wissahickon Creek. Mennonites of Swiss origin reached the area in 1707, while a mass exodus from the Palatinate occurred just two years later. At one point there were said to be 13,000 people on the London docks waiting to leave. From their Germantown nucleus, families moved up the Perkiomen Creek and had by 1720 settled the "German Townships" (Salford, Franconia, and Frederick). Advancing up the "Mennonite Corridor" into

---

[44]The Church of the Brethren was organized in Westphalia, Germany in 1708 and the first migrants arrived in Pennsylvania (Germantown) in 1719. The church in Europe disintegrated and more migrants came to Pennsylvania in the 1720s-30s. More puritanical than the Mennonite faith, the Church of the River Brethren originally located along the Susquehanna in 1770 where they were said to practice baptism by immersion. Later, churches were established in the Bucks-Montgomery area (at Souderton, Silverdale, Graterford, and Stowe).

Bucks County, congregations were formed and meetinghouses and schoolhouses built between the 1730s-50s. The Mennonite settling ground encompassed a zone from Line Lexington to Rockhill and Milford, and from Blooming Glen to Deep Run and Springfield (See Fig.4.1 map).

Here, sequestered from "all the evil and sin which Satan had planted in the world,"[45] they prayed and farmed, dressed in their own way, and practiced beliefs all their own. The use of the German language furthermore "provided a way to promote separation from evil ... a core Anabaptist value."[46] C. Henry Smith in his *Mennonites in History* says that "(the) most they dared ask was simply to be left alone. This conviction became a part of their very being."[47]

The upper townships of Bucks (and nearby Montgomery) provided the dispossessed Mennonite community a place where they could finally put down roots in a near-cloistered agrarian sanctuary that provided both safety and apartness from the many distractions of the world. Here, this close-knit community would be able to live and work in the same place for generations to come. They developed an everyday spirituality based both on scripture and the geography of place, a place secure from public notice that allowed the community to quietly prosper. And prosper they did, in ways and to a degree beyond the other "plain" people. Their modesty and humility did however discourage boastful claims or comparisons.[48]

This "quiet and peaceable life," as described by the Mennonite minister and historian John Ruth, centered on the farmstead and the

---

[45] Rudy Baergen, *The Mennonite Story*, 1981, p.24.

[46] Dawn Ruth Nelson, "Becoming ..." p. 23, *MHEP Quarterly*, Spring, 2009, Volume 12, #1.

[47] C. Henry Smith, *Mennonites in History*, 1907, p. 40-41.

[48] Charlotte Stryker Pervy, *The Bucks County Scrapbook of Old Roads and Towns*, 1948. The author reminds us that the earliest county histories were written by Quakers and naturally focused on the contributions of that community, especially in lower Bucks. The achievements of the upcounty German Lutheran "church people" and the Mennonite "plain people" are sketchily and rather vaguely alluded to, if at all (p. 47).

meetinghouse. An almost sacred attachment to and harmonious relationship with this good, God-given land was a tenet of Mennonite belief. Their sprawling, multi-generational farmhouses reflected a permanence, a commitment to stay ... a commitment perhaps lacking among their more footloose neighbors. Again, John Ruth: "Land and people are always linked in the plain people's mentality ... The condition of the land reflects the character of the people."[49] "Bending low" to work the land and soil and developing a communion with nature were values and practices that set apart not only these world-forsaking people, but this part of Bucks County as well.

Perhaps the most visible expression of the Mennonite culture region was the serviceable and simple meetinghouses, "glorious in their primitive purity." [50] The original log meetinghouses were soon replaced with structures built of sawnwood and/or fieldstone: These buildings, which were of a simple, dignified, architectural design ... are of a severely plain appearance, wholly unadorned. There are not steeples, bells, stained glass windows, or needless ornamentations."[51]

In these stark meetinghouses Old World songs were sung from hymnals ("little tune books") whose fly leafs were often decorated with *"fraktur"* – "a tradition of ornamental calligraphy as old as the Middle Ages" (John Ruth). Bright colors and flourishes were used along with unthreatening images of birds, hearts, and flowers – but never devils or their demon imps. It would appear that such lowly beasts were yet another "needless ornamentation," neither to be feared nor brooded over for very long.

---

[49] John L. Ruth, *A Quiet and Peaceable Life*, 1979, p.56.
[50] D.H. Bender, Introduction (p.8) to C. Henry Smith, *Mennonites in History*, 1907.
[51] Douglas Wenger, p.34-35. Schwenkfelders, Who Were They?

Fig. 4.4 "Plain" Houses of Worship (Top): Wrightstown
Friends Meeting, Arnold Bros. Postcard #7 (circa 1906). (Bottom): Line
Lexington Mennonite Church, Postcard view (1907).

Here in "God's country," the German Lutheran and reformed "church people" harbored more of the Old World superstitions and fears than the "plain people" did; according to Charlotte Stryker Pervy:[52]

> ... (The) church people had retained the old culture rooted in the medieval past which the plain people had rejected along with the world, the devil, and the flesh. With the church people came the arts and crafts, the legends, folkways, and festivals ... the cards, wands and witches, the stories, songs and legends, even the drinking and swearing ...

It's not that the plain people didn't believe in the devil – they did. From an old German hymn sung by the Mennonites: "Consider the anxiety and pain of hell. That Satan not dazzle your eyes with vanity."[53] In Mennonite folklore the oafish but lovable farmer spars with the devil who seeks his soul – but as dimwitted as the farmer is, he usually manages to defeat or at least frustrate the devil.[54] Paul Miller, a Pennsylvania-raised Mennonite pastor, points out that devils and demons don't even appear in the Mennonite Encyclopedia, that they're treated "very lightly if at all." The evil one is greatly diminished in his powers of seduction and harassment. "No Trespassing" signs "... are set against him at every doorway" and when working the fields, he deserves and receives no more than a "quick side wise glance."[55] At least in this part of Bucks County the Kingdom of God clearly controlled the destiny of man, livestock, and crops. Satan was reduced to a pathetic and impotent schemer, a whipped dog skulking behind every bush and rock in the Indian Valley. He was beaten by the power of Christ's sacrifice on the cross. He was defeated by the power of goodness ("*Do not let evil conquer you, but use good to defeat evil*" – 12 Romans). This rebel son (or

---

[52]Charlotte Stryker Pervy, op.cit., p. 49-50.

[53] Caleb Franks, "Spirituality ..." *MHEP Quarterly,* Spring 2009, Volume 12, #1, p. 30.

[54] Adam Kirchhoff collected from residents at a local Mennonite nursing home. "Eileschpijjel" (spelled variously) was the not-too-bright comic bumpkin brought over from the German Rhineland. *Pennsylvania German Legends,* www.kutztown.edu/academics/liberal_arts/anthropology/legend.

[55] Paul M. Miller, *The Devil Did Not Make Me Do It,* 1977, p.20 ... 34.

"naughty boy") is best left to ply his evil ways in (some) far-country pigpen of misery."[56] Not in this domain!

Still other "plain people" settled near the northwestern corner (Milford Township) of Bucks County. These were the Schwenkfelders. Small in number, they were (are) like the Mennonites and Quakers in ways – good farmers who believed in simplicity in dress and in manners and who opposed all war and oath-taking. They too frowned upon outward displays of religion (incense, rituals, and ceremony), preferring a more inner-directed spiritual world and unadorned churches. They were followers of Caspar Schwenckfeld (1489-1561), a preacher, radical reformer, and nobleman who clashed with both the Catholic Church and with Martin Luther over doctrinal issues (including baptism, communion, and the Last Supper). Despite protections given them in Saxony and Silesia (Prussia), Schwenckfeld and his followers were persecuted as heretics and chased as "outlaws" all across Europe by the Jesuits. Luther accused Schwenckfeld of being the "bond servant" of the devil.[57]

Much of the Schwenkfelder community from southern Germany migrated to Pennsylvania in the 1730s. The first group of families arrived in Philadelphia in 1731, with the largest contingent of 180 people (forty families) arriving in 1734. These farmers and craftsmen followed the trail of Mennonite migration up the Skippack and Perkiomen Creeks, occupying the area (the "Goschenhoppen" or "upper district") generally north and west of the Indian Valley. They pushed up the Macoby and Hosensack Creeks into the Upper Perkiomen Valley (to Red Hill, Pennsburg, East Greenville and Palm), just miles from the Bucks County border. From here, they fanned out to the north into Berks and Lehigh Counties (today's Route 29 corridor). Given the dispersed nature of Schwenkfelder settlement and the proximity to Bucks County, it would appear that despite there being no meetinghouse in Bucks, at least some Schwenkfelder (perhaps through intermarriage) did in fact live and farm in the upper end of the county. This was especially true in the

---

[56] Miller, op.cit., 33.
[57] Wenger, op.cit., 82

more isolated hill and valley terrain of Milford Township (e.g. Zion Hill, Spinnerstown, Geryville, and Mumbaurersville).

H. W. Kriebel (*The Schwenkfelders in Pennsylvania*) describes the group's offer in 1734 to buy two thousand acres of farmland in Perkasie Manor (near Chalfont) as a site for their community, but says that "For some reason no sale was made ... because the people (already there) did not wish them to settle there."[58] Kriebel comments that the Schwenkfelders were thus spared "the barbaric cruelty of the revengeful Indian" in the Indian Valley. No available tract of land was found for a community settlement and the Schwenkfelders spread out buying parcels of land here and there in nearby Montgomery, Berks and Lehigh Counties. Here, they and their ancestors "toiled and triumphed in their toil,"[59] becoming weavers and linen makers, wheelwrights and carpenters, millers and distillers (that "mischievous applejack"). In their near history and nearby geography, the Schwenkfelders sought out and found an upright and pious life lived in "the quiet of the land,"[60] just beyond the borders of Bucks County. The Schwenkfelders (a.k.a. "Confessors of the Glory of Christ") numbered about 4,000 at the time of Schwenckfeld's death; 1,800 plus in the1930s; and today have about 3,000 in six congregations in Southeastern Pennsylvania. The Schwenkfelder Library and Heritage Center is located in Pennsburg, just one and a half miles from the Bucks County border.

For centuries and from the British Isles to the Rhineland to Pennsylvania, the old folk devil had worked overtime to insert himself into peoples' daily lives. He thought that he had found an amenable home on the Triassic lands of Bucks County. But now, these plain and gentle farmers had invoked God and his good angels to undermine his credibility. To some, he was nothing but a defeated and powerless imp; to others, he didn't even exist. Not only was his reputation as a folk devil sullied, he was spiritually defrocked. And it all happened so quickly too. He felt like the horror movie corpse just released from a thousand

---

[58] Howard W. Kriebel, *The Schwenkfelders in Pennsylvania*, 1904, p.41.
[59] Kriebel, op cit.p.53.
[60] Kriebel, op cit.p.133.

year curse, decomposing in sixty seconds of melting flesh and crumbling bone in the last few minutes of the film. Investigators would stare with open-mouthed amazement as the creature became a tiny pile of powdery ash. Who needed that. Old World Celtic and Teutonic demonology was now stashed away and forgotten in the attics of the old stone farmhouses. And a time would come when people wouldn't even remember why porch ceilings were once painted blue. What was a poor devil to do?

CHAPTER 5
GRAVEYARD STORY

But ah, How many who once loved along thy shores to roam, Now sleep beneath the graveyard sod, Lain in their final home.

They have gone their short space, they have lived their short day; As a tale that is told they have vanished away.

– Nathan Ely, a "humble Farmer" quoted in an 1850 reminiscence of Cuttalossa Creek, Solebury Township, Bucks County Historical Society, *A Collection of Papers*

It is autumn with all the world, and the stars weep to see it.

– Lord Dunsany, *The Lonely Idol* (1915)

Fig. 5.1 Upcounty, Deep in Thought

This is a sad chapter. Sad, not because it's about graveyards. That might make it melancholy, but not necessarily sad. It's sad because it's about endings … about death and departing and the softly-played violin strains of loneliness. In other words, it's all about life as it was once lived on the Triassic lands in Bucks County.

He was alone. In a sense, of course, he had been alone for all these thousands of years. No one talked with him – and rightly so. But he felt it now more than ever. It was a terrible, profound loneliness, like being utterly alone in the Times Square' crowd when it rang in the New Year. It was a ringing-in-the-ear quiet loneliness that a shopping mall might have at 3 a.m. That's how he felt because he knew that his time in Bucks was almost up. It had been sixty-six autumns and six months since his arrival here. His shopping for souls, here at least, was done. His fun was at an end. He felt like the last Triassic dinosaur.

He also felt very alone now because he was about to leave again. He had been a long time coming to this place. He actually liked Bucks County (indeed, most people did!) and had in fact come to regard it as a comfortable-enough home for all these years. Yet, there was much that remained to be done, but not here. Soon he would be gone, gone with the Indian ghosts and gypsy winds, gone with the passenger pigeons and eight-square schoolhouses. Just plain gone.

He was alone here … in the graveyard. He was upcounty on the German settling ground; amid a tangle of briars and weeds, he was deep in thought, thinking about how westward he should go. He was leaning against a gray granular stone carved in memory of – *"Zum Andenken"* – someone born in Bavaria who had come to rest here in the red Triassic soil of America. All around him, the wind-blown leaves of early autumn danced between the rows of tilting, rotting, and sinking tombstones. They danced around his heels and hooves, taunting him in their excited urgency to be gone. No exorcism was even necessary.

The old folk devil loved graveyards and frequented these places regularly. Old country bone orchards and small family burying grounds down dead-end lanes were his favorites. And the more neglected and forsaken the better. He loved such places not because of any morbid fascination with death or any ghoulish twist of mind. Some thought that he favored them because it was, after all, the devil's mission to make all the world one universal graveyard whose lifeless peace he broke with an awful shriek of triumph. Not quite. Someone once claimed that he liked them because the cold graveyard mud was "the stopper of hell" with the demons of the sulfurous fire pit cavorting just below the decaying bones and boxes. Rather, he was actually a devout student of graveyards and their tombstones because of what they could teach him about people and places. The mawkish sentiments amused him. The exaggerated, retroactive virtuosity of the epitaphs fascinated him. The inscriptions informed him as to peoples' attitudes about life and about him, along with their hidden fears and aspirations.

He was also fascinated by the genealogical couplings and geographical comings and goings. This latter touched an emotional chord in him. He identified with the impermanence, the transient wanderlust that drove people on in their (of course) futile search for an earthly paradise. Old deeds confirm property transfers every five years or so. And still, he thought, this society had the nerve to mythologize the family farmstead and the old home town as if it were anything but ephemeral. Why, they never stayed put long enough to even tend to their graveyards or care about who was buried where. The old settlers were laid to a silent and moldering sleep, their labors done and their houses and families raised. And forgotten. The living moved on. He realized that he had learned much about the county and its people from these sandstone, slate, and granite "open books," these data banks of personal history. The verse was often lousy, but the rest was pretty informative.

The Interview

The year 1886 was three-quarters gone. Autumn had returned, and with it an autumnal air, an air of melancholy and departure. He was alone in the graveyard reading and thinking about the graven sentiments and sayings of another time. It was here on a late September afternoon that the reporter from the *Doylestown Democrat* encountered him. And it was here that the last interview took place. It would be his last appearance here in Bucks County.

"Well, Old Scratch," began the reporter as he whipped out pencil and pad. "Rumor has it that you may be leaving this fine county ... could that be true? And if so, where would you be headed? My editor and our readers are always interested in your latest doings."

There in the twilight world of the graveyard where different worlds met, where long-dead county residents listened in from beneath the silent dust, his Satanic Majesty found himself in a noticeably agreeable and reflective mood. He seemed old and weary, as old as the world and just as weary ... but ready to explain:

"Let me come at it indirectly. Look at it this way: the earliest settlers who lived in Bucks died poor; they were hard-working farmers. So, when they died, they buried each other in a corner of the family farm, in a field out back and under a tree, or maybe in some small patch of common ground if a hamlet or village was nearby. Most despicably, perhaps consecrated church ground was used. There wasn't time for ritual or fanfare, and there really wasn't the money to pay for the stone carver's skill to create design work or fancy inscriptions. In most graveyards you still see these very early stones, really just roughly shaped chunks of native rock plucked right out of the ground, chiseled not very neatly or legibly with only initials and dates: 'E.B., Ag. 17, 1721.' Or 'S.L., Nov. 1770.' Homemade stones like these are now badly weathered and discolored, and downright unreadable. Sad! We'll never know whose life they commemorate. Sadder still, we'll never know where most of the old settlers are even buried; their crude headstones are completely gone. Have you ever wondered about that? You see, the numbers just don't add up. Far more people died here than seem to be buried here. Their gravesites are long since forgotten and lost. Too much coming and going. Families move away and the farms are sold and resold. I've noticed that sometimes the headstones are removed and reused for making stone walls or walkways, and the burial sites plowed under. Nothing's sacred. You see, nothing's permanent. The monumental works of man yield to the territorially ambitious, ever encroaching farmer's plow (and at a much later date bank buildings, pharmacies, and gas stations). One would think that if not the fear, then at least the sanctity of death would deter people from churning up other people's remains to grow bushels of wheat and bales of hay. But no. Maybe it's a vestigial aspect of their tribal ways and days in Europe. Like Celtic warriors, they make light of death.

Look all around you. Wherever you look, you see life, but you really see death, past life recycled through the power of decay and re-birth. Where are all the people who lived, died, and then were buried here over the past two hundred years? They're in the grain you eat to keep from being hungry and in the wood you burn to keep from being cold. 'All flesh is grass,' isn't that what a poet once said? Death sustains life; or as the Buddhists say, 'The cause of life ... is death!' Remove these cracked and chipped old tombstones, allow the graveyards weath-ered old walls to crumble, and what's buried within is quickly reclaimed by nature. A farmer over in Wrightstown once pulled up all the tomb-stones in an old graveyard and along with the surrounding wall had the stone rubble hauled away with the rubbish. Later, he plowed over the graveyard acres and planted grain, but his family would never eat the bread made from the grain grown in that field. No wonder! (No Wonder Bread, either).

But I digress. Professional stone carvers eventually made their services available locally and the stones were machine-cut and shaped; the local slate rocks and sandstones lost appeal to the finer granites and marbles hauled in by train from elsewhere. Later, people were able to spend a bit more money to have biblical citations and homey rhymes carefully lined on the stones. Still, the numbers don't add up. A genera-tion or two goes by and who cares? The broken and tumbled stones are pulled from the earth like so many decayed teeth and left to rot, thrown in a heap beneath a tree, left to disintegrate beneath layers of moldy leaves through seasons and years of rain and frost. Devils have strong feelings about things like this too. God and his angels have no monopoly on the idea of death, the afterlife, and its earthly symbols. Remember

PENNSBURY

P. P.
1660-1696

ROUGH FIELDSTONES

LOWER
SOUTHAMPTON

NOVEMBER
1770

BEDMINSTER

NEW HOPE

IN
Memory of
MARY VANSANT
who died
Feb 5ᵗʰ 1926

J.A.R.

PRE-CIVIL WAR
SIMPLE SLAB STONES

PERKASIE

REVOLUTIONARY WAR
SOLDIERS

Hier ruhet in Gott
Jacob Stout

UPPER
MAKEFIELD

To yᵉ Memory of Capt
James Moore of ye ney
York Artillery, So
e Cornelia
ew York he
m yᵉ 26 A.D
e 24 Years

ABRAHAM
was Bor
1740 a
77:5
Aged
and

MOTHER

WEST
ROCKHILL

ROMANTIC
PERIOD

SARAH
Wife of
WM R.DUAH
DIED DEC.3 1870
IN THE 44ᵗʰ YEAR
OF HER AGE

OUR EMMA

Born March 17,1874
Died Aug. 27,1875

WRIGHTSTOWN

LOWER BUCKS

ROB

NEWTOWN
FRIENDS

Born 9th Mo. 4th 1802
Died 7th Mo. 20th 1974

Fig. 5.2 Bucks County
Tombstones

that half the people buried in these graveyards are mine. Well, maybe not quite half, but they do call these places 'God's Acre' and 'Hell's Half-Acre.' So, I can claim at least one-third.

Bucks County settlers could have learned much from the New England Puritans and the very imagery of death in a folk world. It is pleasing to see the seriousness that New Englanders brought to their 'little cities of the dead.' The acres of gray stone chiseled with skulls and crossbones, the grim reaper with scythe in hands, frightening demons and puffy imps carrying the darts of death, picks and shovels, haunting moon faces vacantly staring from their coffins, death with a laurel wreath triumphantly extinguishing the candle flame of life. Great symbols. Great stuff. An art form in itself. A region's folk art. But even more than that, it reflects how the Puritans felt about death, the devil, and the hereafter. For them, death was a descent into hellfire and brimstone, or at best, a not much better journey into the hands of an angry God. The portal-shaped tombstones were their individual doorways into the terrifying and not at all predictable shadow world beyond the grave. The searing epitaphs and gruesome pictographs were in perfect agreement with their folk beliefs and stern theology.

But their very best and most popular visual device, perhaps what better than anything else expressed the age-old folk fears, was the 'death's head'; these soul effigies were horrifying, wide-eyed and winged skulls and shriveled heads whose empty eye sockets gazed directly out from the cold stone; the message: life is indeed transitory. Rows of skeletal teeth or fossilized frowns that don't have to say it but did: 'Time flies, look at me and remember that you're next, pal.' (In case the stark hollow-eyed motifs didn't convey the message unequivocally enough, epitaphs were added that did: 'As you are now, so once was I, And as I am now, you soon will be'; 'While living men my tomb do view, Remember well – room here there is for you'). Carried to snowy hillsides and sleepy hollows by hearses pulled by horses draped in robes embroidered with these angry, earthy yet ethereal images, generations of New Englanders were buried with their feet to the east, to the rising sun that etched the crisply-carved blank stone faces in shadow and light.

I mention all of this for two reasons. First, some of this tombstone imagery did filter down into the Delaware Valley, and even into Bucks. It came as part of the great, perpetually westward moving wave of Yankee people and culture that swept across Long Island Sound, the Hudson Valley and Highlands, and the Jersey flatlands. Arriving on this side of the Delaware, it was naturally watered down by time and distance and, in the case with gravestone art, lacked any fiery theological underpinning. The portal-shaped stones were perpetuated by second and third generation New Englanders because it was customary or traditional. Death's heads, well, you find a few of these on the Jersey side of the river, but fewer still in Bucks. And even these are more cherubic than grisly. While practically whole villages of land-hungry Yankees transplanted themselves to Bucks, their Puritan faith had lost its hellfire appeal and, besides, the local plain folks would have none of it. Despite the great theological similarities between the two sects, and the fact that they were both highly anti-art in most any form, the Puritans did give themselves over to the expression of their feelings through these icy and graphic mortality symbols. By contrast, the Quaker graveyard can be a very plain place. Whether down upon the outwash plain at Bristol or Falls meeting, or up on the Triassic lands at Newtown or Wrightstown meeting, they're all the same from place to place, from stone to stone: acres of neat, unostentatious, unadorned white sugar cube blocks that virtually disappear beneath a good snowfall, becoming a sea of equal-sized swells on an ocean of white. It's actually quite to be expected of a plain, egalitarian people. The levelling process of Quaker life is reflected in all the level stones. No disrespect intended, but not very fertile ground for a folk devil.

Secondly, you must realize that this is why I left New England (Here, the devil plays down the fact that he was actually booted out). The fear of hell had dulled and a belief in witches and devils had eroded along with both the social and moral power of the Puritan ministry. Hellfire had faded in the light of reason and the fear of hell itself had ebbed. The ghastly tombstone imagery of a rural, yeoman people was likewise replaced by pleasant, artful designs that disarmed both death and hell of any meaning. To me, this was awful. These new styles expressed nothing of the ancient fears of death and the otherworld that should have been there; but this was what the new mercantile class, influenced by things like neoclassicism and romanticism, wanted: decorative funerary urns and willow trees, scrollwork and architectural filigrees, the so-called tree of life and palm branch of victory. Meaningless! Entirely inappropriate! But what can you do? Styles change. I spent my very last years in New England in the granite hills, in the backwaters of Vermont and western Massachusetts where the old ways lingered somewhat longer. But eventually, even there, the hourglasses and death's heads yielded to the willow trees and urns. Graveyards became 'cemeteries'. Prettified places to stroll and even picnic in.

When I came to Bucks I found rather earthy folk beliefs still in place and a more fitting graveyard symbolism still going strong, at least among many of the German farm people here in the upper county. Not only did they believe in me, but on their stones their anonymous carvers chiseled hex signs, the open bible, wishbones, and zodiac signs like waning moons. If you want to find skulls and crossbones, and winged death's heads, you have to look to the red shales and sandstones in the German family graveyards. They even covered their quilts, butter molds, storage chests, and church windows with these same ancient folk symbols. And when they used tulips, lilies, birds, hearts, swastikas, and other mystic symbols from pre-Christian times, even they conveyed an ice water feeling that's anything but airy and romantic. My moods, my mission, my credibility, were all confirmed by their stone carvers and artisans. That's why I frequent places like this. It gives me consolation to know that such symbols and words fall on dead *herrs*.

But now, I see changes even here. Tombstone art is a dying art form. Nobody bothers much with images or designs at all nowadays. Teutonic fears and symbols are fast disappearing. Oh, up here most of them still speak the German language and the local papers still publish in German, you know that. But just look at the way they Americanize or Anglicize their family names; from one row of stones to the next, from one generation to the next, you can see it in how they want posterity to remember them.

Why do they discard the names they were born with? Why do they, here in the most solemn place of all, throw away the names their grandparents proudly carried across the ocean? Yes, greater acceptance into the American mainstream, I guess. So, they adopt shorter, more pronounceable, more easily-spelt English-sounding names. A loathing of things foreign and a desire now to be more 'American'. This is all understandable in a century in which nationalism has been such an important theme. But something is lost in the translation, don't you agree? That same something is lost when the stone carvers begin to inscribe the vital data and epitaphs in English rather than German. And it all bespeaks a larger sense of loss and change – a folk society, a farming region, a devil's sanctuary all falling apart like the old Germans themselves six feet down in their wooden coffins.

Fig.5.3 Anglicization of German Family Names

"It's all very fascinating" said the reporter, "but about yourself, that's what I'm here to find out." The devil replied, "Ah, but if you were listening attentively, it is all about myself (it usually was) and why I feel a need to leave. Let me spell it out more clearly then:

"Look, part of it's the plain people and the temperance people and others who either don't believe I exist or don't appreciate my being here. Because of this, Bucks is no longer any fun, and may never, ever be again. But it's more than this. I'm a folk devil and I do well in folk societies, rural areas where people are more in touch with raw nature – with me and my elements, the mud and dung, the seasons, the wind and lightning, and all that. It's a nice tribute when people speak of dust as 'devil's snow', and when they refer to those deceptive patches of sunshine during stormy weather as the 'devil's smile'. It shows that they believe in me. I tell you though, this place, this Bucks, is fast losing its pre-industrial innocence; technology, commerce, industry, railroads and trolley lines, and the cities are too close now. The feeling of the modern is everywhere. But people are losing touch with the real things, with their folkways, getting themselves walled off from their own land by a giant technological screen that is slipping between them and nature. They think that this is all for the better, that it makes them comfortable, warm, safe, and secure . . .

But you realize, it doesn't!! Worse, it robs people of their passion, their animal lust; they forget how to be sinfully initiative and inventive. It's become all too bland and civilized here. Too much emphasis on decorum, restraint, formality, regimentation of lifestyles. Too calm and too decent for an indecent old devil like me. I tell you, I'm heading west to where there's more excitement and violence. Just look at the nastiness and basic human rottenness in Chicago this past spring – anarchism and hysteria, labor unrest, police battling rioters, strikers getting shot, bombs flying through the air, people getting hung and committing suicide in jail cells. I tell you, that's for me. That's fertile, feral ground. They'll do even better with me out there!"

Towards the end of the interview, his words became tinged with bitterness and sadness, and were whispered so low it was difficult for the reporter to hear his words. What he did hear was this: "What joy have I won through my evil designs? What peace in my soul-wrecking plans? ... (I) have won nothing more than man."[61]

Late September:
The Story is Reported
... and the Road Beckons

So, on that late September day in 1886 the reporter filed his story and it appeared in the Tuesday, September 28th edition of *The Doylestown Democrat*. It ran as a lengthy article in the local affairs column on page one: THE DEVIL LEAVING BUCKS. It was sandwiched in between the news that little Enos Hunsberger died of malignant diphtheria at the age of twelve, and that a local judge was beginning a long business trip to Central America. The judge would be away from three months to several years. One wonders what little Enos did to die after only twelve summers of life, and what the local judge had going in Central America. There are, of course, no answers.

In that same issue it was also reported that the people of Newfoundland were starving because both the crops and the fisheries had failed. It was also reported that the dimensions of heaven had been figured out by a contributing reader (there were 496 zillion cubic feet ... definitely not news to the devil). Other things were reported too: that "sick varmints" had raided several local chicken coops and hen houses; that a "pursuing party" of six muscular men with six-shooters and double-barreled shotguns were combing the countryside in search of horse thieves; that the temperance people were offering a fifty dollar gold piece for the best specimen of a drunkard to be lassoed and brought in; that loathsome afflictions like rheumatism, cholera, runny pink eye, piles, and catarrh could be made better by using Dr. Wright's Speedy

---

[61] As later quoted in the Rev. W.S. Harris, *Sermons by the Devil*, 1904, p. 303.

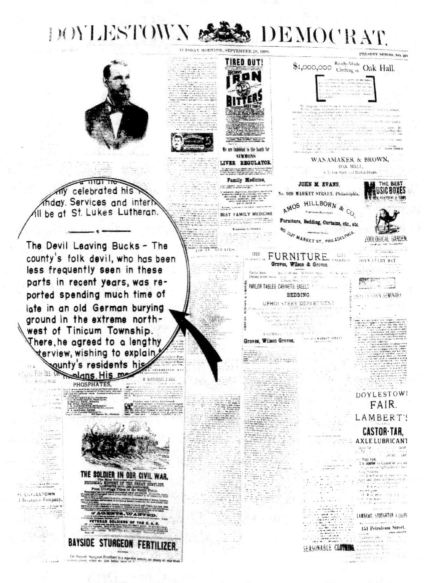

The newspaper clipping reads, in part:

...ny celebrated his ...hday. Services and interi ...ll be at St. Lukes Lutheran.

The Devil Leaving Bucks – The county's folk devil, who has been less frequently seen in these parts in recent years, was reported spending much time of late in an old German burying ground in the extreme northwest of Tinicum Township. There, he agreed to a lengthy ...terview, wishing to explain ...ounty's residents his ...plans. His m...

Fig. 5.4 The Story is Reported (September 28th, 1886)

Cure. Ayer's Sarsaparilla, Spencer's Cornicura, and Ely's Cream Balm. "Early Decay and Loss of Manhood" could be remedied with the use of a discovery made by a South American missionary. And, as described by the newspaper, William White had imprisoned two large snakes inside a glass cage, and called them "his pets." That was quite enough. The devil didn't want to know anymore. He was leaving.

No comfy brimstone bed that night for the devil. The night of the interview he curled up in the rotted-out hollow of an ancient log not far from the Devil's Half-Acre. It was actually the skeleton of a log in whose shade William Penn himself might have stolen an afternoon nap. The devil slept among the squirrels, while worms burrowed in the acidic soil beneath the possibly historical log. A rather large colony of purple martins slept in old woodpecker holes. This too would be their last night in Bucks; in the morning, they would soar into the air and wheel towards South America. For one last night, the devil felt very close to the earth, the good Triassic earth of Bucks. Tongues of St. Elmo's Fire streamed from the brushwood earth and danced in the fields around him. This, the portent of a long journey.

He dreamed whatever devils dream: It was only right to again move; he was simply fulfilling the biblical mission assigned to him in the Book of Job: "Roaming the earth and patrolling it ... going to and fro in the earth and walking up and down in it." In a few years, he thought, the story of his presence here would be related only by the oldest inhabitants. He even doubted whether posterity would be convinced that such a devil as he had ever existed. Like the vanishing graves, all memory of his sojourn would be gone. Even the Durham Cave, for all its great size and beauty, would be gone as the cave itself disappeared little by little.

He dreamed of popes. In Rome, Leo XIII was writing a treatise explaining how to exorcise the devil. No need for that he thought; devils get tired of living in the same place or body for too long and just up and leave of their own accord. In his foreknowledge of the world to be, it rankled him that a pope (John Paul II) would one day proclaim St. Francis the "Patron of the Environment" and that another future pope would dare call himself Pope Francis. Not that he had anything personal against the good saint: in fact, they both loved solitary caves. Both harbored something of a mystic, pagan passion for nature. They had spent many a Michaelmas Day together on a mountaintop where the devil tormented the steadfast saint with all his wicked machinations. But now he fumed because he knew that nobody, not even Francis, was closer to nature than he. Nobody was more in tune with the primal forces, the antediluvian elements of muck and mud than he. He was the earth, the "Prince of this Earth." That night the old folk devil nestled among the squirrels and worms, coffined in decomposing wood. He felt cheated. He felt bad, lower than a snake's chin.

The cheerless morning of September 29th was greeted by cloudy skies and chilly winds. It was again Michaelmas Day in the Old World, a tradition that had little meaning here. It was the day commemorating the Archangel Michael's celestial victory over the Prince of Darkness. In the words of the English Prayer Book, it celebrated the banishment from heaven of the dragon, "that old serpent, called the devil and Satan, which deceiveth the whole world." Festivals and town processions were held in the few places where the deep-rooted observances of the medieval church still survived. The goose was stuffed and cakes were baked. He thought this a fitting enough day for a devil to be gone.

In his vagabond boots and with the wind to his back, he walked across the county, up and down the undulating dirt roads. The feel of an early autumn was definitely in the air. Through the small attic windows of the stone farmhouses he could see summer dresses and straw hats being put into Saratoga trunks; winter flannels were being brought out. And in the fields, the yellow of corn rows and goldenrod had already yielded to the tan of wigwam corn stalks. Orange mounds of pumpkins filled the fields. The roads were busy with buckboards loaded with winter coal and with apples; drivers made their way to the white oak cider presses. Men on porches cleaned squirrel guns and wives in kitchens boiled apple butter and baked rabbit hot-pie. Some sipped apple whiskey. Everyone appeared occupied and no one really paid much heed to the old man in black hoofing his way west. He was no stranger to them, but they didn't have time for him anymore. Scarecrows stood woodenly in the fields, but it was no longer the season for "Christianity's scarecrow." He had outlived his stay and had become as desirable as a barroom clock.

The autumn sky sported V-formations of geese and blackbirds, winging their way south through the heady aromas of clove, cinnamon, and sassafras wafting up from the farmhouse kitchens. He remembered that once the sky was dark with crows until the county treasurer offered to pay three cents apiece for every "crow-scalp" brought to the county seat. He noticed though that there was something else no longer seen or heard. Years before, when he first came to Bucks, the noonday sky would be darkened for hours by literally billions of strong and swift-flying birds – like the roar of a thousand threshing machines, "feathered lightning" or a "living wind" as Aldo Leopold would later describe it. It was the immense and endless flocks of passenger pigeons, once the most prolific of all American birds. Horse teams became frightened by the sound of the flock and grown men stood in awe. Food being scarce in the early years of settlement, great quantities of these pigeons – sent by "the providence of God" – were shot. After all, they (along with the wild turkeys) were boldly and hungrily devouring the seeds the farmers had planted. Farmers organized massive "shoot-offs;" they shot-gunned tens of thousands of these migratory doves in minutes. Their tasty little bodies of iridescent blue were packed in barrels, shipped in railroad box-cars, and sold (at twenty-five cents a dozen) to posh New York restaurants to make the savory delicacy called "pigeon hot-pie." ("He that advances near with one good shot, may kill enough to fill both spit and pot"). The spread of towns and farms and the retreat of woods deprived the birds of their very habitat and food, the beechnut. Their beechnut diet was no longer possible in a world without beechnut trees. When the last one was gone,[62] when greed, cruelty, and indifference had had their day, people wondered where the birds went. The local folks protested. "Who? Us? We didn't do anything!" It was reported that a great wave

---

[62] The last passenger pigeon in Pennsylvania was reportedly shot and killed on October 2, 1895. (as cited in The Auk, January, 1918, Volume 35, #1, p.96).

of remorse swept over the land. A committee of naturalists even offered a five thousand dollar reward to anyone who could find a living passenger pigeon. But it was too late.

The devil felt strangely akin to these about-to-vanish birds, birds whose presence was said to presage "some evil." Now, both they and he had become fading bits of wildness in a land being stripped of danger and mystery.

Far into the future, a mock tombstone would be erected to the memory of the passenger pigeon at the Bronx Zoo's "Animal Graveyard." That, he really didn't need. And, in that future time, one of the area's last passenger pigeons would be stuffed, its body wired, and its eyes replaced with cotton balls. Eternity's cotton balls stare at uncomprehending visitors from the inside of a dirty, finger-smudged glass case at a local museum. That, the devil didn't need either. As the martins drifted south to Brazil, the passenger pigeons drifted ever more faintly to the back of peoples' minds. The devil – to survive – drifted west with the turning of the earth. The north winds began to wail through the browning fields and the soon-to-be naked woods.

He felt like doing some small piece of mischief to mitigate his sadness, and so caused a farmer to be struck in the head (not fatally) by a falling barn beam. Many of the local wells were running dry, and he would of course be blamed for that too. Actually, he had nothing to do with the latter. He felt like uncorking a dramatic parting shot in the couldn't-care-less manner of Rhett Butler: "My dear Bucks, I don't give a damn." But he did. So, he let the very last thing he said to the reporter stand as his advice to the county; with a schoolmarm's wave of a bony index finger, he enigmatically warned that "Time has a way of bringing back what's gone. A far worse evil will take my place; the devil that's seen is better than the devil that ain't."

A traveling medicine man was peddling his cure-all nostrums (the "devil's delusions") from house-to-house that same afternoon; he reported seeing the devil trudging along Windybush Road. This sighting seemed correct. The devil had indeed taken this road and paused at a small roadside graveyard on the wooded shoulder of the road. Here, on a deeply shaded hillside above Dark Hollow Run, he spotted the gravestone of a twenty-three year old man who had died in California, and whose body had been buried out there. But the stone was erected and engraved to his memory … the memory of a restless soul who, like so many millions of others, had joined the great migration to the west. He would forever be remembered here in Bucks. The devil liked the thought of that, and hoped for at least as much.

He was last seen in the gathering dusk, pausing briefly in front of the house with the devil's door-knocker. "You'll miss me much," he mused as he continued on across the heart of the county. He tramped through the railroad cut at Rushland, the damp and earthy smell of the still-wet diabase looming darkly above and alongside of him. And then, his shadowy form was seen reflected only where the rain had puddled between the wooden ties. With the dying of the day, he vanished from Bucks like the wake of a ship … and was seen no more.

Fig. 5.5 Railroad Cut at Rushland

And on April nights daffodils would bloom by the dooryard in the light of the Paschal Moon. Shiny and silver-sided shad would do their death dance in nets of stout linen cord stretched beneath the river's luminescent waters. But in springtimes to come, this fine land would be forever after without its devil. On St. Walpurgis Night when evil beings were abroad and a train of Teutonic deities swept through the sky above these farmlands, the devil would be nowhere in sight. So, not halfway through the story we appear to have lost our main character – or have we? The unforeseen and unexpected make up the life of this world.

Afterwards

Some of what he did and where he went after leaving Bucks can be pieced together from a variety of sources. The news that filtered back was this: he had stayed in the Susquehanna country for a number of years, mixing in warmly and easily with the Pennsylvania "Dutch." There, he was a perfect fit with the cave dragons, phantom horsemen, witches, and other transplanted folklore from the Rhineland and Black Forest. They enticed him to stay by naming places in his honor, but he soon moved on again. He did leave behind many devilish toponyms attached to rock promontories, diabase boulder fields, and gloomy glacial pools and streams.

In 1893 "the old man" was found in a cavern in the woods not far from Chicago. There, he was interviewed by R. Palasco Drant, a traveling reporter for an eastern newspaper. "What a scoop!" said Drant, "I'll interview Satan." That famous interview was eventually published as a book by the Schulte Publishing Company of Chicago under the title *Hell Up To Date*. In it we read that somewhere along the way west the devil had his tail broken in an exciting fight, but as Drant pointed out, it "had been spliced (back on), and, judging from the dexterity with which he handled it, was as good as new." The devil had also picked up a shiny new top hat that he was wearing, and – for some unexplained reason – was buttoning his coat on the wrong side. And, he was now smoking cigarettes which he puffed on beneath a thin, twirly Mr. Magician's mustache. That same year he visited the Columbian Exposition in Chicago where his despicably evil work would later be written about by Erik Larson in *The Devil in the White City* (2003).

After leaving the Midwest, he resurfaced in Montana where many German farmers went to homestead after the Civil War; this made him feel right at home. Here, he rode with vigilante bands in the last great drama of the closing frontier. Galloping across the Triassic redbeds on a great black stallion, his hair and cape flew free in the Montana winds that blew across the graves of Custer's cavalrymen. His teeth grit the dust of the high plains in the dry 1890s. He sported a Remington carbine which now replaced the old six-foot trident left behind in Bucks. His health and spirit were rejuvenated and his allergies were much better. His limp was gone, and he seemed happy.

With the devil gone west, with the county rid of its slandering snake of a folk devil, Bucks – like St. Patrick's Ireland – was placed under an eternally protective eye. In this case, that of the proprietor and founder, William Penn himself. In 1894, though Penn had long since been laid to rest in his Buckinghamshire grave, a thirty-seven-foot tall, 53,000 pound metal replica of him was mounted atop Philadelphia's City Hall. The sculpture was designed by Alexander Calder and was (and still is) the largest stature on any building anywhere in the world. It is also the most visible symbol of the region's Quaker past. From beneath his broad-brimmed Quaker hat, Penn stares out across the center city and into the hazy distance, beyond the acres of rowhouses and through the veil of pollution that ungraciously hangs over northeast Philadelphia. He looks towards the distant *Peaceable Kingdom*, the gently rolling outwash plain and the undulating red ridges and lowlands of Bucks. There, free at last of the evil one, the old settlers lie asleep in silent dust; they rest in "God's Acres."

A Closer Look:
Rushland's "Little Italy"

As this dark-attired stranger was leaving, other "strangers" were just arriving in Bucks County; they were called "the strangers" who came to work and live in a "secret village". Hazel Gover described it this way in the *Bucks County Traveler* magazine in 1954:

> On the Rushland-Wycombe Road (Mill Creek) there is a small settlement known as 'Little Italy' … people have passed the entrance, once a ford, and now a bridge, and wondered what went on among these people who found their way from Italy …

> (February, 1954, p. 10-11)

Though first settled around 1890, it's still labeled "Little Italy" in contemporary street atlases. A group of stone masons and their families arrived from Italy. Temporarily leaving their wives and children in Philadelphia, the men found work at the Rushland quarries, as watchmen on the railroad, and as farm laborers. Eventually, the families came out to Bucks and for a time lived together in tarpaper shacks. To the neighbors' amazement, they planted gardens that thrived in the barren shale. North of Bristol, Bucks' Catholic population had always been small; "papists" were originally excluded from some of the upcounty townships. By the mid-1800s Catholic Churches numbered just 1% of the county total (Charles Trego, *A Geography of Pennsylvania*, 1843). Other than the Irish community at the base of Haycock Mountain, the Italians at Rushland were one of the very few Catholic outposts in this area of "Penn's Woods." Many of their names still appeared in the 1940 Federal Census (below); many remained unemployed by the lingering depression. But they came here to stay, and stay they did … strangers no more.

1940 United States Federal Census Sheet #9-A, 9-B, Pennsylvania
Bucks, Wrightstown, "Unincorporated Place" -- Rushland

Name	Relation										Birthplace
De Furo, Angelo	Head	O	M	W	60	M	No	1			Italy
— Nancy	Wife	1	F	W	54	M	No	1			Italy
DellaMares, Louie	Lodger	6	M	W	59	S	No	1			Italy
Pilla, Michael	Head	O	M	W	72	Wd	No	o			Italy
Pilla, Anthony	Son	2	M	W	30	M	No	Hi	9		Pennsylvania
Mignogna, Anna	Daughter	2	F	W	38	M	No	8	8		Pennsylvania
Pilone, Thomas	Head	O	M	W	53	M	No	1			Italy
— Molly	Wife	1	F	W	43	M	No	6	6		Pennsylvania
Arusso, Peter	Head	O	M	W	75	M	No	1			Italy
— Virginia	Wife	1	F	W	64	M	No	1			Italy

[Extracted/composited from Census sheets]

CHAPTER 6

CURRIER AND IVES,
EAT YOUR HEARTS OUT

(The city) leads the young man to the saloon with its glitter and glare and one more once honest and happy country boy has been ruined ...(on the farm) he is not living next door to crime and is not associated with the imps of Satan.

– *Wycombe Herald,* March 29, 1900

(The early 1900s) was a time when – in the nostalgic memories of some at least – life was lived out in the soft light of a tree-shaded street on a summer afternoon, the clink of ice in the lemonade pitcher, the creak of porch swing – a time of pause and prosperity.

– Richard Lingeman, *Small Town America,* 1981

Imported Holstein Heifers, *Agriculture of Pennsylvania*, 1880.

Imported Holstein Heifers, *Agriculture of Pennsylvania*, 1880

He was gone, but of course the county survived without him. Up until now we've watched the interplay between Bucks County and the old folk devil … the hard times and the good in the marriage of Old World beliefs from the British Isles and Germany and the quest for happiness and success on the great Triassic lowlands. And further, we've witnessed the rejection of those same beliefs by the plain people … and the rather painful consequences for the devil. He had left of his own accord, and the county definitely survived. But what kind of place was this without earthly evil?

Yellowed Pages in a Yellow Castle

How then did this gentle red Triassic world fare without him? What transpired in Bucks after the devil went west? Was he missed or even thought of? Did any person or thing fill the vacuum left by his unexpected departure? We begin to find answers here:

The answers lie stored in the tower of a weathered building that looks like a medieval castle and stands atop a Triassic ridge in the borough and county seat of Doylestown. It was constructed in the years from 1914-16 by the enormously energetic and eccentric anthropologist-historian, Dr. Henry Chapman Mercer. The whimsical building, a weaving together of Mercer's personal fancies and travel fantasies, was the product of shear instinct and much experimentation. And it bears his name: the Mercer Museum. It is of much significance to architects because it was made of poured reinforced concrete strengthened with iron support rods. This was a very novel concept at the time of its construction. The two-foot thick walls enclosed a virtually fireproof building. The walls were a mix of Portland cement, yellow Jersey gravel, and crushed traprock that together give the building a soft, yellow-gray coloring in the late afternoon sun. The iron support rods were actually old pipes gathered up in Philadelphia junkyards. The reinforced walls made rooms and galleries, boxes and vaults stacked one upon another to a height of several stories. The whole rather curious affair was topped off with a Disneyland of dormers and dovecotes, chimney pots and steeples.

"Crazy" said the construction crew. But it was Mercer's crowning achievement, and today stands as one of the more curious creations of a curious mind.

This museum-castle has been filled to its vaulted roof with all the work-a-day tools and cultural ephemera of the American village and farmscape: cigar store Indians, buckboards and buggies, weathervanes and walking canes, flintlocks and house clocks, candle and shoe molds, bath and butter tubs, a gallows and a hearse, and even a wood coffin with a little glass window. And high above, there's a dimly lit gallery of small rooms where ancient, heavy stoveplates are displayed. Their inscriptions are in German and some depict the old folk devil himself. Eventually, a room that became the library was added. And up above

Fig. 6.1. Mercer Museum (detail), Doylestown

the library is the morgue – the newspaper morgue. More than anywhere, here is where the county's long-ago days come to life. It is here, in what one historian called "that undiscovered country, the last resting place of defunct journals,"[63] that the smell and feel of old Bucks County lives.

---

[63] William W. Davis, *History of Bucks County, Pennsylvania*, Vol. 1, p. 223.

The morgue is a monastic-like chamber, a tower room with wood podiums slanted forty-five degrees on which medieval monks in fading light might have transcribed paragraphs to parchment. The room is a cell, a bare-walled and drafty cell that holds captive all the days of the past. The room's only concession to modernity are three fluorescent lights that illuminate the plaster-patched and weather-stained cement walls, ceiling, and gray cement floor. At the front of the room, windows look down on the library just one level below; there, visitors research ancestors and unearth family roots. Other windows face to the outside of the tower, to the town and its streets beyond the wall-enclosed lawn. When evening comes and only the flood-lit lawn lies in view, on a slow night with only the occasional octogenarian cough or sneeze from the library below, on a still night surrounded in this room with the banner-heads and headlines from thousands of bygone days, there's nothing to suggest that it's the twenty-first Century … or that time has really moved past the days the yellowed newspapers were published. It's a 1,500-square foot time machine.

The paper is cracked, crusty, and sweetly dusty like a moldy old hamlet on a rainy day. No digitized images here. The papers rest on olive drab shelves with rumbling brass rollers across which over six hundred volumes and thousands of brittle pages await to give illumination into the minds and souls of old Bucks Countians.

Among these generously-sized newspapers are: the *Wycombe Herald,* "Independent in Politics and Fair in All Things", the penny-priced and unabashedly partisan *Daily Republican* in its speckled black and white binders (like composition books for giants' children); the *Springtown Weekly Times* with its bannerhead plowman and bundled farm produce, befitting a rural readership; and the *New Hope* ("If it Ain't Here, it Didn't Happen") *News* with pages strangely more gray than yellow. And here too are the newspapers published in German that died out either before or on the eve of the devil's departure.

These newspapers reflect a world of "innocent pleasures" in a time labeled "the Good Years" by some historians. With the arrival of electricity, automobiles, movies, and airplanes, and with Theodore Roosevelt in the White House, the national mood was one of much patriotic pride and buoyancy. In its brushes with history, Bucks County was a mirror to the nation. As the *Bristol Daily Courier* reported, rail cars used for Buffalo Bill Cody's "Wild West" shows in Philadelphia were parked along the railroad sidings in Bristol, with show animals being quartered for the winter(s) on local farms in Bristol, Edgely, and Tullytown. The federal government would soon construct Harriman, a shipyard on the Delaware River in Bristol Borough where dozens of vessels were built during World War I; included in the plan was a residential village for 12,000 workers that featured different styles and sizes of houses along with stores, parks, schools and playgrounds … clearly a foreshadowing of much greater changes to come. And soon after this cataclysmic "Great War" the county's remaining German language newspapers would – understandably – disappear from circulation.

It Was a Picture-Perfect World

It was a world that vividly springs to life in the vintage newspapers preserved in the morgue: described here are Arbor Day activities, the ceremonial planting of oak and elm saplings. It was a time of picnic groves and country fairs. Picnic groves with dance pavilions, Sousa band concerts with patriotic tunes and gasoline calliopes "piercing the night with mellifluous strains." German clubs and "Swastika Societies" with their blankets spread on the grassy earth amid barrels of dill pickles, buckets of oysters, dumplings and black bread, and kegs of Schlitz beer. Village and township fairs with wheels of fortune, Suffragette Party booths, and shiny new Hook & Ladder vehicles wheeled out by the fire company to be admired. Fire company parades led by shoeless little boys with dogs. It was an age of summer camps and camp meetings, of temperance societies and anti-saloon leagues, and an age of intemperance when saloon-keepers were seen as "the devil's servants."

It was a time of "upcountry" summer boarding houses, boarding houses where guests drank Dr. Pepper and Moxie ("Make Mine Moxie" – "a delicious blend of bitter and sweet"). It was a rustic world of summer idlers and Philadelphia money, a fresh air haven for distressed city-dwellers. Linked daily to the city by many trains and trolleys, city-dwellers were whisked across the outwash plain in just thirty-four minutes, past Wanamaker billboards and tin signs on barnboards extolling the virtues of Dr. Schenck's marvelous prescriptions and other patent medicines. The area's appeal was that of healthy and desirable rural scenery guaranteeing a change for the better in quality of air and surroundings. "Salubrious countryside" hawked the railroad company propagandists. Whole resort towns with summer cottages, rows of bungalows, and denominational tent camps and "Spiritualist" resorts sprang up. Boarding houses and three-decked layer cake hotels with names like "Old Turk's Head," "Red Lion," and "Old Black Bear" sprouted on the fertile earth, complete with cool arbors and shady groves. There were free-admission amusement parks built by the trolley companies at the end of their tracks. They were named "Eden," "Forest Park," and "Neshaminy Falls Grove." They were miniature Coney Islands that entertained thousands of visitors, both city day trippers and locals.

It was a time of baseball teams and home town rivalries, the scores from the Bucks County Baseball League prominently reported at the top of page one alongside the news of distant wars and labor unrest in the coal fields to the north. Even the frequently successful Philadelphia Athletics, under management of the great Connie Mack, played second string to the local clubs. It was a real world "Field of Dreams," bathed in the light of Thomas Kincaid.

It was a time of trolleys. Summer trolleys and evening trolleys, yellow and green trolleys with cane seats and pot-bellied stoves, "convenient though uncertain" trolleys that breezed noisy picnic parties and day-trippers to the picnic groves and dance pavilions, past "the beautiful and rolling country ... past fine estates with manicured lawns." Trolleys carrying strawberry pickers and squirrel hunters; trolleys carrying little boys with big bags full of copperheads and black snakes collected under the rock ledges along the creeks; the snakes were taken to laboratories in the city where their venom was extracted for medicinal uses. The little boys were paid thirty-five cents a head. It was a time of trolley line tentacles too, clutching tentacles that downgraded the countryside to the status of a suburb, that transformed mere fields into pretty suburban "station" villages. It all depending on one's point of view!

It was a front porch world, a lemonade world of rope swings and cane rocking chairs. Families, in this presumably happier age of family solidarity, sat together and watched the night arrive. The nights were illuminated with Japanese paper lanterns. There were dogs and bicycles and more dogs; dogs were everywhere. "Artesian" ice cream made from "the purest water in the world" was indulged in below huge shade trees and was dripped onto lazy swaying hammocks. There was pride in the faces of people dressed in summer whites, standing at attention on their Victorian front porches beneath the striped canvas awnings and under their parasols with Chantilly lace covers. Positioned in front of the porches were the objects of their immodesty – the latest fifteen mph "runabouts," the benzene buggies that would one day help destroy this indolent front porch world. The town's first motor car was usually sported about by the local banker or doctor, but soon enough, the (Ford) motorcar for the masses would usher in the car-crazed, carbon ex- haust(ed) "worldawheel" with all "the economic and social evils rising from a motor mad public."[64] But for a while at least, there would still be horse-drawn hayrides on summer evenings and horse-drawn sleigh rides on winter nights.

It was also a world of work. A postcard world of faded hues where young clerks and bearded artisans in white shirts with rolled-up sleeves and baggy, crumpled trousers posed with hands on hips beneath the porch roofs of wood-framed buildings: general stores, feed mills, stove and tinware shops. Small town tradesmen with bloodstained butchers' smocks and blacksmiths' leather aprons, men with pocket watches and bib overalls, their hair slicked down for the photographer's visit. It was a world of idle times between jobs. Afternoons were spent gossiping about crops and politics, playing checkers on the post office porch, or circled around wood stoves or cracker barrels. Old men played cards on railway station platforms, horses hitched nearby bobbed their heads in the feedbags and swished the flies from their tails – thus slightly blurring

---

[64] Wallace Nutting, *Pennsylvania Beautiful*, p.246.

the old slow process glass plate photographs. City-bound milkcans awaited the city-bound steam trains. And off to the side of hundreds of such bucolic porches and platforms, are the blurred images of people going about their long-forgotten errands.

The county ("the North County") was still essentially rural, with the farm population denser than that of many boroughs and villages. It remained a world of farm folk and farm work with the rhythms of the days and seasons revolving about the auctioning-off of cattle and horses, the slaughtering of porkers, and the threshing and reaping of hay. All these activities were colorfully detailed in the newspapers, in both English and German. The National Farm School (later Delaware Valley University) was founded in Doylestown Township in 1888, quickly becoming a valuable area resource for "the honorable, useful and most independent of all callings – agriculture." There were Farmers' Institutes ("Lyceums") and farm clubs, agricultural societies and granges, and "Crop Committees." Records of their undertakings and meetings were reported in the local press. Daily ads were run for new poultry incubators, improved new hog troughs, steel cow stanchions, Waterloo Boy Three-Plow tractors, and "Sneezo" eyeglasses that "can't be sneezed off" – not even with your head in the hog trough. All the important questions of the farmers' day were asked and answered by the newspapers (such as "How do you prevent overfeeding of little pigs?" "Is alsike clove a desirable crop?" and "What causes vertigo in poultry?")

The county's agriculture had now progressed far beyond the subsistence-based "patch farming" of earlier times. Specialty crops had been experimented with by "judicious and industrious agriculturist(s)"[65] and were found to do well: rye for whiskey distillation; wine grapes for palette and pleasure (indeed, the grape vine is shown on both the Penn family crest and the official seal of Bucks County); sugar cane for conversion to molasses; mulberry trees for silk; and Merino sheep for wool. These episodes were generally short-lived and played out mostly in the lower townships and boroughs (Bensalem, Morrisville, and Yardley). Tobacco was grown in fields around Quakertown and Perkasie; cigars

---

[65] Charles Trego, op.cit., p. 197.

were rolled by women and children in red brick factories and then displayed for sale in wood boxes with names like White Ash and King Clay ("2 For 15 Cents"). Wild horses were imported from the West to be "broken in" and harnessed to planting and harvesting machinery. By the 1890s, alfalfa and clover were planted to feed the growing numbers of horses.

But it was dairying that was clearly becoming the leading agricultural activity. Guernseys were being pastured in Bensalem as early as the 1830s. By 1900 Holsteins and Jerseys were the county's top dairy breeds. The county's first silo (for winter food storage) was reported to have been built in 1880 in Lumberville; attached to the silos were the massive dairy barns, sheltering two dozen or more cows and tons of hay and straw. Horse-drawn milk delivery wagons became a common sight; when railroad lines were extended into the county, milk and cream were produced for a larger market. Refrigerated railroad cars were first exhibited at the Centennial Exposition in 1876 and this innovation facilitated the county's shift to an even larger regional market from Trenton to Philadelphia.

World War I brought changes to the county, as it did to the rest of the country. Fuelless Mondays and coal shortages were shared by all. Daylight Savings Time was adopted in 1918 as an energy-saving strategy that also provided the farmers with a little more worklight at nightfall. And when the evening light finally dimmed, they went about their chores in barn and field illuminated with the glow of pumpkin lanterns whose soft incandescence would later be captured on canvas by countless artists in search of rural nostalgia. All in all, it was picture perfect, except .....

Black Crape in a Land of Red Soil

..... when it wasn't. And it wasn't always Currier & Ives perfect. There weren't always "Old Home Weeks" with hot apple pie and chilled glasses of Coca-Cola on warm summer evenings. Arbor Days had to share the news with the damage wrought by Chestnut Blight.

Nostalgia was originally thought to be a neurological disease caused by demons.[66] But in this rural world the thin veneer of nostalgia can barely conceal the hardships and cruelties of everyday life. This was a violent and often unpredictable world of endless drudgery where freak accidents were a common occurrence and mortality rates were obscenely high. Moreover, it was a world of lasting mourning and melancholia, a time when the memory and shared grief of the "world of death" shaped by the Civil War remained omnipresent still.[67]

Boredom and isolation at the end of long farm roads produced an inordinate amount of depression, alcoholism, and suicide on solitary, not-yet electrified farmsteads. Lonely spinsters and bachelors lived in a world where life expectancy was hardly fifty years. Death, either self-inflicted or accidental, was close at hand. The menace of filthy chicken yards and swarms of flies that bred on manure piles brought sickness to the adolescents who worked the farms. Desperation bred worse – some people just ended it all by putting sticks of dynamite in their mouths or gun barrels to their heads. This was done out behind the barn. And with no more passenger pigeons to shotgun, they shot gunned each other at a very angry rate.

Vagrants and peddlers were (infrequently) found dead along the county highways; sometimes their bodies were found dumped into the deserted lime kilns. Others disappeared in blizzards, only to be found in the spring thaw. Fingers were lost on the trolley tracks. The trolleys themselves carried sand boxes in case the pot-bellied stoves tipped over; if they didn't, the sand boxes might be used for vomiting caused by the sideward sway of the cars. Feet were run over and mashed by ice wagon wheels. Heads were bashed by falling barn beams (though nobody bothered to blame the devil anymore). Faces were seared and horribly scarred when, having fallen asleep while reading, heads fell against hot stove plates and pipes. Stoves tipped over and there were fires, fires

---

[66] Johannes Hoffer, a Swiss doctor, coined the term "nostalgia" in 1688. The *New York Times*, July 9th, 2013.
[67] See: Drew Gilpin Faust, *This Republic of Suffering*, N.Y. Alfred Knopf, 2008. The Civil War "...nurtured (a) widely shared grief well into the next century." (p. 170).

everywhere. Barns and church buildings were incinerated. If they weren't carried away by angry flood waters, covered bridges were struck by lightning and burned. Lightning struck farmers, knocking them from their wagons. Wagons of clove seed and timothy were mired in the spring mud, and everything was always "besmirched" with mud and carriage harnesses always needed to be cleaned. And when winter sleigh bells tingled, sleighs were upset spilling sausage and scrapple all over the Christmas card snowscape.

Perhaps the worst accidents were those related to the competition among the horse-drawn vehicles, the electrified trolleys, and the "autoists" in their new-fangled motorcars. It was a time of transition when the rules of the road (and the roads themselves) were very slippery. Horse wagons collided with motorcars with alarming frequency or were struck broadside and dragged horrible distances by trolleys. Horse teams panicked at the sight of cars and the sound of honking horns. Horse team drivers became confused, not knowing whether to pull to the left or right of oncoming motor vehicles. Drivers ended up with fractured ribs and demolished wagons ("the big farm wagon was overturned and the old man dragged under it for some distance"). All of this was dutifully reported upon in the local newspapers.

And it was a time of far too early and unexpected deaths; periodic outbreaks of typhoid and diphtheria took their toll, but so too did childhood diseases. Guardian Angels worked overtime, and still young boys and girls died of scarlet fever. It wasn't all 'Baby Parades' with silver cups judiciously bestowed upon the cutest, smallest, and plumpest Bucks County babies. An unfair number of infants are listed in the daily obituaries; a sad number of parents choosing to place reclining lambs on the graves of "Our Baby." At a time when the infant mortality rate was eight times what it is today, baby parades were for the survivors only.

Not so premature or unexpected were the deaths of thousands of "grizzled and weakened" Union Army veterans of the 104th Pennsylvania volunteers. Soon, there would be hardly any left at all, all laid to rest beneath their GAR medallions in hillside and roadside cemeteries. Dogs bayed mournfully on many a night and doorknockers tied with black crape bouquets were a common sight.

It was a time of comings and goings, and not only the comings and goings of babies and old soldiers. Gas mains and telephone lines were coming in, as were state highways and gasoline filling stations. The old sixteen to eighteen-foot wide farm-to-market roads were being widened and macadamized and the farmers taken out of the mud. The downside: with road widening countless historic buildings and even whole hamlets were lost to the wrecking ball. Steel bridges were replacing the wooden variety. Inscriptions were chiseled onto large stone tablets set into the walls of even very small bridges that spanned the small creeks that meandered across the Triassic lowland: "Constructed 1913" and "Rebuilt and Repaired 1916." The names of the county commissioners and the repairmen were inscribed as well ... reflecting a civility and pride in work seemingly out of place in the modern world.

What was already being called "suburbia" was beginning to cast a longer and larger shadow over the countryside. The county's geography was regarded as healthy and generally agreeable. And more and more the railroad spur lines carried not just milk but an ever expanding daily cadre of urban-suburban commuters. Was this progress or spoliation? As described in the local newspapers, the pleasantly cultivated land of big barns and hard-working farm folk was starting to "succumb to urban progress" and "fall victim to suburbia." William S. Hemsing, the Souderton diarist, lamented: "It is sad that the old woods must go. They must make room for building lots which are at present scarce." [68] The county grew from 68,000 in 1880 to 82,000 by 1920, an increase of 17% over four decades. This was in part due to the growing influx of suburbanites. Immigrant labor was also a factor. Cheap labor was needed to do farm work at harvest time, to lay railroad and trolley tracks, to pave the roads and build the bridges, to landscape the wealthier peoples' estates, and do a thousand other jobs.

---

[68] William S. Hemsing, *Diaries,* October 1, 1885.

Population gain might have been greater, but this was an era of at least some rural decline. Thousands of people were being lured to the emerging Western farmbelts and to the virgin farmlands of western Canada. "California letters" addressed to friends and relatives back East were printed in the local newspapers; these letters described the "veritable but not perfect Paradise" of delights beyond the Sierras. For the price of a ten-cent stamp and an envelope addressed to the Los Angeles Chamber of Commerce, any Pennsylvanian could receive all the details. Many did and many went, shedding pasts, ancestors, and debts. There were moreover an impressive number of "vanishing" people too. Some may have gone to California, maybe to the gold fields of the Yukon or Australia. Or maybe just to Chicago. From newspaper reports, it appears that scores of "runaway" husbands simply told their wives that they were going out for a little walk after supper ("Just going for a walk on the Triassic lowland, dear"); they never returned. Of course, they had previously withdrawn all six hundred dollars from the family bank account before vanishing into the Bucks County night. Again, the town gossip mill was fed with grist.

But here, as in most rural areas, the real tragedy of the countryside was the bleeding out of the younger generation of farm-born men and women. Never again would so many Americans live on farms and in small towns. A combination of circumstances was proving fatal to the farmlands. The magnetic pull of city lights contrasted with the dullness and lack of opportunity in rural areas. State and local agricultural societies, through their farm journals, tried to slow the city-bound wave with stories illustrating the horrors of the ashcan tenements and immigrant slums. 4-H clubs were begun to provide a sense of purpose and meaning to young peoples' work on the farms. The local press did its part in attempting to convince young adults to stay at home in the county; to wit, a 1900 editorial from the *Wycombe Herald*:

Young man, stick to the farm … (why) leave (a) good home on the farm, with all its pleasant surroundings, good companionship and healthfulness for a so-called home in the city, with all its vice and crime … Now is the time for sensible young men to obtain good homes, amid all the beauties of nature, surrounded by influences good and pure … the happy, independent life of a farmer … (there is) no excuse for being idle in these prosperous times.

Those not drawn away by the enticements of the big city came back from the battlefields of Europe with wounds, medals, and expanded horizons. Farm and hamlet provincialism was left in the trenches. Never again would life in the *Peaceable Kingdom* offer enough excitement and opportunity, wine and champagne. Like falling teardrops, patches of white plaster flaked and fell from the walls of the now abandoned farmhouses, exposing the fieldstones to the winters of a new century. Without a younger generation, the crossroads hamlets and smaller villages (Poverty Corners, Pickpocket, Jugtown, and Frogtown) were doomed.

Meanwhile, the good Dr. Mercer was building his museum and stocking it with his collection of hand-crafted tools and toys of a fading rural world ("Tools of the Nation Maker"). A depopulated folk world. The Bucks that would be no more. Mercer did take a break from his museum building to explore "a large apparently artificial mound" that caused a seventy-five by three hundred-foot bump out on the Triassic lowland. Since the time of the devil's arrival, it was believed (by some) that the fourteen-foot high mound might perhaps be "the unexplained and mysterious work of unknown men." More specifically, it might possibly be a "Giant's Grave," the burial site of an over-sized long dead American Indian. Soon, an aura of the occult and a web of folklore entwined itself to the mound. To many, it brought to mind the Biblical passage about "giants in the earth." This shroud of mystery was dispelled one summer morning in 1916 when Dr. Mercer and his work crew arrived at the site with picks and shovels. Determined once and for all to end the wild speculation about the "grave," Mercer carefully mapped the ground with an archaeologist's precision while the workmen dug a series of five-foot deep cross-trenches. Result: rotted shale! Nothing more than a weathered outcrop, a stratified ridge of shale. The excavation "thus disprove(ed) the possibility of human construction."[69] Satisfied that the mystery had been solved, Mercer and his crew – perhaps after a few rounds of brew to quench a thirst worked up beneath a hot August sun – went back to building the museum. There would be no over-sized, mummified American Indian for the museum to display. There was, moreover, a further loss: the Triassic earth had again yielded up some of its secrets. No rotted logs with a sleeping devil; rotted shale, but no sleeping giant. The natural innocence of a folk world was lessened. The unknown had become scientifically proven. The "Giant's Grave" became the grave of superstition and myth.[70]

It was a picture postcard world; it was a lemonade world; it was a front porch world. It was a picture postcard world about to change dramatically. It was a lemonade world about to turn sour. It was a front porch world about to lose it front porches, its front porch innocence and neighborliness. It had of course already its reason for blue porch ceilings. He was gone. The old eight-square schoolhouses had become obsolete; without purpose and abandoned, they simply deteriorated and were torn down: "the old ruins are in fact going to decay." Some were recycled into chicken houses; the more fortunate few became artist's studios (a sign of the times to come). On one level this corner of the world survived; and it survived without any devil or earthly evil. And a

---

[69] For a full account of the excavation, see: Dr. Henry C. Mercer, "An Investigation of the Giant's Grave," Bucks County Historical Society, *A Collection of Papers*, Volume 5, 1926.

[70] This episode in Bucks County history was echoed in a rash of similar such "humbug" mysteries about digging up "giants in the earth"(Genesis 6:4) in late 19th and early 20th century rural America. The most famous case was that of the Cardiff Giant hoax, an ancient ten-foot "petrified giant" excavated in upstate New York. The "giant" turned out to be a cleverly carved block of gypsum made to look like a man.

golden pastoral world it was … at least when viewed through the vaseline-coated and rose-tinted lens of nostalgia. What lies buried in the newspaper morgue reveals a darker, more somber side of rural life. Some things might be downright devilish without any input from a near-at-hand demon.

Then, during the winter of 1909, the neighboring Jersey Devil crossed the Delaware River and visited the now devil-less Bucks. Prior to this, he had pretty much stayed on his side of the river valley, respecting the Bucks' devil's turf. Astonishingly, it was all reported by the local press.[71] He was seen flying diagonally across the river towards Bristol. He traipsed around the town for a while, causing much consternation, and leaving his calling card: hoof prints frozen in the snow and on the snow-covered porch roofs (there were no blue porch ceilings in this old Quaker town to warn him away). He moped around the lower county craning his "snaky neck" and leering curiously through farmhouse windows before disappearing in the vicinity of Buckingham Mountain. This visit inspired some deservedly anonymous verse (*"Oh the Devil's loose in Bucks, and the folks have seen his track, they're keeping up their courage now with jugs of applejack ..."*). This is not all he inspired. It's not known how long his stay in Bucks lasted, but it was obviously the Jersey Devil (and not the Bucks Devil) who animated an event some years later. In the spring of 1913 the *Bristol Daily Courier* reported that a "little colored girl" had tried to kill her playmate by lacing her toast with rat poison – then known as "the Devil's paste." "It tastes like matches smell" said the intended victim. "I guess the devil must have gotten into me" said the "little colored girl." This was clearly the Jersey Devil's work, for in the very next issue of the same newspaper it was reported that a dark and sparkling-eyed stranger was seen riding beneath the boundless blue arc of the Montana sky, galloping across the plains in the company of witches. He had adopted the alias "Desperado Duke." But from the accounts given, it was obvious who he really was.

---

[71] See: Sara Maynard Clark, *"The Night the Devil Came to Bristol,"* Bucks County Traveler, November 1957, p. 38-9.

These events mark the very last recorded appearances of any folk devil in Bucks. And we see that the old (though rejuvenated) Bucks devil was still far away. But something else was starting to happen now. What was demonic and evil no longer prowled these Triassic Redlands in funereal costume and physical form. Evil was becoming a disembodied, abstract force more sinister and powerful than simple folk beliefs and more reflective of a rapidly suburbanizing twentieth century. "Old Scratch" had warned of this when he departed for the West in 1886. Soon, "the devil not seen" would be coming into the land.

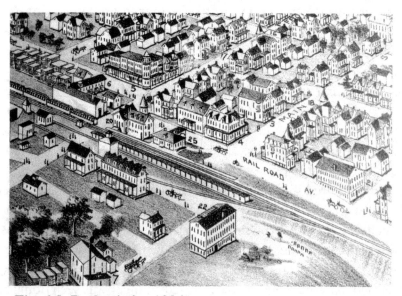

Fig. 6.2 Perkasie in 1894
Detail from Drawing by T.M. Fowler. Published by Fowler and Moyer
(Author's collection)

A Closer Look: Swept Away by History

Nothing better symbolizes this vanished (and still vanishing) picture perfect rural world than the wooden covered bridge. Bucks County had over fifty at one time, most since swept away by floods and fire, by the rising tide of history. A dozen remain today, including the oldest – the 93-foot long South Perkasie Bridge. Built in 1832 of white pine and oak with latticework sides, it survives in Lenape Park, borough of Perkasie (*See Photos below by Jonathan Neuber*). In order to save it, it was moved from its original location in 1958. It is operated by the Perkasie Historical Society. The county's covered bridges are mapped and described at the Bucks County Covered Bridge Society's web site: http://www.buckscountycbs.org/.

CHAPTER 7

ROOTS IN THE EARTH

It probably was a good day for us to meet to talk about erosion control, for (with heavy rains) some of our land (was) going down the stream to the river.

– P Alston Waring, Solebury farmer in *Roots in the Earth*, p. 88

Fig. 7.1 Soil Conservation Service teaching a class of "Vo Ag" Future Farmers on a 75 year-old terrace on James Iden Smith's farm in Buckingham Township. Late 1930's, SCS Glass Plate Slide #Pa.40638. *(Author's Collection)*

Gold!

The old California Hotel (1849) in Richland Township was reportedly named for the California gold rush, and gold nuggets were reportedly found in Pidcock Creek near where it enters the Delaware River. And from time to time, trace amounts of gold have been reportedly found in river gravels and in the hard bedrock of the Reading Prong and the Penn Ridge formations. This is all "reportedly." The county's nearest brush with an actual gold strike seems to have occurred in the early 1900's in West Rockhill Township. There was a mine dug 90 feet down on the southern side of the "ridge" (Ridge Road) near the Naceville crossroads. It did yield "some, but not a lot" of gold before it was flooded out between 1910-12. And that was that. Lost to memory, except for a map designation: Gold Mine Road." Precious metals were never the county's most valuable resource; that, rather, was always what Mennonite historian John Landis Ruth would later call "the gift of the soil." [72]

Just two miles from "Gold Mine Road" is the village of Argus.[73] The settlement dates to the early 1700s when pioneer German farmers came up the Perkiomen Creek into Rockhill Township. With difficulty, the "Rhinelanders" cleared and ploughed a few acres of land and planted crops such as corn, oats, and hay. A patch ("patch farming") of flax and/or hemp was also planted. A home garden and orchard eventually bordered a small log cabin. One such log house, predating by decades the establishment of the township in 1740, remained occupied into the twentieth century and became a symbol of both the antiquity and durability of agriculture in this area. It also became something of a tourist

---

[72] John Landis Ruth, *"Recalling Our Landscape,"* Franconia Mennonite Meeting, Lecture, November 28, 2009.

[73] "Argus" has various meanings in Greek mythology. This one is perhaps the most appropriate to an agricultural area: a primordial giant with a hundred eyes that saw in every direction; his job was to be awake and watchful as the guardian of young cows ("heifer-nymphs").

attraction as described in the *Town and Town and Country* newspaper, 1904:[74]

> Tourists traveling near Argus … who happen to pass the roman-
> tic Souder log cabin … stop (for) a few moments and take a look
> at the oldest and most curious structure in Bucks County. How
> old this log cabin is no living person is able to tell … it has
> (perhaps) faced the storms of more than 200 winters. Its present
> inhabitants … Mr. and Mrs. Noah Souder … are well advanced
> in years, both having passed the four-score mark … (Mrs.
> Souder) still helped her husband last summer to make all the
> hay on their 20 acre farm. She is hale and hearty and still able
> to enjoy a good smoke of Virginia long-cut in her clay pipe …
> She appears at the front gate with the pipe in her mouth in the
> accompanying picture. (*See below*: Fig.7.2)

[74] *Town and Country*, published in Pennsburg, Montgomery County, Pa., Saturday, April 9th, 1904. Schwenkfelder Library and Museum, Pennsburg.

Today, Argus is a collection of some dozen fieldstone and wood frame houses, a linear village on a semi-secluded road (Allentown Road) surrounded by farm fields and state game lands. A country inn and tavern ("wine bar") now occupies the old hotel (1754). A German Lutheran church and large churchyard with many ancient burials lies along boulder-strewn Ridge Valley Creek. It gives an oldish feel (and appeal) to this corner of the county where the artifacts of an agrarian past seem never far from the surface … a surface still extensively "rooted in the earth." (*Continued on p. 125*)

A Closer Look
Never Far Beneath the Surface

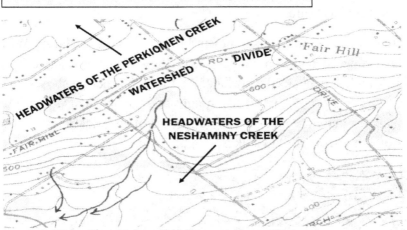

Detail of Hilltown Township from: Telford topographic map sheet, U.S. Geological Survey, 1:24,000 Scale; 20 foot Contour Interval

In Hilltown Township, Fairhill Road sits atop a high ridge that crosses the township lengthwise. It's a watershed divide between creeks that flow south to the Neshaminy and those that flow north to the Perkiomen. Not a quarter of a mile separates the ground where both creeks originate.

(Continued...)

At one time, this was Indian land that was later patented to the Welsh; later still, their "estates" or "plantations" were acquired by a succession of many different landowners, mostly German. There were black slaves and "redemptioners," their burying grounds long since ploughed up, mowed over, and built upon. Long, two-story stone houses were built along the Bethlehem Pike, along with stores, blacksmith shops, tanneries, and wayside inns and taverns. Generations of Rosenbergers (German Mennonites) farmed this land; dairy cows populated the hillside fields. Eventually, the homesteads were abandoned and sat vacant during the Great Depression. In the post-war years they were bought for a song ... though furnaces (and in some cases, electricity) had to be installed. By the 1950s-60s suburban style brick capes were built and the roads were finally paved. Much of the area (open fields and horse farms) is still classified as "rural."

Here, the agrarian past is never far beneath the surface. With trowel and metal detector, a collection of farm-related artifacts can be found just inches beneath the surface. As the photo below shows, this includes wire, doorknobs, iron rods, hinges and latches, nails of various sizes, chains, a penknife and bicycle bell, coins of an indeterminate age, and (incongruously) railroad spikes.

William Penn himself had welcomed the Germans (both "church" and "plain" people) because of their "sober" and industrious ways, especially when these ways were applied to farming. Here (in Rockhill and Hilltown) "it was good to farm, good to live, good to bring up (children)."[75] There was a moral character to family farming, to laboring with little between the land and God's blue sky, to treating the soil well. Great wagonloads of hay were driven to Philadelphia (for carriage horses) and steaming loads of manure came back to fertilize the fields of Bucks. The stern work ethic of the German farmers is credited with "the prevention of soil erosion (and) the balanced rotation of crops"[76] ... and this was at a very early date. Their sound agricultural practices were well known and widely used into the late 1800s as itemized in the *Report of the Pennsylvania Department of Agriculture* (1897): five year crop rotations and proper tillage to prevent soil exhaustion, the use of windbreaks to aid water retention, control of crop and dairy diseases through sanitary measures, "sub-irrigation" for moisture control, the benefits of fallowing, etc. The educational importance of local granges was understood by all. Farmers who hoped to avoid "the same beaten track" taken by their fathers and grandfathers had to have an understanding of markets and operate their farms as a business. Cooperation among local farmers was already an established practice, especially among the Mennonites and other "plain" sects in the more religiously conservative areas.[77] Not that mistakes weren't made or that all farmers were always guided by a sense of moral stewardship toward the land. "Some farmers never learned to understand the soil and their land wore out rapidly." Gradually, the land itself left as "countless tons of topsoil washed ... down to the Neshaminy Creek, into the Delaware, and out to sea." By the beginning of the twentieth century an estimated

---

[75] P.Alston Waring and Walter Teller, *Roots in the Earth*, N.Y.: Harper & Brothers, 1943, p. 6.
[76] Arthur Graeff and John Hostetler, *"Pennsylvania German Culture,"* Mennonite Historical Society Bulletin, April 1956, Vol. XVII, #2, p. 1.
[77] *Report of the Pennsylvania Department of Agriculture*, Harrisburg, Pa. 1897, p. 444.

half of the county's topsoil had been lost in a "cumulative and wholly preventable waste."[78]

By the 1920s-30s farming in Bucks had become less family-based and less traditional in its practices; fewer, larger, and more commercial and specialty agribusinesses were becoming the norm. Since 1880 the number of farms had fallen from 6,493 to 4,299; and the area in farming had declined from 95% to 65% of the county.

The Rockhills were once the center of a cigar-making industry that stretched from Quakertown to Sellersville and Perkasie. Field tobacco and back alley barns to store and cure the crop were common. Though the area was still producing eleven million cigars as late as 1932, the industry had peaked and was diminishing. Growing competition from cigarettes made with tobacco from the southern piedmont was the reason. Dairying (with Holstein-Friesian breeds) remained the most prevalent farm activity because of the nearby urban milk market. Poultry production ranked second to dairying, satisfying those same markets with fresh eggs. "Truck farms" ranked third and were located along the river terraces and on the outwash plain. The county in fact ranked number one in Pennsylvania in the value of truck crops, especially corn and tomatoes. And Bucks farms had "no difficulty in getting the foreign element in the cities to work in the truck fields."[79] And though not "agriculture" in the strictest sense, Prohibition encouraged the county to play an active role in the making of illegal alcohol. Until the end of Prohibition in 1933 many barns and basements in the upper county were used in bootlegging. Field crops like rye and corn were mashed and mixed with brown sugar and other ingredients to make whiskey. Local people were arrested and fined, speakeasies were raided, and Federal agents prowled the woods looking for illegal stills.[80] But by the early 1930s there were other problems …

---

[78] All quoted materials in this paragraph are from: Waring & Teller, op. cit., p.9-10.

[79] R.T.A. Burke and others, *Soil Survey, Bucks County, Pennsylvania*, Washington, D.C.: U.S. Department of Agriculture, Series 1936, #25, p.3.

[80] For a concise account of Bucks County in the Prohibition era see: Hilary Bentman, *When Booze Was Banned*, The Intelligencer, November 29, 2010, p. 1-2.

Our Great Agricultural Sickness

With the onset of the Depression, Bucks County farms found themselves as subject to the vagaries of the economy and nature as any in America. Past land and soil abuse, the accumulated results of man-induced erosion compounded by the destructive forces of wind and rain, caught up with the farmers. It resulted in what Louis Bromfield (author and agricultural innovator whose "Malabar" farm in Ohio was used as a test case for soil conservation practices) called "our great agricultural sickness ... agriculture in this nation is sick and has been since the end of the boom that followed the First World War."[81] Alston Waring, the Solebury Township farmer, noted how "the rapidly changing circumstances of rural life" led to "insecurity (in) our own lives." Waring, describing "the beauty and the struggle that is (farming)" in Bucks County, continues:[82]

> To be a farmer ... is not to live in rural seclusion. It is living in the midst of American life. And American life is none too easy ... We farmers have known economic depression for the last twenty years.

After fourteen years as a poultry man, Waring became convinced that country and city were co-dependent and ought to understand each other better and cooperate more. [83]

In *Roots in the Earth* Waring reminded readers that in Bucks County, Quaker and German agricultural traditions were based on "fairly high standards of husbandry," yet conceded that local farmers did take much from the soil "in their effort to turn a penny."[84] Learning

---

[81] Louis Bromfield, *Foreward*, Waring & Teller, op. cit., p.vii.
[82] Waring & Teller, op. cit., p.23.
[83] Bern Ikeler, *P. Alston Waring: "Productive Acres," Bucks County Traveler*, February, 1952, p. 21-23.
[84] Waring & Teller, op. cit., p.13.

the ways of the land was never easy and rural life was no "pastoral heaven." Mistakes had led to a "terrible poverty among farmers" … and now, through more work and struggle, the time had come to correct those mistakes.

When Soils Go …

Louis Bromfield wrote about the necessity of building a less exploitative and more durable future agriculture; moreover, he noted that "the men of the future (were) already farming in the present."[85]

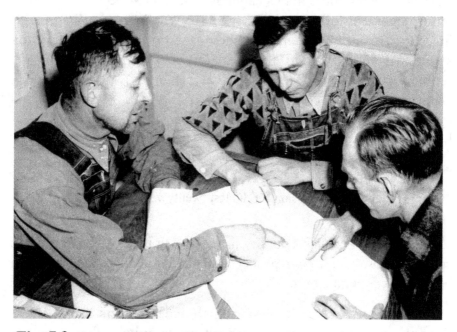

Fig. 7.3 Farmers (Charles Wendig, Herman Otte, and P. A. Waring) "Look Over Soil Conservation Map." Late 1930's. SCS Glass Plate Slide (Unnumbered). (*Author's Collection*)

---

[85] Louis Bromfield, op. cit., p.4.

"It probably was a good day for us to meet to talk about erosion control, for (with heavy rains) some of our land (was) going down the stream to the river." So wrote P. Alston Waring of his meeting with his neighbors who together were working almost eight hundred acres of farmland and woodlot in the Honey Hollow watershed in Solebury.[86] The land was part of William Penn's original land grants and had been farmed for over two centuries. It had been foolishly exploited, and as Waring said, it was time to "(make) our peace with nature."[87]

The practicality of working as a group would make land use management and erosion control easier and far better than going it alone (Cooperation among neighbors had, in fact, long been standard practice with the Mennonite farms in the Indian Valley). It was furthermore realized that advice and technical assistance from the U.S. Soil Conservation Service (SCS) would be invaluable. Consequently, an SCS agent did a survey, drew up a plan, and worked with the farmers to protect soil, water, and wildlife. This was most significant in that the success of this cooperative venture in Bucks County became the prototype conservation showplace for thousands of other American watersheds.

A further revolution brought about by watershed conservation was a change in the very appearance of the county's farmlands. The old, inflexible pattern of squared-off corners and property lines (the ancient system of metes and bounds ... so favored by the devil) was altered in favor of "the easy flowing curves of contoured fields."[88] The soil was nailed down like "the skin of the earth" and erosion better controlled.

---

[86] There were others, other farmers whose lands were not in this particular watershed. Most notably: James Iden Smith (1887–1977) of Buckingham Township. "(A) sad loss to Bucks County" intoned *The Daily Intelligencer* on the death of James Iden Smith: "He was born and grew up on a rolling farm in Pineville ... for generations, he crusaded for preservation of the land, conservation and ecology ... He was an innovator in the early use of farm machinery and pioneered harvesters ... However, he was skilled in the old ways ... Despite changes in farming, he continued the practice of organic building and nurturing of the soil." (October 5, 1977). (Also See Fig. 7.1)
[87] Waring & Teller, op. cit., p. 84.
[88] Waring & Teller, op. cit., p.181

Pennsylvania's governor Gifford Pinchot (1931-35) actively worked to improve the lives of those who lived in rural areas like Bucks County. A step or two in time ahead of FDR's New Deal programs (and seeing job creation as preferable to charity) Pinchot set up emergency work relief camps throughout the state. Other than replanting trees on clear-cut forest lands, much of the work involved roads: upgrading state highways and especially building and paving county roads "to get the farmers out of the mud."[89] These narrow macadamized roads ("Pinchot Roads") threaded their way into previously isolated county districts, opening these areas to urban markets.

In spite of the national depression, the county exhibited a very busy optimism during the decade. Population more than held its own, growing a solid 11% from 97,000 to over 107,000. The farms produced a respectable million dollars in cash crops. The New Deal established at least nine public works projects in the county including parks, a water works (Sellersville), a prison wall (Doylestown), and most particularly the reconstruction of William Penn's manor house in Pennsbury. Governor Pinchot presided over a ceremony at which he, on behalf of the state, accepted the deed of ownership to a forty-mile stretch of the Delaware Canal in Bucks County. With declining barge traffic and revenues, the Lehigh Coal and Navigation Company was finished moving anthracite by canal in 1931. Much to the governor's approval, the old workaday canal and towpath would become a recreational and sightseeing resource for the public.[90]

---

[89] Char Miller, *Gifford Pinchot and the Making of Modern Environmentalism,* Washington, D.C.: Island Press, 2001, p. 318.

[90] See: *A Timeline of Bucks County History, 1600's-1900's.* mercermuseum.org. Gov. Pinchot named the canal property Roosevelt State Park in honor of his friend and fellow conservationist, Theodore Roosevelt. It was later changed to the Delaware Canal State Park (1989).

"What fresh hell is this?"

The time was right; the opportunities were there. Money and the arts were about to "discover" Bucks County. As Wallace Nutting said, "(its) gentle rolling charm" provided the "ideal country life." The county was "(as) old, as finished, as pleasing as any of the counties in the state …"

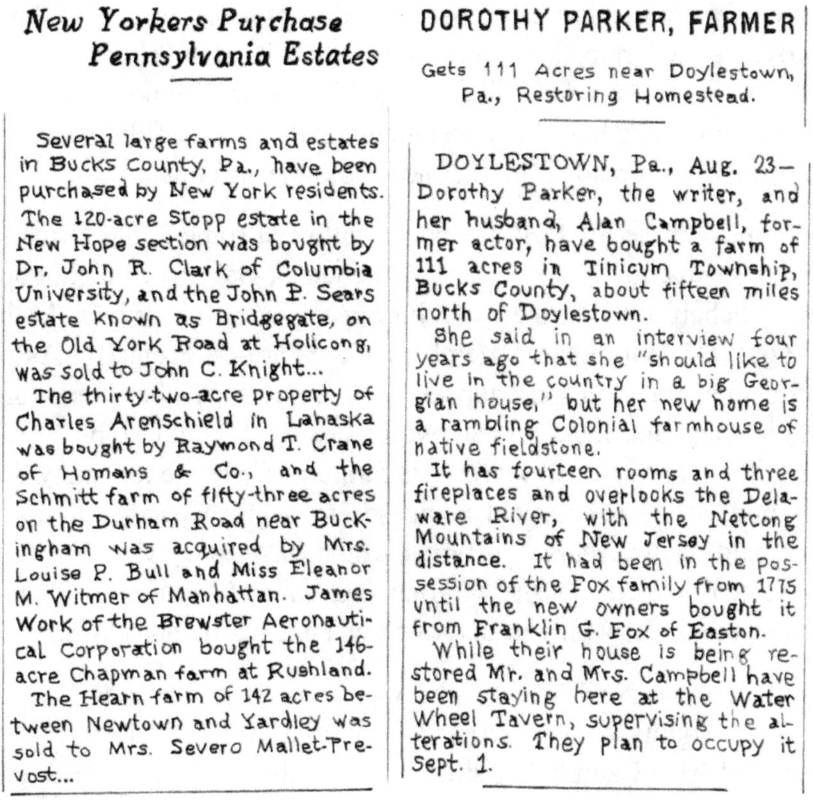

New Yorkers Purchase Pennsylvania Estates

Several large farms and estates in Bucks County, Pa., have been purchased by New York residents. The 120-acre Stopp estate in the New Hope section was bought by Dr. John R. Clark of Columbia University, and the John P. Sears estate known as Bridgegate, on the Old York Road at Holicong, was sold to John C. Knight...

The thirty-two-acre property of Charles Arenschield in Lahaska was bought by Raymond T. Crane of Homans & Co., and the Schmitt farm of fifty-three acres on the Durham Road near Buckingham was acquired by Mrs. Louise P. Bull and Miss Eleanor M. Witmer of Manhattan. James Work of the Brewster Aeronautical Corporation bought the 146-acre Chapman farm at Rushland.

The Hearn farm of 142 acres between Newtown and Yardley was sold to Mrs. Severo Mallet-Prevost...

DOROTHY PARKER, FARMER

Gets 111 Acres near Doylestown, Pa., Restoring Homestead.

DOYLESTOWN, Pa., Aug. 23— Dorothy Parker, the writer, and her husband, Alan Campbell, former actor, have bought a farm of 111 acres in Tinicum Township, Bucks County, about fifteen miles north of Doylestown.

She said in an interview four years ago that she "should like to live in the country in a big Georgian house," but her new home is a rambling Colonial farmhouse of native fieldstone.

It has fourteen rooms and three fireplaces and overlooks the Delaware River, with the Netcong Mountains of New Jersey in the distance. It had been in the possession of the Fox family from 1715 until the new owners bought it from Franklin G. Fox of Easton.

While their house is being restored Mr. and Mrs. Campbell have been staying here at the Water Wheel Tavern, supervising the alterations. They plan to occupy it Sept. 1.

Fig. 7.4 *"Special to The New York Times"* Author's sketch of news articles: May 31, 1935 (left) and August 24, 1936 (right).

And almost daily, The *New York Times* described "the growing Bucks County colony of artists and other celebrities" flocking to the area.[91] There were too many to name and many actually preferred the anonymity of "back woods" rural Bucks. The *Times* did, however, name a few on May 31, 1935 (*See above*).

It could make one absolutely giddy with delight – finding, buying for a song, and fixing up a fieldstone farmhouse down a dead end lane … one with a big, walk-in fireplace and a date stone from the 1700s, with several acres that looked across a meadow or had a river view. And, of course, a patio terrace for entertaining. And a bay barn (livestock optional) that could and would be converted into a fine studio. A furnace and insulation would have to be installed, but that was doable. It was all the rage! And what made it all the more possible was this:

In the summer of 1934 the county allowed some 3,000 farms to be put on the auction block for tax delinquency. Governor Pinchot appealed on behalf of the farmers, but his appeals were ignored. On Monday, August 6th, four hundred members of the Farmers Protective Association demonstrated at the courthouse in Doylestown, but were confronted by state and local police "with sidearms and riot clubs." "We can do nothing about it," observed one farmer; "There are too many police around."[92]The county did acquiesce to a grace period; if taxes weren't paid in two years, the farms would have to be vacated. And many were. Bucks of old, the agrarian *Peaceable Kingdom*, was fated to become the country playground of New York wealth and fame.

One famous New Yorker who was eager to join friends already living in the county was the writer Dorothy Parker. The "acerbic wit" and husband Alan Campbell visited Bucks in the summer of 1936 and decided to buy ("for a steal" at $4,500) a run-down 1750 farmhouse on 111 acres near Pipersville. They sunk thousands of dollars into the house, adding electricity and indoor plumbing. Curiously or perhaps just in jest The *New York Times* described her as a "farmer" (*See*: Fig. 7.4),

---

[91] The *New York Times*, May 31, 1935.
[92] The *New York Times*, August 7, 1934.

while her biographer said that "Dottie" wanted to plant "roots" in Bucks County.[93] Marion Meade titled her 1987 biography *"What Fresh Hell is This?"* after an oft-quoted line attributed to Dorothy Parker whenever she answered the doorbell or the telephone.[94] Bucks County ... a "fresh hell"?

Foreshadowings

Napoleon Hill (1883-1970) was a best-selling motivational author and lecturer in the 1930s; this popular "success guru" and advisor to President Franklin Roosevelt managed to snag an interview with his Satanic Majesty in 1938 in which the devil boasted of having brought about the miseries of the Great War and the Great Depression.[95] Through his power and cunning this self-described "abstract force" further claimed to have ensnared and controlled 98% of earthbound humanity. This was obviously not the old folk devil of Old World superstition. This rather was a slick salesman and showman, a purveyor of greed, avarice, and fear who stalked the world. Would he soon turn his attention to Bucks County? And how would he appear? In his own words:[96]

> My physical appearance? ... I have no physical body. I would be handicapped by such an encumbrance ... I consist of negative energy, and I live in the minds of people who fear me ... I am no beast with a forked tongue and a split tail.

---

[93] Biographer Marion Meade as quoted by the *Dorothy Parker Society* at www.dorothyparker.com/dot23.htm.

[94] See: Wikiquote and Everything2.com. Art Bergman also used the line as the title of a 1995 alternative rock music album.

[95] The interview appeared in book form in 1938, but was considered too controversial at that time; it was released by Sterling Press of New York in 2011.

[96] Napoleon Hill, *Outwitting the Devil*, p. 59-60. Did Hill interview a real or imagined devil? In his own words: "...the devil that I interviewed may have been real, just as he claimed to be, or he may have been the creation of my own imagination. Whichever he was, whether real or imaginary, is of little importance compared with the nature of the information conveyed through the interview." (p. 55-56).

Pulp fiction and sci-fi writer Kendall Crossen worked for the WPA in the 1930s and contributed to the *New York City Guidebook* produced by the Federal Writers' Project in 1939. Less famously, he also wrote *Satan Comes Calling* in 1940. The main character in this story leaves the comfort of his Bucks County farmhouse to partake of the fun, excitement and exhilaration of New York. There, however, he finds Satan going about his perniciously evil ways.[97] Would this clearly urban (urbane) and boastful devil now follow the money trail to Bucks ... along with the growing legion of New Yorkers with their wealth, talent, and fame?

---

[97] Kendall Crossen (aka Bennett Barlay), *Satan Comes Calling*, New York: Red Star News Company, 1940.

CHAPTER 8

THE DEVIL MUCH
PREFERS MINK

So, let us, right now, give this group and its milieus a name. The name ... is Exurbanite; its habitat, the Exurbs. The exurb is generally further from New York than the suburb ...

   –   A.C. Spectorsky, *The Exurbanites, 1955*

In the world outside Bucks County, there seems to be a great many people who think that Bucks County is in New Hope. This is not true; New Hope is in Bucks County, although the statement bears some qualification ... New Hope is in Bucks County to the same extent that Monaco is in France.

   –Timothy Weed, *"Livelier than Ever,"*
   Bucks County Traveler, July 1956

A SLICE OF **HELL**

They came flocking into Bucks County like locusts—artists and writers and the flannel-suited execs from Madison Avenue and Radio City. All were looking for a paradise away from the rat race. What they found was something a lot different....

For example, take Bil... to set up a quiet hor... happen to Bill's wife... the TV studio? How... her wild and despe...

And these are just... refugees who cam... search of high jin... with them all the... they were leavin... in such a grab b... lay smoldering.

Here is a nov... and packed...

Fig. 8.1 *The Devil in Bucks County* by Edmund Schiddel

Giant Cardinal Edition Jacket (1960) by Pocket Books, Inc.

50¢

GIANT CARDINAL EDITION

G C·83

A SHOCKING NOVEL ABOUT A SLICE OF EXURBIA FAMOUS FROM MANHATTAN TO BEVERLY HILLS

The Devil in Bucks County

Edmund Schiddel

THE COMPLETE BOOK

He is broad-shouldered and naked. Her torn blue nightgown has slipped from her shoulders and rides high about her thighs. Dracula-like, he plants a hungry kiss on her neck; her eyes are closed and her ruby red lips are pursed in expectation. Her head is thrust backwards and her mane of blonde hair reaches down to her waist and matches the gold of her wedding band. He is not her husband, but he is about to ravage her and exultingly satisfy "her wild and desperate longings." In the dark room, their anatomies will intertwine on the white sheets. Welcome to Bucks County!

This adulterous liaison between a bakery truck deliveryman and a neglected housewife serves as the jacket illustration for Edmund Schiddel's (1909-1982) novel *The Devil in Bucks County.* It was published by Simon & Schuster in 1959. The artwork actually appears on the cover of the Pocket Books edition, which was released in paperback in 1960 ... when a 450-page paperback sold for only fifty cents. The passionate bedroom scene between the bakery boy and the Bucks County housewife is overprinted with sensational hype: "A shocking novel about a slice of exurbia famous from Manhattan to Beverly Hills." The "high jinx" and "smoldering" scandals played out in the old stone farmhouses are alluded to on the back cover, while the drinking, whoring, and wife-swapping are further glamorized between quotes from the *New York Times* ("Shocking, vivid, valid ...") and the *Philadelphia Bulletin* ("The last word on Bucks County ..."). Red letters in the title are cleverly pointed, like the devil's pointy tail.

The Devil in Bucks County was Edmund Schiddel's first novel in his Bucks County trilogy. *Scandal's Child* was published in 1962, and lastly *The Good and Bad Weather* in 1965. Schiddel was a local writer who fictionalized the "unusually repellent" people and their lifestyles who lived in the New Hope area. His depiction was strongly objected to by some. In *The Good and Bad Weather* ("Hotter than Harlow" according to the jacket) the main protagonist is "Tavio," the wanderer. He's described as a "swaggering, arrogant (tattooed) stud ..." who appears to have more than a bit of the devil in him.

I suppose it now seems pretty shallow and silly, the type of sleazy come-on that was used to sell cheap paperbacks at a time when the paperback market in America was absolutely booming with sleaze and depravity as cultural and legal restraints were swept away.[98]

The arousing scene on the cover of *The Devil in Bucks County* might unfortunately lead the prospective reader to judge the book to be of no greater depth or meaning than a thousand other titillating "night readers" with lurid covers and formulaic storylines that screamed for attention on the paperback racks of drug stores and train stations. But there's more here than sleaze and soft core sex; there's symbolism and even sensitivity in this particular (peculiar?) slice of exurbia where the dark side of life in scandalous Bucks is exposed … isn't there Mr. Schiddel? Besides, who or what was this "devil" in Bucks County? Hadn't he left? Had he returned only to play the role of a crumby bread truck Casanova? Not likely.

Somewhere West of the Hudson

A good place to find answers to these questions is New Hope. New Hope is a Pennsylvania village that sits on a long and narrow river terrace composed of sands and gravels washed down the Delaware Valley by the last great glacial meltoff. The village faces a quarter-mile wide river from its quarter-mile wide floodplain. Main Street runs the length of the village and has but three or four cross streets that fall steeply from a wooded 200-300 foot-high Triassic ridge to the west of town. (*See:* Fig.8.2)

---

[98] In 1959 the U.S. Court of Appeals decided in favor of the publication of D.H. Lawrence's notorious *Lady Chatterly's Lover* on the grounds that it had "redeeming social or literary value." Thus ended the "Chatterly ban;" the door was opened for the publication of other works like *Tropic of Cancer* and *Fanny Hill*.

Fig. 8.2 Looking West on Mechanic St., New Hope, Pa.
1950's Postcard *(Author's Collection)*

Beyond the village outskirts lies the rich and rolling farm country of Solebury Township. Runs called Rabbit and Dark Hollow define the mile-long, three-square mile village at its upper and lower ends. But it's the larger creek with the American Indian name "Aquetong" that defines the town's history and explains something of the circumstances and changes that brought Schiddel's devil to Bucks County. The Aquetong rises three miles to the west in a great natural spring (Ingham Spring), a fissure in the sedimentary beds that releases an enormous volume of clear, cold water. The water flows down a willow-shaded ravine through New Hope to the Delaware. Along its course, and especially in New Hope, its sweep had been a source of mill power for centuries. New Hope spent the better part of its history as a sweaty little mill and canal town. The raw materials and products of the various flour, flaxseed oil, lumber, tin and iron casting mills were carried up and down the canal by barges. The junction of the Aquetong and the canal was the nerve center of the busiest industrial community in the valley. But that prosperity based on the clatter and hum of the mills all faded away with changes in modes of transportation. By the late nineteenth-century the village was on the brink of obscurity, exhausted and in an economic sink. It languished, apathetically crawling through an extended period of agricultural decline and nearby rural abandonment. A saving grace was needed.

What saved New Hope and brought about its rebirth – and what eventually led to the return of the devil – was another geographic plus: an advantageous location on what since colonial times had been a major river crossing and the major thoroughfare from New York to Philadelphia. A ferry house and tavern were on site as early as the 1720s, providing bed and whiskey before the ferry crossing to the Jersey shore. From there, the York Road became the King's Highway, carrying stagecoaches along an old Indian trail to points north. By the 1920s-30s this historic route, paved for motor cars and lined with roadside filling stations, wayside taverns, and small tourist cabins, served as one of the great migratory trails of the growing American road and roadster culture. Macadamized (as it would later be McDonaldized) state "rowt" 202 snaked up across the rubbish dumps of the Newark meadows and led to lower Manhattan via the glistening white-tiled tube of the Holland Tunnel. It opened a floodgate. And the footlight people from the Great White Way, the literary lights from Greenwich Village, and later the TV and Madison Avenue advertising men in their light gray suits, all "found" Bucks. This would happen in the course of a motor excursion before the Saturday matinee, on a long weekend drive into the "country." What they actually found was New Hope and its Solebury farmscape:[99]

> (They) went for an automobile ride into unexplored territory somewhere west of the Hudson; as chance would have it, the road taken was Route 202 to Flemington and thence across the Delaware; one glimpse of those farmhouses with stone walls two feet thick, one phrase dropped by a real estate dealer about land up for grabs at $25 an acre, and the first sale had been consummated.

---

[99] A.C. Spectorsky, *The Exurbanites,* New York: J.B. Lippincott, 1955; p. 49.

In the late 1920s-early 1930s much of Bucks was still outside the radius of the yet-to-be developed automobile suburb. It was a region of diminished farmland, semi-isolated service hamlets and villages, and occasionally larger towns. All were going about their rather prosaic existence. For example, look at Bristol Borough: Big news in this very old canal and river town was the opening of a soap factory and the raiding of the "house of ill repute." The commonplaces were sauerkraut suppers and card parties, bowling leagues with bowling scores prominently reported in the local newspaper. Even then, Bristol went about its solidly blue collar existence. Brick row houses by the trolley tracks were being converted into summer bungalows, workers were being hired and fired at the furniture factories, Italian immigrants were opening barber shops, while some others were dodging water bills and burning buildings to collect the insurance. People watched lots of movies at the nickelodeon; in 1927 it was ten cents a show to see Ken Maynard play the dare-devil Don Juan in *The Unknown Cavalier.* The movie *Devil's Island* was billed as a drama about the strangest marriage market in the world. Bristolians also watched *Wings of the Storm"* which was described as a "Touching human story of a Girl, a Man, and a Dog." This show also featured Chief Mohawk and Little Papoose live on stage performing a number of "native dances" between the featured film and a "funny reel" called *Dummy Love.* All this, or only this, while New Hope was about to be anointed with Broadway glitter and New York chic.

While Bristol's merchants were attracting window shoppers with marked down, out-of-date "New York Clothes," New Hope was attracting the New Yorkers who wore not any of those clothes, but the latest in mink. Not that there was anything wrong with the lives that people lived in Bristol and other such real places; the point is that the type of lifestyle and entertainment found in Bristol was obviously of no appeal to the people busy "finding" New Hope by way of Route 202. Bristol and New Hope were just moving to a different rhythm, listening to a different drummer. A dichotomy was forming in the county between the blue collar working class at the lower end and the upcounty mink collar crowd. Of course, the devil much preferred mink.

From One Village to Another

By the 1920s New York's Greenwich Village was already losing some of its "Bohemian" appeal. The rebel artists' studios and literary tea-rooms and taprooms were being squeezed out by the more well-to-do white collar newcomers and tourists. The end of the all-night intellectual conversations and, especially, the cheap rents forced many an artist to the outlands. Bucks County was part of that outland. Actually, the changes being felt in Bucks had begun sometime before. Attracted by the untended and untenanted fields and farms, by the idle and deserted farm buildings that were home to five or more generations of farm families, artists and writers had already "found" Bucks by the late nineteenth century. "Expats" arriving on the outland were lured here by precisely those things Greenwich Village once possessed, but had lost: inexpensive rooms, low taxes, and a comparative quiet. Here, they could set up their easels and writing tables and work more affordably than they could in Greenwich Village lofts and brownstone attics.

It was the same disrepaired buildings, barns, and mills that provided the artists with a most picturesque subject matter. The peace and serenity of the countryside allowed them their concentration and moods. Their creative spirits were free to flourish here. Bucks was also the ideal locale for the artists because it was between the famous Philadelphia art academies and the New York dealers and galleries.

As early as the 1870s-80s, and long before artists gravitated to the New Hope area on the Delaware, a "colony" of painters and writers from New York spent several summers exploring and celebrating the aesthetic pleasures of the Neshaminy and Perkiomen Creeks. "Lovers of the wild" stayed in cabins and bungalows along the creek banks and sung their praises of nature in verse, in prose, and on canvas.[100]

The "Pennsylvania Impressionist School" of painting had its beginnings in 1898 when William Lathrop rented the miller's house across the road from Phillips Mill. The old canal and an assortment of run-

---

[100] George MacReynolds gives a nice description of this "colony" in his *Places Names in Bucks County* under "Neshaminy Creek" on p. 256 ff.

down structures abounded in the area, thus supplying Lathrop (and others)[101] with their subject matter. Critics accuse the Bucks "art colony" of never having developed the spark and dynamism of a Hudson River School. They painted the everyday and commonplace ... and not the sublime and romantic ... not the Palisades and the Highlands of the Hudson. Furthermore, they never earned a national reputation because their works were regarded as regional, repetitive, and really not very original renditions of the same old stone houses, barns, and mills. This was, after all, a time of urban gusto when the teeming tenements and ashcan alleyways of the big city demanded attention.

Some even thought of the Bucks "art colony" as a collection of dropouts from a more vital and vigorous urban school, preferring summer hillsides and haystacks to the backyards and rooftops of Greenwich Village. They painted the trivia of the countryside instead of the trivia of the city. That was their sin. This "School of Placidity," this "Copycat School" of Delaware Valley "dabblers" would include on their canvases extinct covered bridges that were simply dittoes from old photographs, dead pheasants and rabbits that hung from weathered gray barnboards, and autumn pastures with early winter moons. They kept churning it out for years. It was a tritely pleasant rural nostalgia; but nothing profound or innovative here. All this, according to its detractors. These artists were said to lack the anguish and self-torture that "real" artists felt; the anguish that would have allowed them to paint pigeons perched on the window ledges of tenements. These local artists who "peddled their work (wherever there was hanging space) – hotel lobbies, the 'Sho-A-Rama' clothesline show, roadside dogwagons" were roundly trashed by Edmund Schiddel:[102]

---

[101] The New -Solebury "art colony" would come to include Daniel Garber, Edward Redfield, John Folinsbee, Harry Leith-Ross, Robert Spencer, and Cortland Butterfield ... among others.
[102] Edmund Schiddel, *The Devil in Bucks County*, pp. 167-71.

The art of the region never really reflected the conflict of the times, though the years since 1900, when people began speaking of a 'Delaware Valley School' were as full of conflict as any in history ... (they) painted barns and landscapes, and usually there were barns in the landscapes ... the trouble with most Bucks artists was that the main current of Western painting had by-passed them ... the sterility of the county's art, the preoccupation with snow scenes, the inevitable bridges and barns, the academic still lifes, reflected a lack of struggle; half the county's artists had never had to fight for anything, and the placidity of their palettes showed it; their lives, too, lacked the challenges which encourage new forms and methods.

But, in fact, these artists who dressed in slouch hats and sat with their palettes and easels along the old canal, along the river and the river road, have achieved a reputation far beyond the valley itself; their works may now fetch prices in the six-figure range and be exhibited at the Metropolitan, the Corcoran, and the Philadelphia Museum of Art. Furthermore, what the "New Hope Artist and Professional Colony" did accomplish (and this returns us to our story line and the devil) was this: As had happened elsewhere (at the falls of the Passaic River, in the Hudson Highlands, and at Philadelphia's Fairmount waterworks) what was once a bustling scene of commercial and industrial activity began to be interpreted aesthetically; and, with the patina of time and the soft, muted strokes of the artist's brush, was reinvented as an industrial aesthetic. The derelict features of a prior industrial age gradually faded back to nature. The quarries, limekilns, mills, and even the farm fields became the objects of a sentimentalized, elegiac world. Though these Bucks artists may not have reflected the torment and excitement of the urban landscape, they did record the vanishing *Peaceable Kingdom* in such a way, a longed-for and memory-rich way, that what they painted confirmed the desirability of seeing and living in the very area they painted.

In this, their success paved the way for other changes. Bucks was now stamped with a certified national attractiveness. During the Great

Depression, many found the county a cheap (or at least cheaper) place to live and work than elsewhere. Hard times forced local families to become dependent on rentals. By the 1930s the small cooperative community of a dozen or so serious artists had morphed into something else. At least one hundred and eighty "artists" were said to be in residence in the area by then. Many no doubt were more attracted by the potential for partying and socializing than by the lessened potential for painting the less tranquil and more crowded hamlets and hillsides. Art students came and rented homes (converted pig sties became studios) to be near their mentors. Dilettantes and cocktail circuit artists arrived. "Clothesline" art replaced the real thing. Soon there were so many artists that rivalries and schisms developed between "traditionalists," "modernists," and "independentists." True artists were scattered further upcounty and to the back-country. Commercial artists welded stronger ties to the city, to New York, which was now just an easy commute. When Henry Miller visited New Hope in 1945 ("somewhat of a slumbering European village), he found "no hope" there for the genuine artist:[103]

> The only artists who were not leading a dog's life were the commercial artists; they had beautiful homes, beautiful brushes, beautiful models. The others were living like ex-convicts …A corn-fed hog enjoys a better life than a creative writer, painter …

Spring Fever Plows No Furrows, But "Bucks Fever" …

Both the "real" and the commercial artists brought a high level of name recognition to the county. Now, it was just "Bucks;" no need for Bucks County, Pa. This recognition set the stage for the coming of the glamorous people and all the sparkle and gaiety they would bring with them. For a while it was believed (or feared) that the county might

---

[103] Henry Miller, *The Air-Conditioned Nightmare*, New York: A New Direction Book, p. 16.

become "Hollywood East." By the early 1930s tantalizing but un-founded rumors circulated that some big, unnamed west coast studio was scouting out a suitably scenic 4,000 acres in the New Hope area. (Indeed, scenes in the 1914 serial *The Perils of Pauline* had been filmed locally ... the heroine being roped to the tracks on a railroad trestle). But "Hollywood East" it was not to be; "Broadway South" it **was** to be. Schiddel described the arrival of the playwrights and producers, the stage actors and actresses, along with all the "camp-followers." Cele-brated or not so celebrated, they had all contracted "Bucks fever" and would soon acquire their very own vintage farmhouses. "It was Broad-wayites who brought the first, 'transported' life, living in much the same way they had on East Seventy-third Street or in the Village in New York, one major difference being that they ate and drank on their flag-stone terraces instead of at restaurants ..."[104]

A young James Michener watched the influx of this same nou-veau riche Shubert Alley element, and wrote of the disdain the "natives" felt for them:[105]

...Distinguished men and women from New York theatrical life discovered our magnificent farms, and for the next forty years one after another of the old places fell into alien hands. I was a boy at the time this invasion began and I can remember the bitterness with which we watched the outlanders arrive with their inflated bankrolls and their station wagons: George S. Kaufman, the playwright; S.J. Perelman, who thought he was funny; Pearl Buck, who wrote all those books about China; Oscar Hammerstein, who was mixed up with musical comedies; Moss Hart, who wrote and directed plays ... we watched them all come and of each we suspected the worst.

Hart had come to visit Kaufman. One day while traveling through the county with Harpo Marx he bought seventy-two acres and stayed in

---

[104] Edmund Schiddel, op. cit., p.110.
[105] James Michener, *Report of the County Chairman*, New York: Random House, 1961, p. 73.

Bucks for the next seventeen years. Hammerstein bought a farm, raised cows, and had an inspirational view of the rolling Bucks hills and fields before his window. It was here that he wrote the lyrics for the hit musical *Oklahoma*. He also collaborated with Richard Rogers on *South Pacific*, which was based on the "native" James Michener's *Tales of the South Pacific*. The actress Helen Hayes stayed for a while at the New Hope Inn (though her home remained in Rockland County in the Hudson Valley), and Lilian Gish and Sidney Blackburn were among the then famous who came to Bucks.

With all the accumulated talent and fame gravitating around Bucks, the New York press began to refer to the county as the "Genius Belt." A county home in Bucks was the Holy Grail for the New York elite. Sitting at the typewriter in a rundown farmhouse or converted chicken coop, a writer could find both a retreat from the noisy pandemonium of the city and (hopefully) inspiration from the Black Angus grazing on the hillside outside the window. Local realtors encouraged the rush to Bucks and helped emboss the name "Bucks County" in the national consciousness by placing enticing advertisements in the *New York Times*; James Michener noted how such ads spread "the illusion that Bucks County was a paradise ... the fame of Bucks County was due in large part to (realtors') inspired shenanigans."[106] They took the bait and in 1937 alone more than forty farms were sold to New Yorkers.

When the old playhouse had its gala opening in a rebuilt and renovated grist mill on the banks of the Aquetong in 1939, New Hope had begun to ride the wave of Broadway notoriety; Edward Everett Horton was on stage and Orson Welles and Burgess Meredith were in attendance. It was experimental theatre and the unproven plays just might end up on Broadway. And it was proven Broadway plays in a rustic setting. It was young actors and actresses just starting out, doing their apprenticeships. But the "straw hat circuit" drew established stars too: Diana Barrymore, Zazu Pitts, Jackie Cooper, Hermione Gingold, Bert Lahr, Arthur Treacher, and Bela Lugosi. And later came Grace Kelly,

---

[106] James Michener, Introduction to *The Genius Belt, The Story of the Arts in Bucks County, Pennsylvania,* Penn State, Pa.: Penn State Press, 1997, p.8.

Liza Minelli, and Merv Griffin. With all these famous names associated with it, the converted mill quickly achieved a reputation as perhaps the finest summer stage in America. The quality of productions, the goings on between this one and that one, the late night card games and drinking bouts, were reported on by big city columnists including Dorothy Parker. Her house guests, friends of these house guests, and friends of the friends of the house guests – a chain of at least sixty, it was said – all took out mortgages so they might breathe the same country air as the celebrities. Glitter thus accrued to the once unpretentious farmlands and mill town. Legends were made. More "outlanders" and "aliens" poured in. And the devil awaited his opportunity.

Despite the surface glitter, there was something evil in the wings, a nasty shadow that stalked the fly gallery, waiting. Waiting! In 1936 a film starring Jackie Cooper and Mickey Rooney made the rounds at the local theatres; it was titled *The Devil is a Sissy*. Despite what was implied in the title, clearly he was not. He was no harmless wimp. Now he was a rejuvenated, voracious abstraction carried in on the winds of exurbanization. And his time was, again, near at hand.

The stars and star-makers, the agents and publicists, and all the other hangers-on probably didn't notice it. They were no doubt too absorbed in the endless routine of play rehearsals and opening and closing night parties, brunches and lunches, and the back and forth trips to New York. But they themselves had introduced an essential change in lifestyle and landscape that would forever more characterize this part of the county. The *Facts For Farm Folks* column, the *Timely Tips Farm Calendar*, and the agricultural lime ads were pushed aside by the play and movie review columns, by party recipe and *menu maneuver* columns on how to feed and please the bevy of hungry city folk which has just arrived at your door. Calloused city hands came to "putter around the barn," while honest farm labor became a thing of the past. The air was filled with resentment and gloom. The rural way of life, as Michener observed, was ending. Animosity developed between "the poor honest residents of the county and the rich debauched strangers who swept in." Michener continues:[107]

> ... We were powerless to keep them out, and our farms were no longer productive, and in time Bucks County became world famous as a center for intellectual bohemianism, not that Kaufman, Perelman, Buck and Hammerstein ever engaged in any of it. They rather disappointed us by staying properly at home on their farms just as if they had been stuffy Bucks Countians all their lives. It was the hangers-on that made Bucks County, and especially the lovely old town of New Hope, notorious. The area was flooded with artists and writers and revolutionaries and people who never took baths. A disproportionate number of homosexuals arrived and people who read poetry aloud and listened to high-fidelity music at all hours of the night.

In the autumn of 1938 farmers across the river in Grovers Mill, near Princeton, New Jersey were arming themselves with shotguns and pitchforks in fear of H.G. Wells Martians; Orson Welles' famous Halloween radio broadcast had described their arrival. But here in Bucks, it wasn't fear of Martians, but fear of the people and things Michener had catalogued ... fear of losing the ancestral earth to outsiders and to taxes. This may have led terribly "despondent" farmers to hang themselves from barn rafters and "blow out their brains" with frequency and shotguns. As it would on many another occasion, the *New Hope News* reported "Isaac Swope, 37, committed suicide by hanging himself in the barn ... (he) had seemed in particularly good spirits and had plowed the entire day."

"This Peculiar Panorama"

Mr. Schiddel created the same image of local peoples' lives being affected by changes they could neither understand nor cope with; he

---

[107] James Michener, *Report of the County Chairman*, p.74.

did so in a perhaps more subtle and touching way. That these "natural" changes were not only inevitable and unfortunate, but something more foreboding, became the symbolism and meaning of his "devil." The old German farmers, the "real" Pennsylvanians, could in the past fend off the foul fiend with simple devices like blue porch ceilings and hex signs. Not this time; not this new evil. It was a pernicious and pervasive cancer that fed on the lives of the "simple, unpretentious people who farmed ..." There is a mini-morality play here that pits the show-boating city people ("those dreadful people moving in everywhere") against the un-ostentatious old-timers. It's no wonder that *The Devil in Bucks County* caused quite a scandal when it first appeared in print. It kicked up a lot of Triassic dirt. New Hope and its population were described in a rather uncomplimentary way: shop windows filled with cheap junk, trucks filled with crushed stone roaring down Main Street rattling the window panes that displayed the cheap junk; café bars filled with "luncheon la-dies" gulping down martinis and whiskey sours; bored and wild di-vorcees cruising the streets "just begging for it;" people who wanted to rub against art, "big or little A, take your choice" (Art who?). "Bucks ha(d) everything." A whole devil's brigade of gaudy characters who had all "heard something about Bucks" and simply had to be part of it. This even included "cancelled" gay priests.

Otto and Emma Hutchnecker were certainly up against it. This is the old farm couple used to represent the real people. They are not perverted, not out of the ordinary, not plastic stage people. But theirs is a tragic fate. Emma is a house lady for a city family (the same family whose wife/mother is being seduced on the book jacket ... an act that results in the family's toilet being hopelessly clogged with a used con-dom). But Otto's fate is even worse; he's dying from an unnamed sick-ness:

> Otto and I planted dogwoods at the edge of that field ...
> we looked at them together, watched them grow and bloom
> in spring and turn red in fall. They meant something. The
> new people who bought the field, when they cleared, cut
> them ... somehow it seems Otto's sickness began about
> that time.

Some three hundred pages later, in a tear-wrenching passage, the aged German farmer dies; Otto dies by the window that overlooks the fields they once worked, fields that like poor Emma's heart would soon be sunless and cold as all the years of her widowhood:[108]

> He turned his head to her … life draining into death at last … the light went from his eyes, his head dropped forward and he was still … wordless and without sound in the room that was now quiet.

As Emma weeps and binds his body in linen strips as was still the custom among rural Germans, the reader comes to realize that what has died is not only Otto, but a whole way of life. Agrarian tradition, a panorama of plowed ridges and fields, a loving closeness to the ancient Triassic earth in which Otto will be buried. All this is in its twilight as "Big City" life, the devil of exurbanization, sweeps across and conquers the red-soiled farmscape, "lemonad-ing" the "real" Pennsylvanians into insignificance. We're never told whether his soul departed the house through the *"seelenfenster,"* the small soul window sometimes built into the gable end; or whether Emma followed the German custom of placing a garland of rosemary around the neck of the deceased to keep the devil away. If she didn't, it's really quite understandable. The devil, the growth, had already invaded Otto's body and Otto's land. This was the new "devil" in Bucks.

Satan and the "Subspecies"

Exurbanization? So that's the devil of it! That's the diabolical force that now slithered into the county. That's the guise he now affected. Interestingly, he took up residence in the Solebury hills, not far from where the old folk devil himself had dwelt. To quote one of Schiddel's characters, "Haven't you read Spectorsky?" Auguste Compte Spectorsky, the man who coined the word "exurb;" he introduced it into

---

[108] All of the above quoted material is from Edmund Schiddel, op.cit. pp. 13 and 336.

the language in 1955 to describe those parts of the American landscape like the Solebury-New Hope area. Further, the very same Spectorsky who defined the existence of a "mink curtain" devil.

Spectorsky was born in Paris of American parents. In the 1950s he was writing magazine articles about skiing and lifestyles for new homemakers and was regarded as something of an East Coast sophisticate. But when he died in 1972 the *New York Times* obituary writer said that "He had somewhat more substance than the public realized." He considered himself a "communicator." He was the associate publisher and advertising director at *Playboy* magazine when it first appeared on the newsstands as a thin, eighty-page newcomer. Living in Manhattan, but intimately familiar with the sylvan hills of Bucks, Spectorsky claimed "exurbanite status" for himself. His now classic work on American culture was published in 1955 under the title *The Exurbanites.* Geographically and sociologically he located this new class of people, this new "subspecies," in its proper setting; in so doing, he added a new root word and its derivatives to our vocabulary: "So, let us, right now, give this group and its milieus a name. The name … is Exurbanite; its habitat, the Exurbs. The exurb is generally further from New York than the suburb."[109] In "a wistful search for roots, for the realization of a dream, for a home" the exurbanite leapfrogged the "dull and demure domesticity" of the suburbs where "he could never be happy" to pastures further afield where his more flamboyant lifestyle could be satisfied. The journey of "these short-haul expatriates" out of and away from the city ("ex") to where the suburbs peter out is traced through the decades to the 1950s when a definable (though spotty) exurban ring surrounded New York City at a distance of between twenty-five and sixty miles. The home turf of this new "subspecies" was Rockland County west of the Hudson River, Fairfield County in southwestern Connecticut, parts of Long Island's north shore, scattered "outposts" in the Princeton area, and most especially, Bucks County's Solebury-New Hope area. Though

---

[109] A.C. Spectorsky, op. cit., p.4.

the exurbanite lifestyle is grounded in these lairs, its life support system winds back to "the city" via the highways and rail lines:[110]

> ... The new exurbanite is a displaced New Yorker. He has moved from the city to the country ... (but) he will never quite completely permit himself to be absorbed into his new surroundings; he will never acclimate ... spiritually; he will always be urban, an irreconcilable whose step, after walking a hundred country lanes, is still steadiest when it returns to the ... crowded crosswalks of Madison Avenue.

Spectorsky chronicles the first waves of displaced New Yorkers arriving in the new exurb; these were the artists and theatre people coming in as early as 1930s-40s, thus inaugurating the county's "golden age." But then, the tsunami: by the late 1940s-50s it was those on the fringe of the commercial arts, the "big slick" magazine advertising executives, the newspaper publishers and columnists, the illustrator-photographers, the writers of TV and radio jingles, and the army of junior executives. All were (or pretended to be) "movers and shakers" of ideas and trendsetters. These "up-and-coming eager beavers," these upwardly mobile "symbol manipulator(s) ... (merchants) of dreams for the rest of the nation," declared Bucks one of their exurban "capitals" and in the process overshadowed much of the earlier artistic and theatrical atmosphere. These exiles from the rat race, these pseudo-farmers jar loose the more contemplative privacy of the artists. They add nothing to the glamour parade. These in fact are Schiddel's wife-swappers and heavy drinkers; these are the people of questionable worth who bring down what Spectorsky called the "mink curtain" of exclusivity and seclusion on this part of Bucks:[111]

---

[110] Ibid., p. 6 ... 7.
[111] A.C.Spectorsky, op. cit., p.55 ... 61.

.… The exurbanites who, when they get home, are like as not to stretch a chain across their driveways. They are home as in a burrow, and want no part of any human companionship until it is forced on them by the morrow they remain secluded, declining to entertain or to be entertained (their) privacy is, by and large, respected.

Turning inward, turning his back to the area he has so recently invaded, the well-heeled period executive is caricatured in *The Exurbanites* by the cartoonist Robert Osborn; dripping with New York money and conceit, this smug and spiffy devil is shown below (Fig. 8.3).

Fig. 8.3 Spectorsky's Devil
Spiffy and conceited, hooved and with tail
(Author's sketch after Robert Osborn, p.44
in *The Exurbanites*)

So there it is, or there he is! Schiddel's devil, the debonair New York smelling of expensive cigars and with the feel of mink. Spectorsky's devil of exurban growth. This evil force appeared to have cancerated farmers like old Otto (a victory he could probably not have achieved in the 1800s); moreover, in his new junior executive guise, he ruined New Hope's attempt to remain a splendidly isolated colony of struggling artists in the hinterland.

New Hope did however remain a center of theatrical activity throughout the 1950s; the big names continued to grace the playhouse stage: Zero Mostel, Walter Mathau, Jack Klugman, Angela Lansbury, Gene Rayburn, Paul Lynde, and so many others. In 1955 Dave Garroway affirmed the playhouse's national status by featuring it on the *Today* show. That same year the hurricane-induced flooding in the valley caused muddy, debris-choked waters to rise several inches above the level of the stage and four feet above the tops of the parking meters out on Main Street. This did little to dampen the enthusiasm of theatre lovers. While the playhouse lived a quality life of its own, more and more the quality of the town and its surroundings was questioned. Budd Schulberg, the film writer, novelist (*What Makes Sammy Run?*), and TV producer found a quiet place to read and write in Solebury Township. He lived and worked there for five years and came to realize that Bucks was more than just an annex of Beverly Hills ... still, he did concede that by 1953 the county had become a "suburb of Hollywood where writers, directors, and actors retired to vegetate and hide out ..."[112]

During the 1950s there was much road-building in the area and the town itself lost the tall old trees that lined Main Street; they were gassed by the exhaust from convoys of quarry trucks that passed through town. According to one resident, the town had also become "seedy in spots, corny in others, like a gentle old lady in a Bikini bathing suit!" To be polite, the town had hit the doldrums; to be impolite, as one writer was, the town became "a sink of iniquity and neurosis." Speaking impolitely, Schiddel summarized New Hope's downhill slide this way:

---

[112] Budd Schulberg (1914-2009) as quoted in "Schulberg and the County," *Bucks County Traveler*, March 1953, p. 7.

"even the ... whores had taken off, business was so bad."[113]Chintzy commercialism, a gewgaw and gimcrack air, had cheapened a town that aspired to be more than a tourist trap. It was called tawdry and tainted; it was compared to an over-the-hill starlet living in a boarding house with only her memories and wearing a bit too much bad makeup and bargain store perfume to help keep alive the illusion of charm.

By the early 1960s Schiddel continued his tormenting critique of "Failure Beach ... a town of losers." It is tempting to quote further from Schiddel's colorful word thrashing; giving into that temptation:[114]

> ... He saw Olympia (New Hope) as unusually repellent ... the (artsy-craftsy) lower bowel of exurban art ... the middle aged and elderly moving in droves through the streets, searching for a Bohemia now as rare as the o-o bird ... They seemed so many replicas of human beings ... But whatever might be said against the place, it seemed to offer potentialities for people of little importance or talent. Balding minor actors ... fled here, making the scene any way they could, and skipped the hairpiece.

The town was cursed by "moral failure" and "wasted lives" and really needed some panache. Its appeal had withered and its population had actually dropped to fewer than a thousand residents by 1960 (down ten percent in the 1950s).

There was a different kind of life in New Hope now; it seemed to have a decidedly impaired quality to it. This was captured "with savage frankness" by Stuart James in his 1963 novel *Devil's Workshop* (*See:* Fig. 8.4), originally published in 1961 as *Bucks County Report*.[115]

---

[113] Edmund Schiddel, op. cit., p. 124.

[114] Edmund Schiddel, *The Good and Bad Weather*, New York: Simon and Schuster, 1965, p. 363.

[115] In the heyday of paperback sleaze, publishers would frequently change a book title and cover to create a more scintillating product that just might sell better the second time around. Manhattan-based Midwood (Tower) radically juiced-up the dullish-

When a famous sexologist and his research team visit the town (called "Walkers Ferry") and its environs to take the sexual temperature of the female population, they find an appalling collection of frustrated and neglected housewives seducing the lawn boys while their husbands work in the city (seducing their secretaries). "The town was known from coast to coast as the hub of a cultural center, and as a hangout for odd-balls"[116] where lesbians hosted alcohol-fueled house parties and the local police harassed the "pansies." Not good! A workshop in sex addiction and human depravity. In sum, the "usual quota" of exurban moral dereliction. The devil's own New Hope.

Fig. 8.4 Same Book, Same Author; Different Title and Cover
(Left) Stuart James, *Bucks County Report*, Midwood #F77, 1961;
(Right) Stuart James, *Devil's Workship*, Midwood #F301, 1963.

---

sounding *Bucks County Report* (#F77) with only words on the cover of this 1961 edition to the far more provocative cover (or barely covered) *Devil's Workshop* with its translucent nudity in the 1963 edition (#F301).
[116] Stuart James, *Bucks County Report* (*Devil's Workshop*), New York: Midwood (Tower) Publication, 1961, p. 33.

Something Sad and Hostile Abroad

Though exurbia played the part of the black-caped, mustachioed villain in the piece, ultimately exurbia itself was seen threatened by something larger, more earth-shaking and earth-moving, more diabolical still. As Spectorsky observed of Rockland County's hilly Triassic exurb in 1955, "there hangs over it a hush of brooding expectancy." The immensity of imminent change produced a "neurotically fatalistic charm," an "exurban sadness." Exurbia was only ephemeral. And Rockland's pleasant exurb was about to be engulfed by a rapidly spreading suburbia that was pushing its way across the Hudson River via the just-completed Tappan Zee Bridge and New York State Thruway. Much of what pertained to Rockland's vulnerable exurbia and its vestiges of theatrical grandeur was true of Bucks' exurbia as well:[117]

> The benign atmosphere is threatened; there is something hostile abroad. Here, where so many plays have been written ... there is an autumnal sadness. If you bend an ear attentively, you may be able to hear a distant sound, as if from the sky, the sound of a violin string breaking, melancholy. Silence ensues, broken by the sound of a distant bulldozer, by the sound of a dozen, two-dozen, six-dozen ranch houses and split levels being reared overnight.

The development of Bucks County's "mink curtain" exurb involved no great number of people, nor did it substantially imperil or alter the rest of the expansive region of nearby hills and ridges. It took the half century from 1900-50 for the county's population to double (to 144,000). Spectorsky's real devil was in fact gathering steam below the Langhorne Ridge, down on the outwash plain. It was unstoppable, brooding, and cataclysmic. The county's population was about to double again – but this time in only a very few years. It may have seemed desirable to some, but to others it was the worst and most sinister transformation Bucks would ever experience.

---

[117] A. C. Spectorsky, op. cit., p.73.

Pearl Buck's house is located in the relative seclusion of rural Hilltown Township. From here, she wrote about Chinese field workers living on *The Good Earth* (1931). On the other side of the county and along the river, Bucks County's good Triassic earth was being transformed (in a not unpleasant way) into the mink curtain exurb. And at the other (lower) end of the county, the good earth awaited the onslaught of the great American suburb.

At this time, some New Hope artists had begun experimenting with Colorforms; "professional (artists) do terrific things with it ... (that) really has to be seen to be appreciated."[118] What had to be appreciated too was that at the very same time these static-cling, die-cut vinyl images and shapes were invented (1951)[119] and popularized, thousands of little "Baby Boomers" were also doing amazing things with their new plastic toy as they played on the radiant-heated floors of their new homes. Monumental change was on the good earth's horizon ... and it would be called Levittown.

---

[118] *Bucks County Traveler*, November-December, 1952, p. 34.
[119] Colorforms were invented by Harry and Pat Kislevitz in their New York City apartment.

CHAPTER 9

LEVITTOWN: FALSE FIRE

Only a couple of years ago, Pennsylvania's Bucks County ... was a quiet farm country ... Now, with a speed appropriate to this jet atomic era, this sleepy hollow is becoming the nation's newest big urban center. — *New York Times, June 29,*

'Progress' in the form of steel mills and 'model' communities of pre-fabricated housing, is transforming the whole character of the locality.

–Audubon Davis, *Bucks County Traveler*, October 1952

The devil of it is ... (it's like) Lucifer's shabby victory in Eden.

– John Keats describing the new American suburb in *The Crack in the Picture Window*, 1956

Levittown Deed (portion), Appletree Hill, Nov. 5, 1953 (*Author's Collection*)

The February 2, 1948 cover of *Life* magazine pictured a scarfed and mittened five year old farm boy amid the snowdrifts of Rockville, Maine; he smiled for the camera into a warm winter sun. Inside the magazine, that same winter sun – but this time an infernal sun – shone on a group of Palestinian Jews crawling through a crossfire of Arab bullets. Between the Maine farm boy and the soon-to-be Israelis, between the warmth and scorching heat of the sun, appeared a full-length, illustrated article by *Time* magazine editor Whittaker Chambers, entitled *"The Devil."*

It seems that Chambers came upon the devil at a New Year's Eve party in a swank New York nightclub and eavesdropped on one of the demon's conversations. The Devil, who said that he'd been "underground" for a while, expressed delight in a world where man's intellectual pride had brought him to the point of being capable of self-extermination through either the plutonium bomb ("of which, frankly, I am a little tired of hearing," said the devil) or bacteriological annihilation. While he took much pleasure in these additions to humanity's arsenal of perfidious toys, the well-spring of this mid-twentieth century devil was his city-slick, metropolitan *savoir-faire*. He had become the suavely-dressed stranger with the deep Miami tan. He looked "distinguished, relaxed, urbane." He was now Madison Avenue dapper; he eschewed all those "years of fighting dim-witted peasants with horns and hoofs and tricks that a sideshow huckster would be ashamed of." He was now the slumlord and pimp, the big city omnivore and corruptor of the countryside, "which in other times had been the reservoir from which exhausted cultures replenished their faith and forces." This "Prince of Evil" was thus no joke; he drew the person he was conversing with to a window:[120]

> … to a window which overlooked the city and the harbor. Said
> Satan, "Behold the world! Behold my handiwork! … Below
> them the sheer walls of the buildings of Rockefeller Center, ab-
> stracting glittering with their geometry of electrically lighted

---

[120] Whittaker Chambers, "The Devil," *Life,* February 2, 1948, p. 81.

windows, plunged gray and chasmic to the city at their base. "A profound architecture," said the Devil. "We have a view of Hell rather like it."

Writing in the *New York Folklore Quarterly* in 1952, Louis C. Jones regretted that "The Devil seems not to come among us anymore ..." Not among the upstate farm hamlets that is. But Jones cautioned readers "not to belittle the amount of deviltry that is going on in our day ..." To many, that devilish and corrupting force was now the gangrenous tentacles of land development itself that was spreading a "crushing sameness" of "nothing-down paradise(s)" across the country(side).[121]

More specifically, it was the suburban fringes, the suburbanizing, coalescing fringes within the great East Coast Megalopolitan corridor. The years between 1948 and 1952 had witnessed the successful building and growth of what better than anything had come to personify the devil of suburban sprawl and mall(s): the large-scale, pre-planned instant city that Levitt & Sons had created on Long Island, New York. That the country would be destroyed by the bomb was a possibility; that the countryside would be destroyed by the baby boom bomb and its "babyvilles" was a fact. And the cause of it all, the devil of it all, could clearly be read in the curving, muddy streets of the new Levittown and Levittown-like communities.

The Levitts were known as "the Henry Fords of the building industry;" the Levitt firm had gained valuable experience constructing a large number of navy barracks during World War II. That war and the preceding depression had stalled suburban growth, bottling up suburbanizing energies; these energies were about to be released. By the end of the war the nation's maternity wards began greeting the vanguard of the baby boomer hordes. With the government bringing home-buying within the reach of many through VA and FHA mortgages, the Levitts answered the patriotic call by changing the topography of Long Island. Their first daring version of Levittown U.S.A. featured Cape Cod-style "little nests" with four rooms and an unfinished attic for young families

---

[121] John Keats, *The Crack in the Picture Window*, New York: Ballantine Books, 1956.

built upon what had been potato fields near the Grumman and Republic aviation plants. The instant suburb was a great success. "We were pleasantly bewildered" said Bill Levitt. It helped solve the nursery problems of the late 1940s and made home-owners of those who would have never become home-owners. Very soon the demand for no-frills, low cost Levitt houses turned the builder's vision to another developable, pastoral spot along the Atlantic Seaboard. The old *Peaceable Kingdom*, that flat and fertile outwash plain of the Quakers, was being targeted for the nation's biggest pre-planned town since Washington D.C. was laid out by Pierre L'Enfant in 1800.

Bucolic with Broccoli

On the eve of the suburban boom Bucks County farms were themselves booming – the agricultural work force was 10,000 strong and there were 3,750 farms ranking the county first among all American counties in growing summer vegetables. Though one-third of the farmhouses still didn't have telephones, radios were almost universal. A popular new 6:30 a.m. radio program called *"Down on the Farm"* on WBUX (1570 on your radio dial!) "carried vital information to the Bucks County farmer." [122]

Fig. 9.1 Future Farmers of America broadcasting on WBUX Radio in Quakertown (Bucks County School Director's Association), 1951

[122] Paul Blanshard Jr., "Boom Times for Bucks Farmers," *Bucks County Traveler,* January 1954, p. 9ff.

Quakertown area farmer George Doane foresaw no great change in farming at his end of the county; and the *Bucks County Traveler* magazine drew a picture of the "healthy, expanding farm economy." But down below Langhorne it was another matter entirely – farming was indeed doomed: "… what happens when the irresistible force of industrial progress meets the immovable object of an agricultural tradition … farming is doomed south of the Pennsylvania Railroad (lower sixth of the county) …"[123]

Before the arrival of the builders it was open farmland and woods, a metes and bounds patchwork of green and tan rectangles, squares, and parallelograms. The well-drained soil of the outwash plain was producing asparagus, spinach, turnips, parsnips, cucumbers … and a whole lot of broccoli. Though no longer the sheltered *Peaceable Kingdom* of Quaker days, it was still a relatively unspoiled market garden for the nearby cities. If no longer a somnolent pastoral world, it was still quite rural: narrow roads lined with clumps of age-old trees whose leaves rustled in the breezes that blew in from the river; trees old enough to have listened to conversations between William Penn and the American Indians; bare exposed earth; ancient stone houses without electricity or water; and livestock enough to have attracted city folk with children getting their first close look at real cows. Veterans who had seen atomic bombed and blitzed cities in Japan and in Europe had decided to raise families away from "ground zero;" *Life* and *Look* magazines described it as "defense by decentralization." Less abstractly, veterans with small but growing families living in small city houses and apartments came to picnic and sightsee. Day trippers in their Nash Ramblers and Ford Ranch Wagons explored the land of green earth and blue sky. Bill Levitt said: "Think big … you have to have nerve … you have to think big."[124] A part of this can be yours!

[123] ibid.

[124] Bill Levitt as quoted in James Michener, *Report of the County Chairman*, New York: Random House, 1961, pp.42-43.

"Big Steel"

"Big Steel" was also thinking big. The U.S. Steel Corp-oration announced plans in 1950 to construct a $400 million mill in Falls Township, lower Bucks County. The corporation purchased nearly 3,000 acres of (former) farmland along the Delaware River. These were good times for the American steel industry and here on the outwash plain a perfect geography had jelled: location at the head of navigation with easy access to iron ore from Labrador and Venezuela, proximity to major markets, and a willing and skilled labor force. Some 8,000 workers and their families would locate here, needing housing and schools, and places to shop. U.S. Steel's Fairless Works began operating in late 1952 and a planned community of 1,500+ prefabricated houses (Fairless Hills)[125]was built with a $50 million loan from U.S. Steel. And there was more – with the outbreak of the Korean War, lower Bucks was designated a "critical" defense area; other companies located here as well (Kaiser Metals which made parts for over 400 B-57 (Canberra) jet bombers). The industrialization and suburbanization of the lower county had begun and the fate of the farmlands was sealed; Bucks would quickly become a sprawling, polluting Pittsburgh with a million people.[126] Up-county, it was rumored that some of the "gentlemen farmers," the Broadway types, artists and writers, might be leaving a no longer bucolic Bucks. Few if any did; realtors calmed jittery nerves by assuring them that "the territory above the industrial region will remain rural and pleasant ..."[127] Thus, massive Korean War industrial output was wedded together with the immediate need for mass-produced housing. And so it came to be ...

---

[125] Benjamin W. Fairless was the president of U.S. Steel. The company would operate in lower Bucks County for nearly 40 years, ending operations in 1991.

[126] The lower county had in fact had a long history of industrialization centered especially on Bristol Borough: ship-building, woolen and carpet mills, Warner sand and gravel. (Nearby, and just across the river, was the massive GM plant in West Trenton).

[127] Frederick Walker, "Industrialism in Bucks County," *Bucks County Traveler*, October, 1952, p. 10.

A (Very) Marketable Dream

Textbook theory and planning became a reality. While younger brother Alfred handled the architectural details, and while a staff of one hundred engineers brought forth from their drawing boards this "prototype of a new kind of twentieth-century American living," the ground itself was readied. Farmers were bought out, being paid an average of $1,800 per acre for an aggregate of 5,560 acres. A few stubborn farmers refused to sell, but for those who did, it was far more money under the pillow than they would ever have realized in farming. Though care was taken to "work around" old burial grounds,[128] at least four pre-existing graveyards of family vaults were left untouched during construction and are today concealed by stone walls and thick bushes. "Unwanted" farm buildings, structures that decades hence might have been the idol of local historical societies, were simply cleared away; it seemingly perturbed no one in the early 1950's to see colonial era farmhouses dynamited and bulldozed, frame structures ignited and the ancient wood set ablaze with cans of gasoline hurled through the windows. Newsreel footage showing sad gray acres of burning buildings and cellar holes, explosive charges being detonated and three hundred-year old trees being uprooted, might have led some to think that someone had mistakenly spliced in battlefield footage from the European war. Poor *Peaceable Kingdom*!

The prepared ground was then "miraculously" leveled by the bulldozers … with some difficulty due to the heavy gravelly content of the outwash soils. But once readied (in early 1952) lawns were seeded and trees were staked. Foundation slabs were laid, sewer lines and water mains were dug, and telephone lines and poles were placed in the backyards (though Levitt would have preferred them buried underground). All this was done simultaneously. Bill Levitt was somewhat appalled that the existing municipal services were, to him, on a scale approaching that of 1900. (Or maybe Triassic times). When the utilities and streets

---

[128] Levittown Relics website: http://home.comcast.net/~Levittownrelics/facts/index. The actual locations are listed as "Fact #14" at this site.

were ready, "one of the most colossal acts ever of mortal creation" (according to the *New York Times*) was about to be witnessed.

The "Colossus of Levittown" was about to be born. A rail yard was built. A saw mill was set up to pre-cut the lumber. A forest of wood was cut up. Forty-eight trainloads of materials were hauled up to the rail yard each morning. Miles of bricks and appliance crates were stacked up, because each dream house would have an all-electric kitchen with an array of GE and Bendix appliances (that's 17,000 eight-cubic foot refrigerators!). With the builders' high speed construction schedule and assembly line techniques, one house was pieced together and erected in a 26-step building process that took just 16 minutes to complete. Quicker than it took to bake a cake, another stark and simple two-bedroom house, not unlike the southern California bungalows of the early 1900s, had wondrously risen on the plain. "Another day, another forty houses," proclaimed the laborers. Another 200 per week, 5,000 in the first year. Levitt supervised the construction of his community from an old stone "mansion" on a nearby hill; he was careful to point out though, and advertised prominently, that this "scientific model of the perfectly planned suburban community" consisted of fine and desirable houses, and not jerry-built "barracks" or Monopoly-board bungalows as had been unfairly rumored:

> ... Every house, every road, every facility had been
> planned and planned and planned ... Levittown is perma-
> nent and, God willing, will grow and live on long after the
> word 'defense' is forgotten.

Even before the first nail was driven, before the first house was finished, another little scene was played out: it was a cool and dreary weekend in the 1951 pre-Christmas season and a long, curious line of prospective buyers formed to see the model houses and enter the sales office on Bristol Pike. The men, dressed respectfully in their best (or only) topcoats and ties, the women in their Lana Turner coiffures and Sunday furs, came to see what Levitt was billing as "America's Best Value." The right publicity and advertising had already produced an atmosphere of enthusiasm and acceptability. There was no question that

Fig. 9.2 Modern Miracle This Is Levittown, Pa.
The Mayrose Co. Publishers, Linden, New Jersey. Period Postcard (Author's Collection)

they liked what they saw and had to choose from: several appliance-stocked models with sliding aluminum doors and Thermopane insulated picture windows ranging in price from $9,000 to $17,000. The typical Levittowner model required no down payment from veteran defense workers and only six hundred dollars for veterans. And the monthly mortgage was an amazing sixty dollars (And, "Wow, a backyard for the kids" and radiant, slab heating to warm the backsides of boomer babies, put comfortably to sleep on the floor). Before the day was done, 75,000 people, a good many of them pregnant or soon to be, had swarmed the sales office, transacting $2 million in business. In the first week, $5 million was transacted with the bank that Levitt had brought down from New York to handle the mortgages. It was said that the paperwork could be completed in just three minutes. Never again would the path to suburban homeownership be paved with such easy terms.

A Monday In 1952

It was Monday, the 23rd of June, 1952 and armies were stalemated somewhere north of the 38th parallel in the Korean Peninsula. The U.S. 45th Infantry Division was killing Chinese troops near Chorwon, and a Filipino battalion was holding its position in hand-to-hand combat with other Chinese. Half a world away, it was Monday in the northeastern Megalopolis and Robin Roberts and the Philadelphia Phillies were watching the raindrops wash out their scheduled baseball game with the Chicago Cubs; meanwhile, Jim Hearn and the New York Giants watched the same thing happen to their game with Cincinnati at the Polo Grounds. It was raining all along the East Coast ... and Cincinnati had just changed its team name from Reds to Redlegs so that no one would think Ted Kluszewski and his teammates were communists.

Deep within the rainy East Coast corridor, sixty five miles from New York and twenty five miles from Philadelphia, it was Monday in lower Bucks County and Joe Shugart from Detroit along with his wife and children were among the first families to move into their new Levittown house.[129] Joe, crewcut and smiling, his wife and their baby both smiling, and their young son, smiling beneath his baseball cap visor – here indeed was the postwar "Happy Days" generation, cut neatly from the Ozzie & Harriet mold. They had just settled the title papers and received their house keys; they stood proudly posed for the news photographer beside their luxury brick fireplace and still-packed cardboard boxes. Above the *New York Times* news photo[130] could be seen the "feverish" last minute activity of the construction crews as they put the finishing touches on scores of other houses and driveways. All around Joe's house, Levittown's "first families" were claiming their 85 by 115-

---

[129] According to the *"Levittown Relics"* website, the first official residents were John and Philomena Dougherty who moved into the Stonybrook section on June 23, 1952. Other families may have "occupied" their houses earlier ("under cover of darkness"), but Bill Levitt for years sent Mrs. Dougherty flowers on the anniversary of her family's move. "Levittown Facts #5," *Levittown Relics:* http://home.comcast.net~Levittownrelics/facts/index.

[130] The *New York Times*, Real Estate Section, p. 1, June 29, 1952.

foot piece of paradise. For some, this new home was to be their honeymoon suite; still amazed by it all, they camped out on the floor that first night and dined on cold cereal and pickles. They were young (then) and they worked in steel or in the defense plants. They were from lower middle class backgrounds and were drawn here from near and far ... from Philadelphia's crowded neighborhoods or Pittsburgh's, from Mahanoy City, Scranton, Wilkes-Barre and countless coal patch towns in the upstate anthracite country, and from New York and Trenton. The men and women of the new suburban frontier were described quite magnanimously by the local press:[131]

> Like their early American ancestors who blazed a covered-wagon trail across the continent, a group of twentieth-century families will 'pioneer' a new community when they become the first to move into Bucks County's new development, Levittown, today and tomorrow.

It was on that same Monday and ninety miles away in the South Bronx; a seven year old was trying to find the missing piece to complete his shoebox baseball card collection. The missing card being Enos "Country" Slaughter. He was the right fielder for the St. Louis Cardinals in 1952, and more importantly, he was the #65 card in the Topps bubblegum baseball card set. That afternoon the seven year old had made several trips past the Irish and German corner bars to the mom-and-pop candy store where he invested the last few pennies he had found in the dust beneath his bed in another pack of cards. But it was fruitless; Enos Slaughter still eluded him. His last chance this day would be the spontaneous trading and flipping sessions on the apartment house stoops after the evening curb ball game. When the light that filtered down between the walk-up tenements (tenements faced with reddish Triassic building stone!) became came too dim to see the Spaldeen (a pink rubber ball that blended in all too well with the factory wall where "off-the-point" was played) piles of cards wrapped in rubber bands were brought from dungaree pockets for bartering. Somewhere in this red and pink

---

[131] *Bristol Courier*, June 23, 1952.

world of street games and Triassic stone would surely be found an Enos Slaughter.

But there would be no curb ball that night. No groups of boys with stacks of baseball cards bulging in their back pockets. And no Enos Slaughters. It had been happening for quite some time, but this night, as never before, its awful magnitude impressed itself upon him. His South Bronx neighborhood was being dismantled building by building, block by block. Friends were moving away day by day. The vacant, brick and glass strewn lots now outnumbered the apartments. Tommy's father had found a job in Nyack; Johnny's family had moved to a house on Staten Island; and Ronnie's parents had found their dream somewhere on the farmlands of southeastern Pennsylvania. The cruel politics of urban renewal (This was a "slum" and slums needed to be torn down) and the new sociology of suburban sprawl (a.k.a. "white flight") were beyond his comprehension. His red Triassic world of five-story apartments and front stoops was as much a victim of government, baby suburbs, and cars as the rolling red-earthed farmlands ninety miles away. He knew only that there was no one left to play with. There were no Enos Slaughters to be found. Only emptied-out apartment shells and deserted streets.

The following night Joe Shugart and his family may have watched the Milton Berle show on their new DuMont seven-inch TV in the comfort of their new Levittown home. But the seven-year old in the South Bronx was instead transfixed by the gaunt black and white figure in black cassock with cape and waistband who had telegenically begun to captivate viewers with a half hour show on another network. Rather than the actual message, it was the image itself of a sometimes angry, sometimes compassionate Catholic bishop with his chalk and blackboard diagrams that mesmerized him. Fulton J. Sheen's message of hope and perfect love in a suffering world eluded him. He gathered though that "that wicked man – Satan" was alive and out there in the stygian darkness with men named Marx and Stalin. The bishop described the "horrible face of Satan," the face that filled the world with despair and demonic disruption; but there was hope in that "without the devil, there could be no saints."[132]   But there was more anger than hope in the bishop's coal-dark eyes when he spoke of communist governments and the power of wickedness, of "our great problem" with communism, scavengers, manure, and the death of decaying civilizations. The seven year old didn't know what all this was, but it sure sounded serious. He certainly didn't associate communism with the loss of his friends, with the Cincinnati Reds, or with the impossibility of finding an Enos Slaughter baseball card. But others knew exactly what communism was and where to find it. Or at least they thought they did.

Punishment for "Cardboard Canyon"

While the new Levittown was orderly and meticulously becoming a city of 70,000 people and 17,000 houses on the outwash plain, much of the rest of the county – the rolling farm country on the Triassic lands – still remained for the moment a relatively unchanged backwater of rural seclusion. But Levittown symbolized the metamorphosis the entire county was destined to undergo. The "overdevelopment" of lower Bucks was reflected in the 113% growth rate the county experienced in the 1950s. And this was viewed by some "old-timers" with fear and contempt. The assembled panoply of row on serpentine row of "boxes on a slab" brought creeping claustrophobia to the land-wealthier up-county residents. Vicious things were said and thought of the new community. James Michener, reflecting on Levittown's early days, saw it this way:[133]

---

[132] Bishop Fulton *"Life is Worth Living,"* February, 1952. YouTube videos (3 parts) on "The Demonic in the World Today." Speaking of saints (and in the context of Bucks County) Mother (now Saint) Katherine Drexel became the county's first saint in the year 2000 for her work in founding and leading the Sisters of the Blessed Sacrament at a convent in Cornwell's Heights, Bensalem Township. She died in 1955 after devoting a lifetime to the welfare and education of minorities and the poor. Interestingly, Bishop Sheen himself is now a candidate for sainthood.
[133] James Michener, *Report of the County Chairman*, New York: Random House, 1961, p. 140.

... The rumors ... circulated in my end of the county. This gossip leveled (several) charges at Levittown. It was a rural slum with people crowded together like rabbits. It was filled with undesirable elements from the big cities, which meant Jews and Catholics with special emphasis on Italians. Unions were known to be strong (here) and engaged in evil work. The area was crawling with communists who had even dared to name a public school after J. Robert Oppenheimer.

The charges, both general and specific, were many: the development was said to personify the shabbiness and monotony of the new American suburb stigmatized by musical verses like "ticky-tacky little boxes." Acres of cheap slapboard construction had usurped the fine farmland, chasing away the farmers, as well as the artists and writers who thrived on the good vibrations of an unsullied and secluded rural milieu. Or so it was argued. Good old Bucks, "the one-time millionaires' country playground," had been democratized and downgraded to a teeming middle class "fertility valley" with overcrowded two shift-a-day elementary schools (Joke: One school child to another: "Are you new here, too?"; "No, I've been here two days!").

It was, of course, assumed that "culture" could flourish only in the more culturally rarified atmosphere of places like New Hope and Solebury. Some readers of the *Bucks County Traveler* magazine did, however, complain about the fawning attention always accorded the New Hope arts and playhouse community at the expense of "culture-less" Levittown. The magazine did correct itself (in the mid-1950s) with several revealing stories about the "dream-city" in the lower county, in fact praising the work of the Levittown Opera Company, the Color Camera Club, the String Orchestra, and the fifty-member Artists Association. It was pointed out that while most Levittown artists considered themselves "Sunday amateurs," many in the group had fine arts degrees and created "really professional work" ... heroic pieces of sculpture and paintings produced in their converted carports. Bill Levitt himself encouraged the cultural scene by letting the artists use an old surviving farmhouse (the Watts farm) for their meetings. Nor was live theatre ignored – the Levittown Players staged productions geared to young families with themes like expectant motherhood and babysitting.

Furthermore, the design itself was said to be poorly conceived. Too much open space was given over to streets and roads, rather than to gardens and green-lined pedestrianways. The seventy miles of winding roads created a world ruled by DeSotos, Hudsons, and Studebakers; a world ruled by men with car keys who commuted daily to distant jobs, leaving behind matriarchal households where much boredom resulted from an inability to go anywhere or do anything with a growing brood of kids. There weren't enough green spaces, bike paths, neighborhood play areas and stores within walking distance.

All the streets and all the houses looked alike right down to the cracked, Thermopane picture windows, thus producing a maze of confusion. Relatives and friends who braved the dust and dirt, became easily lost when they came out to visit. Children and dogs got lost all the time. Husbands, even with help from the police, couldn't find their way home in the evening … or worse, ended up in the wrong look-alike house in the wrong bed with the wrong look-alike wife. The symbiosis of sin and suburbia was thus explained. Not only did all the streets and houses look alike, all the people and what they did was monotonously the same. The same Tupperware parties and the same cheese dip in the same but different living rooms. Stiflingly similar cocktail parties with everyone hurriedly poisoning themselves with martinis. Or so it was said.

In his classic 1956 suburban critique (*The Crack in the Picture Window*) author John Keats brutally described "the evil (of) development life" in these "future slums:" [134]

---

[134] John Keats, *The Crack in the Picture Window*, New York: Ballantine Books, 1956, p. 156-57.

... the cheapest and easiest step to a life of numb horror ... to the abyss of boredom and conformity ... the simple fact is, look-alike people act alike in look-alike houses and they all go burbing off together down their peculiar roads to inanity.

He cameos the world created by the "builders (with) little red eyes" through the eyes of a typical homemaker:[135]

(Mary) stood looking out her picture window and for the first time became aware of the picture window across the treeless street ... she ran to her door and tore it open, looking up and down the block. And everywhere she looked, she saw houses like her own, row on row of them, the same, the same, the same ...

The landscape Mary surveys with sudden fear has become "a straitjacket for (her) soul."[136]

The truth of course was rather different. Bill Levitt's father and the company founder, Abraham, had said that "Houses are for the people, not critics ..." While Levittown, Long Island, was all Cape Cods, in Bucks County Levitt planned the "perfect community" with six different house models (Ranchers, Country Clubbers, Levittowners, Jubilees, Colonials, and Pennsylvanians) in seven different colors – meaning that the exact same house would appear only once in forty-two times.

A one class (low class, at that), like-minded community on a grand scale ...yes, that's Levittown! Everybody was young, of more or less the same educational and social background, and motivated by the same vision of upward mobility. And everybody was white. Blacks were excluded from this "apartheid dreamworld" until almost 1960 when they were unhappily accepted along with other growing pains like

---

[135] John Keats, *op. cit.*, p. 115-16.
[136] John Keats, op. cit., p.157.

crime, drugs, and teenage restlessness. And it wasn't just racial segregation. A built-in part of this new suburb was a separating out through a geographic "caste system." As originally conceived, Levittown was to integrate different price models on the same streets in the same sections. But, in fact, each differently priced model was built exclusively in different sections, thus creating blue collar "shantytowns" among the Ranchers and Levittowners, middle income areas with Jubilees in the intermediate-priced sections, and white collar managerial enclaves where the higher-priced Country Clubbers were built. As urbanologist Lewis Mumford summarized it, "mechanically, it is admirably done. Socially, the design is backwards."

The new town was also thought to have too much of an army post atmosphere. It was like Rin Tin Tin's army post out on the Great Plains where the wind and rain lashed away at the runty saplings and washed away the grassless lawns in rivers of mud. Enthusiasm amid the mud. Mud-splattered running boards and pant legs hiked up to avoid the omnipresent mud. In fact, the first Levittowners took much pride in their "pioneering" effort and peppered their talk with echoes of frontier-day bravado. The analogy was strengthened by the prime time TV shows young families watched in their family room dens: from the early 1950s *Death Valley Days* to the late 1950s *Wagon Train* pioneer families were led west by the likes of Major Seth Adams. Maybe the 1955 anthology *Frontier* said it best: as pale blue ovals of light flickered from thousands of TV screens on Sunday nights, Levittowners (along with a legion of other suburban pioneers) were greeted with these opening lines: "This is the land of beginning again. This is the story of men and women facing the frontier." And so it was. Not vicariously, and not out on the western Plains, but here, moving out to the "ranch," living in a Rancher, on the great outwash plain.

So there it was. Evil lived in Levittown and reds were under the beds in every Jubilee, in the closets of all the Ranchers. After all, look at the way these Levittowners were always sharing baby cribs, lawn mowers, barbecue tools and fondue pots; the way they were forming baby-sitting clubs (or collectives?). Wasn't this the very essence of a

THE MOST PERFECTLY PLANNED COMMUNITY IN AMERICA!

Levittown

Fig. 9.4 Country Clubber and Levittowner Models
Levitt and Sons ad, Bristol (Pa.) Courier, Friday,
December 7, 1951.

communally-sharing communist society? And hadn't the Levitt family come from Russia? The post war "Red Scare" had found another target. Demonic and un-American forces had been transposed from the red-painted fireplaces on the Triassic countryside to the red brick fireplaces of the new Country Clubbers. Nor did it help allay communist fears when, several years later, Soviet leader Nikita Khrushchev announced his intention to see Levittown (at the urging of President Eisenhower). Was it really to observe the American way of life at its best? Or was there something more sinister at play? These questions were answered to nobody's satisfaction since the closest the "chubby premier" came to Levittown's "fine homes" was the tracks of the Pennsylvania Railroad. "Here he comes ... there he goes" headlined the local newspaper as the premier's fifteen-car train sped by at seventy five mph.

No welcome wagons were rolled out for Levittown. Viewed from the other side of the Langhorne Ridge, the changes brought about by Levittown were simply undesirable. Among these were changes in the county's ethnic makeup and, in all likelihood, switches in voting preferences from Republican to Democrat. And there were the fears that this atrocious "fresh air slum" would destroy the aesthetic integrity of the lower county. Upcounty newspapers cited the "horrid, jerry-built" houses that insulted the landscape. It was possible that in ten to fifteen years Bucks would look like Paterson, New Jersey. They called it "tent city" and "vice city." Like some cheap sci-fi monster, "shack city" had been spawned of the black smoke and coke ovens of the nearby pollution mill. Bucolic Bucks was doomed! Those who grew up in Levittown in the 1950s remember the snotty attitude and taunts: "Hey kid, go home to cardboard canyon;" "Your house will fall apart and blow away;" "Tarpaper and spit! That's all them houses are." So, not everybody was pleased with the modern miracle, the American dream town.

And it didn't stop with nasty attitudes and stupid taunts. Parts of the development were at first denied electric power by local officials. The stalwart farmers refused to provide juice for Levittown's houses (for all those "city people") until Levitt's lawyers stepped in to have the lights turned on. Levittown was also emasculated from the very beginning: "Gerrymandered in advance" as the political scientist would say, and as James Michener did say. Though what was called Levittown quickly grew to a city of 70,000 (the state's tenth largest city), its political and municipal existence was denied. "The canny old-time citizens" of Bucks, as Michener said, realized the imminent power of a place that size in a county of just 144,000 people. Thus, they stubbornly refused to let the new development coalesce into a major central place, to incorporate into a single entity. Instead, on the map and on the ground, this enormous community came into existence as a set of small pieces (forty one sections), "actually a rambling collection of four fragments (Falls, Middletown, Tullytown, and Bristol Township) ... a group of four contiguous rural communities, each governed in a separate manner and all governed as if they were unimportant rural villages." The locals, fearful of losing not only their individuality but their individual tax base, made Levittown pay for having sprouted like an unholy weed in their farm fields.

Red Hell or Blue Heaven?

Did the super suburb deserve such an unneighborly greeting? Was it all that Satanical a force as some had said? Was it a veiled communist threat to the American way of life? Was it an affront to the landscape of the *Peaceable Kingdom* it had so abruptly invaded? A resounding "Yes," at least according to the early critics. The allegedly malevolent arrival of Levittown in a pastoral Eden, along with the attempts made to politically emasculate it, were part of a wider scattershot criticism of the postwar suburbia.

Levittown was criticized for being a bare and sterile landscape where the do's and don'ts were tightly circumscribed by company rules. The (in)famous "Deed Restrictions"[137] mandated that no moving vans were to be pulled beneath the carports. That no family was to have more

---

[137] The "Homeowners Guide" for new Levittowners, including the "restrictions," can be found online at: home.comcast.net/-Levittownrelics/homeguide/index.htm.

than two pets. That pets and young children were to be "penned in" with a good thorny barberry shrub, but NO FABRICATED FENCES WILL BE PERMITTED. It was forbidden to change the color of any house without permission from Mr. Levitt. A fine could be imposed for not mowing the lawn once a week ... or when the grass was three inches high. No unsightly working peoples' wash was to be displayed on wash-lines. No such lines were in fact allowed ... only rotary drying racks; and these were never to be used on weekends. Oh, the clonelike bland-ness, the enforced conformity and uniformity. Who needed it! Besides, it was all so restrictive. It was most surely like the heavy-handed, free-dom-denying standards that a village council in Soviet Russia might employ to govern the miserable, overregulated lives of the peasants.

But what is being described here is Levittown as perceived from the outside, an ill-informed outside. Miles away, and with much dismay and apprehension, the development was seen quite threateningly. A threat to an agrarian universe that was already starting to crumble. If this Levittown was a success, then would there not be more? Many more. The old Triassic earth of metes and bounds and furlonged fields and covered bridges would be gobbled up by "Megalopolitan sprawl." Perhaps there was also some measure of envy; the snug, convenience-packed little houses looked pretty good from within the walls of the cold and drafty fieldstone mausoleums that stood like pale white monuments to a now-dissolving agrarian past. Perhaps. Perhaps most of the critics never even got close enough to differentiate between a Country Clubber and a Rancher. The peripatetic James Michener took matters in hand: "I decided that I knew nothing about this huge suburbia that had erupted in my backyard." So, unlike most, he decided to journey into deepest Levittown to observe the beast firsthand:[138]

---

[138] James Michener, op. cit., p. 141.

> I noticed with approval the neat plantings of arborvitae and yew at the corners of the blocks … 'This may be a slum,' I mused, 'but it's the best-kept one I ever saw.' The houses were neat and well-cared for. Enough variation had been introduced to avoid monotony, and paint was everywhere in evidence. Driveways were trimmed and such automobiles as I saw tended to be new … I thought: 'I've been in a whole lot of suburbs that didn't look this good.

Michener noted that the houses themselves were commodious and well-planned, and that both parents and children appeared healthy and friendly. "Not a single rumor I had heard about Levittown was true, and everything I had hoped to find here was present: the happiness of people who were living better than they used to."

In fact, as Michener found, the distant stereotype was plainly false. To those who lived it, life in Levittown was really small town America, if not on a grander scale. And they loved it. Neighborliness seems to have been a valued trait that was brought by many who had come from the upstate coal country and from big city neighborhoods. The fact that there were at first no telephones further stimulated frequent visiting. Levittown was conceived of as a collection of family-oriented neighborhoods done on a human scale, with people encouraged to identify with their section and their section's softball teams and schools. Circumferential drives delimited the perimeter of each section and were intended to further community spirit in each of the forty one "instant" neighborhoods. The *Bucks County Traveler* found "sociability" to be "the most prevalent occupation in the community."[139] A coziness in these sections was furthered through the use of bucolic-sounding names such as Crabtree Hollow, Forsythia Gate, Magnolia Hill, Snowball Gate, Upper Orchard, and thirty-six others. When Levittown marked its fourth Christmas in 1955, the *Bucks County Traveler* (ordinarily more focused on the upper county) heaped praise on the huge community of

---

[139] The *Bucks County Traveler*, December, 1955, p. 70.

"comparative strangers" for having made a "wonderful social adjustment," creating a true home with "a relaxed kind of living." In fact, festively decorated for the holidays, Levittown was (almost) Bucks County picturesque:[140]

> One of the most breathtaking sights in the county this time of year is a night view from the top of the Levittown Parkway ... (the homes) glittering like an open treasure chest of jewels ... spread out below.

Boredom? Monotony? Pre-fabricated blandness? Not here. Not then. There were backyard barbecues and block parties. There were community baseball diamonds, five Olympic-size swimming pools, a lake (from which construction material had been excavated), and two shopping centers. And quite quickly, the company rulebook was set aside and the houses repainted; houses grew up and out, carports became studios or workshops, and eventually no two houses looked the same at all. The one-third acre properties were landscaped beyond the twelve trees and assorted bushes provided by the developer, beyond the eight million dollars Levitt was said to have spent on landscaping. With a growing number of children and pets (hurtling kids on cardboard sleds that slid down hills and into picnic tables and wandering dogs that trampled gardens) fences were inevitable. Fences may have closed off the green rolling vistas that Levitt had wanted, but miles of fencing had a way of making good neighbors better neighbors.

Shopping centers were soon built where Santa could be visited before Christmas. Playgrounds were built within walking distance, and contrary to what the critics had claimed, the new town did originally attempt to de-emphasize the auto. Much more recently, the local columnist J.D. Mullane explained it this way:[141]

> They point fingers at suburban templates like Levittown, and say it was 'built for the car.' Nonsense. Levittown is deliberately planned to be 'internodal.' That is, it accommodated all

[140] Ibid., p. 68.
[141] J.D. Mullane, *The Intelligencer* "Commentary," April 29, 2010.

manner of transportation choices, from walking (nearly 300 miles of sidewalks) and biking, to rail, bus, and car ... The builder wanted to encourage walking so neighbor would get to know neighbor. He said so.

As to the charge(s) that Levittown was a uniform, one-class community: Nonsense. Levittown attracted people of very limited means as well as a solid middle class. There were riff-raff and those who could care less if their community looked like an inner city slum. But there were also professional and well-educated people who had a strong and visible pride in ownership. Levittown also afforded this human cross-section the opportunity to trade up over the years, to go for a larger house in a more expensive section ... thus destroying the myth of the one-class monolith.

Though the houses were rumored to have the life expectancy of a career in pro hockey, and though rumors had spread upcounty that Levittown had been washed away by the devastating barrage of East Coast hurricanes in the mid-1950s (Connie, Diane, and Hazel), the truth was otherwise. Building experience and years were proving these down-to-earth, unpretentious houses to be durable. (In fact, the Levittowner model had won *Home and Gardens* five star house of the month award.) Levittown proved itself to itself and to the doubters during those hurricanes: while wind and flood damage brought havoc to much of the Delaware Valley (killing eighty eight people, washing away covered bridges, and doing seventy five million dollars in property damage in Pennsylvania alone), Levittown emerged with a few toppled trees and TV antennas ... but with its extra strength three-tab asbestos shingles and siding largely intact. And yet, the rumors – those pernicious rumors – that basementless Levittown's basements had all been inundated, persisted.

Midsummer Fires ... But No Hellfires Here

From Hollywood to Washington many things and many people were accused of being evil in the 1950s, evil either through their alleged or real association with Communism or with the devil, or both. It was the nature of the times. All the while Levittown was grooving to the beat of the "Devil's music" – rock with its "savage rhythms." Lyrics with obvious sexual double entendres were carried on the airwaves in direct challenge to the mellow strains of Glenn Miller. Levittown was rocking 'round the clock in blue suede shoes. It was also part of the nation's first TV-addicted generation. There were fifteen million TV sets in the country at the time of Levittown's birth. These fifteen million "electronic babysitters," these new family members, were in the view of some starting to exert a dangerously immoral influence on the society by diminishing family life and encouraging youthful delinquency. The unholy alliance of two evils, rock 'n roll and TV, was made official in 1957 when Dick Clark's *American Bandstand* began broadcasting from nearby Philadelphia. The parents and schoolteachers in Levittown may have fumed along with their counterparts in other new suburbs, but the army of young eyes glued to a "Whole Lotta Shakin' Goin' On" on their small black and white DuMont screens helped create secure and well-paying jobs for TV producers and Madison Avenue admen who were able to migrate to Bucks (certainly not lower Bucks!), finding new homes in the exurbia of the 1950s-60s.

All across lower Bucks County Levittown-like developments would soon spring up. (For example, "The Villages" at Neshaminy Woods – "Bucks County Homesteads in Natural Wooded Settings ... Literature on request."). But were Levittown and its imitators, children of pent-up post-war housing demands and then consumer *par excellence* of the '50s culture, manifestations of something evil? Had the old folk devil himself returned to howl down Joe Shugart's chimney and scamper across the yard in blue suede shoes? Was he the cause of the high infidelity and high fidelity? Rather, was the devil a more abstract incarnation of evil as symbolized by Whittaker Chambers' slick, urbane demon? Was he the force behind the engorging, obscene sprawl of this crowded new American "main street and crossroads," this ever enlarging monster with Levittown and Bucks already ingested in the belly of the Megalopolis? Was there a hint of anything Satanical in the way Levittown supposedly snatched away farmland, helping to smother once green fields beneath a spreading carpet of development? Was there anything diabolically threatening in the very way Levittown looked and acted?

On all charges and in answer to all questions, a resounding "No!" Levittown accommodated over 70,000 people on less than 6,000 acres of land; that's a miniscule 1 ½% of the county's total land area. That number of people were allowed to work on their American dream in a concentrated yet roomy enclave that – for the time being at least – let the rest of the county retain its blessed rurality. There would be other truly devilish forces to come, but for now, this baby boom nursery, this blue heaven, this place in which city people could feel the earth again (if only in their gardens, backyards, and lawns) was more a godsend than the rest of the county would care to have admitted. "It was a gift," one Levittowner wistfully recalls, a gift to the World War II and Korean War generations from Bill Levitt.

Of course, the "ultimate suburb" had and would always have its problems. The willow trees that Levitt planted by everybody's back door proved to be a poor choice. The trees' roots clasped and crunched the crunchable sewer pipes, requiring many Levittowners to later pay the cost of excavating and removing the willow trees. The willow, graveyard symbol of eternity that it was, was nothing more than an eternal pain in the (gr)ass. Then there was the inconvenience of the bath water being too hot and bathroom floor tiles burning the feet … but not because it was built atop hell. The fires of Levittown were not brought up from the nether regions as the rumor mill insisted. Instead, as James

Michener observed of the young development, here were the good fires of a new life, a new generation:[142]

> None of the myths about Levittown, of course, were true. I have rarely known a better group of citizens nor one with which I would be more willingly associated. They represent one of the strongest reservoirs in our society and I wish there were a hundred Levittowns across the country instead of only three major ones on Long Island, Bucks County, and (Willingboro) New Jersey. I myself would be most happy to live in one, and if in older life I found it necessary to sell the home I now occupy, I would think first of a good Levittown. I don't want the genteel section of some tired old city or the rural chauvinism of some house in which George Washington may have rested. I want the midsummer fires of a Levittown, for here live the people with vitality.

---

[142] James Michener, op. cit., p. 150.

A Closer Look: Levittown Pioneer

Robert C. Ford is shown in June of 2012 signing the Levittown sixty-year anniversary banner at the Bolton Mansion, Holly Drive. "Bob" Ford is a combat veteran of the Korean War who has lived in Levittown since the early 1950s. He remembers standing in line to buy his first Levittown house: "The line was so long, I couldn't believe it ... that there were that many veterans." He was interviewed in his Levittown home on May 23rd, 2014:

"I grew up in Philadelphia and had been living in an apartment in Willow Grove – with three young children. I heard about the sample (Levitt) house set up on Route 13. For $88 a month, we bought a house (a Levittowner) in the Violetwood section. It had three bedrooms and came with asbestos siding; but I put vertical strips over it to make it look like a Tudor. It was a great place for my family to move to.

(Cont'd ...)

And then there was all the dust ... that was before they put the land-scaping in. Levitt's brother Alfred was in charge of the landscaping. They planted a lot of fruit trees and they were OK. But the willow tree(s) in back of the house later did damage to the underground lines. Levitt wanted everything underground.

Later, we found a good deal on a Country Clubber in Snowball Gate. It was convenient to everything and everywhere: the playgrounds and pools. And Levitt built quite a few schools too. And it was only an hour and a half from the (Jersey) shore.

It (Levittown) was a quickly-built, ready-made community, but nothing wrong with that. I've been in construction my whole life. And I know it was well put together ... and then remodeled and changed over the years. Hurricanes and all, Levittown survived it.

I can't think of anything but good things to say about Levittown. It was Levitt's gift to the veterans and to the county."

CHAPTER 10

THE "DEVILOPERS" ...
OR THE CASE OF
THE VANISHING COWS

In the construction business. Responsible for building towers and ramparts. Can also help destroy the power of others ... When he appears in human form, he can be recognized by his loud, croaking voice.

–Description of the devil "Malphas" from: "Know Your Enemy: A Dossier of Demons Known to be Operating on Earth," in Louis Stewart, *Life Forces*, 1980

Now the farms that are left can't afford city taxes. They want out, that's quite easy to see. But the people who moved from the city won't let them, it's country they've come out to see.

Chorus: So the song of Bucks gets sadder it seems, and the writers won't let it alone. Each new verse that they add, tells of damage they've done. It won't end till there's nothing at all.

–Mark Osterman, *The Song of Bucks County* (1977)

OK. It does seem silly or perhaps a bit too cute. That is, the kind of play-on-words device a big city tabloid might use with lurid "pix" of the latest crime victim to sell its daily rag sheet. "**Devilopers**" that is. But look, it does express how many people feel about the county. It expresses what many residents feel has been the greatest problem and the greatest danger to both landscape and lifestyle in recent times. It you still don't care for it, take out your taxicab yellow #2 pencil, scratch out the chapter title, and substitute the more elegiac: "Land of the Lonely Barn Ramps." The less serious reader might prefer: "There'll Never be Another Moo."

Triassic Daydream

The daredevil Evil Knevil might have enjoyed growing up in Bucks County. For a little tyke on a motorbike with a lust for roaring up hills and vaulting through empty air, he would have loved the Triassic lowlands. Before challenging Mack trucks and river gorges, there would be hundreds of such hills (or, in the more utilitarian sense, "ramps") for him to practice on, at first soaring up and over a row of six or more chickens, building up to a file of a dozen pigs slobbing up their grub from the feed trough, and eventually leaping the assembled ranks of rusting farm machinery. These ramps, barn ramps, are as ubiquitous a part of the Bucks farmscape as prairie dog mounds in Kansas or crayfish "castles" in the Louisiana bayous. They are barn ramps without their barns. They are part of a rusting, vanishing landscape. And like blue porch ceilings without a folk devil, they have lost their very meaning.

If noticed at all by the casual traveler, the grass and weed-covered barn ramps are often taken for granted or assumed to be something other than what they are – geologic abnormalities or the burial mounds of an ancient civilization perhaps. But, they were actually an important structural element of the nineteenth-century barn, an imposing evidence of regional folk culture rapidly disappearing. Yet these barns and their ramps are still numerous enough to give a visually strong historic and scenic quality to the land. The barn ramps are part of what has variably been called the Pennsylvania barn, the German barn, the forebay or

Fig. 10.1 Banked Barn With Ramp, Tinicum Township *(Author's Photo)*

overshot barn, the Swiss bridge barn, or the banked barn. All are correct in that the banked, two-level structure with projecting forebay was a borrowing of building techniques brought from central Europe. It was initially associated with only areas of German (or Swiss German) settlement in Pennsylvania, but was soon 'Americanized' and adopted by other rural cultures. These barns are "as splendid as the edges of American towns are horrible" says the landscape architect and critic Ian Nairn; "they constitute the one great example of instinctive design in present-day America ..."[143]

Successor to smaller and earlier "English" style barns, the "great" barns of German design were built "like palaces," often as much as sixty

---

[143] Ian Nairn, *The American Landscape, A Critical View,* New York: Random House, 1965, p.21.

by one hundred feet in size – usually several times larger than the adjacent farmhouse. This attests both to the farm prosperity of the region in times past and to the care attended the livestock. Built into the bank of a rolling hill to a height of two levels, they were supported by a heavy skeleton of thick, pegged and joined timbers cut from oak trees. The upper level frame of wooden boards was painted red with an iron oxide pigment, while the lower stone masonry was done up with a white, lead-based paint or with a lime whitewash. A cantilevered wooden forebay on the second floor ran the full length of the barn and projected six or more feet beyond the lower level. It provided additional storage space and protected the lower walls and stable doors from snow and rain; it also protected the sunny, usually south-facing barnyard (much as the forebay in medieval houses protected the lower doors and walls from the elements). While the livestock were quartered and fed in this enclosed yard and in ground level stalls, hay and grain were stored on the upper level. The storage lofts were aired and grain kept cool either by windows or ventilation slits in the stone gable ends, or both.

To the north side and opposite the barnyard, the lower and upper levels were connected by an earthen ramp or bridge. An inclined cartway built of soil and rubble to a height of six or more feet, the ramp was often sided with drywall or mortared stone masonry. (Sometimes, the German farmers excavated a space beneath the ramp; shorn up with timbers, but otherwise dirt-walled, this "secret" area became a superb cold storage crypt – an herb, potato, root, and mushroom cellar). The ramp itself led to the second story doors, doors framed in white trim, the "devil doors." They were doors of massive dimensions that either slid open or swung wide to accommodate wagons carrying grain to the huge storage area on the upper level. There, the grain was threshed and winnowed on the floor and fed through trapdoors and wooden sluice boxes to the livestock below. Looking back on the old days, days of horse-drawn wagons and "when the horse rested, you rested; the new machines don't ever rest."

There emerges from all of this a highly functional and beautiful piece of American folk architecture.[144] But, in many cases now, the characteristic ramps are all that remains. They're seen along roadsides and out in the fields, wherever there once were barns. Forlorn and overgrown with grass and weeds, they are slowly leveled by erosion to the level of the Triassic earth around them. Like sand castles whose identifiable shapes and edges turn to rounded lumps before disappearing entirely, they are one more testament to the impermanency, the temporariness of the human landscape. As a ruin, these abruptly truncated ramps to nowhere have probably as much romantic, dream-inducing quality as the castle drawbridges in Ivanhoe's merry England: ghost images and auras made of sweat and animal scents in the shimmering haze of August afternoons; images and auras not of knights and horses in clanking, sun-reflecting armor crossing moats, but of farmers and livestock trudging up ramps; the livestock long since gone to the slaughterhouse. Farmers, horses, and wagons loaded only to the weight that a horse could pull up the incline, long lines of each, generations long, all wearily marching up the old barn ramp or "bridge," and onto the threshing room floor. The trudging and sweating stops when the last horse and wagon go crashing down the terminated ramp; the screaming, neighing, and whir of the wheels in the empty air above the bellied-up wagon bring the daydream to a jarring halt as well.

The Fate of the Earth's Own

Although some collapsed or had their roofs ripped off in the violent hurricane winds of the 1950s, they hardly ever just fell down; these barns were built too well for that. But one day an Amish group from Lancaster County came and dismantled one, taking the venerable boards back home to use in expanding one of their very prosperous-looking barns further west on the Triassic lowland (or perhaps way out in Ohio

---

[144] For a full description of the origins and appearance of the Pennsylvania German barn and farmstead, see: Amos Long, *The Pennsylvania German Family Farm,* Breinigsville, Pa.: The Pennsylvania German Society, 1972).

or Kansas). One night a Solebury barn went up in smoke and flames, lighting the sky for miles around with its reddish glow. Lightning? Spontaneous combustion? Or just a careless butt after a lusty, late night tryst in the hayloft? No matter, another lost barn. Another day, park rangers helped raze another barn in a county park because it had become a hangout for idle teens, a vandalized and graffitied mockery of its former self. With busted floorboards and broken ladders leading to sideless lofts, it had become a danger to trespassers. The barn needed to go. On yet another day, yet another great barn was stripped of its pineboard siding and its skeleton picked clean of its tightly-fitting oak beams and rafters. They were sold to a dealer in New York who in turn resold them as "genuine, worm-eaten, weathered Pennsylvania barnboards." They ended up as paneling in a trendy Manhattan pub whose décor also featured stained glass windows and London street signs. And so it went throughout the years … one after another into the hundreds and into the thousands. Eventually even the stone foundations are bulldozed and hauled away to begin new lives as fireplaces, new "old" stone walls, and suburban walkways. And what's left? The only thing that seems to have no recyclable value – the lonely barn ramps.

Although this was and is the fate of many barn ramps across parts of still rural Bucks, in areas like Spectorsky's "mink curtain" exurb, wealth and creative talent have gone to work at conversions. (What also denotes an exurb is that everyone seems to have a brother-uncle-cousin who works as an architect or interior designer). "Barns" become "homes" after X thousands of dollars are spent on plumbing, wiring, insulation, picture windows, sliding glass doors, and solar panels. The final touch is the latest model BMW parked on the barn ramp. The "Land of the Lonely Barn Ramp" becomes the charming, speculative exurban fringe.

When county residents were surveyed on what they liked least about the county (*See:* Appendix D), many zeroed in on the developers and the "massive amount of development." If evil is alive and present, its guise for many is that of the "abominable" and "detestable" wheelers and dealers of land and the builders of housing tracts, industrial parks, and the countless mini-malls (mauls). The bitter feelings voiced about the "invasion of our magnificent countryside by developers who don't give a damn" is a feeling not unique to Bucks. It's a feeling shared by people on any metropolitan fringe who see the "countryside" beyond the suburbs being consumed by hurried growth, by constant and unending growth. An older way of life, one with an almost legendary wholesomeness, is seen disintegrating. Its most obvious symbols – the barn, the farmstead, and its precious open space sadly vanish. Lost beauty and value are replaced by nothing (much). And in Bucks, more than elsewhere, the loss of an agrarian world is regarded with more than just a passing nostalgia. Because it was so mythologized on canvas by so many artists and because it was America's first and only *Peaceable Kingdom*, what the developers do is colored by anger: "housing developments are creeping up ... growing out of the soil like alien beings and spreading like cancer." Whether viewed from Levittown or from the "mink curtain" exurbs, "the building disease" is described in much the same terms: developers who "sit like vultures, waiting ...;" developers who "bribe, threaten, and cheat" the farmers out of their land, and developers who "care nothing for the land, only for the money that jingles in their pockets." A local politician censures a county where developers "rule" and where they want to "make the beautiful hills of Bucks County into Northeast Philadelphia." The "hustle-a-buck developer" is seen as the devil incarnate, a master marauder who, with admen, lawyers, and engineers pillages and plunders. A devil who pockets not peoples' souls, but their land. Land, the very soul of Bucks.

A Rippling Wave across an Ocean of Earth

This latter-day devil in developer's clothing (developer in devil's clothing?) is comfortably at home on the speculative exurban fringe. This is his turf, his Triassic sandbox and playpen. This is the very cutting edge of the metropolis, the new flesh of the Megalopolis where the forces of growth and change are most evident. This is where Spectorsky found a "benign atmosphere" threatened by something hostile. In the end, an "autumnal sadness" prevails. This modern day exurban fringe is vastly different from the old "mink curtain" exurb, and actually twists the meaning of the term. It's not a hiding place for money and talent and there's no air of exclusivity and seclusion about it. It is an area of very hot real estate speculation that lies on the outer edge of the suburbs. It's a twilight land that's recently ceased being one thing – farmed land – but hasn't yet become what it will become when the economy and the housing market allow, i.e., suburban sprawl. In Bucks, farms lie to one side along with vestiges of the older, wealthier exurb … while on the other side are the suburban tracts, industrial parks, and malls both big and small.

It's a short-lived, rather ephemeral thing, or place. There are no *"Welcome to Exurbia"* signs posted along the roadsides by local Chambers of Commerce. But there are signs. It's a slippery, amorphous geographical entity with no clear boundaries. Worse, when attempting to map it, it's found to be constantly on the move like a belt of drought marching across the Sahara. Particularly in Bucks where growth was especially rapid in the second half of the twentieth century, the exurban fringe became a moving blur, a shapeless locust swarm that daily consumed whatever greenery and open space, barns and barn ramps that happened to lie in its path. Nonetheless, an attempt to locate and map this fringe was undertaken by geography students at the local college. These intrepid students were recruited as "field observers" and were literally told to go out and observe the fields, to record changes in land use, especially the telltale signs suggesting the end of agriculture: overgrown, weedy, or abandoned fields, rusting farm equipment, real estate billboards, boarded up stone houses, disappearing barns and silos. And the blaring roadside pronouncements: "Coming Real Soon, Another fifty-acre mini-mall." The twilight of the exurban landscape is signaled by the arrival of the survey crews to stake out the fields … with bulldozers anxiously waiting. When a combination of these visual prompts

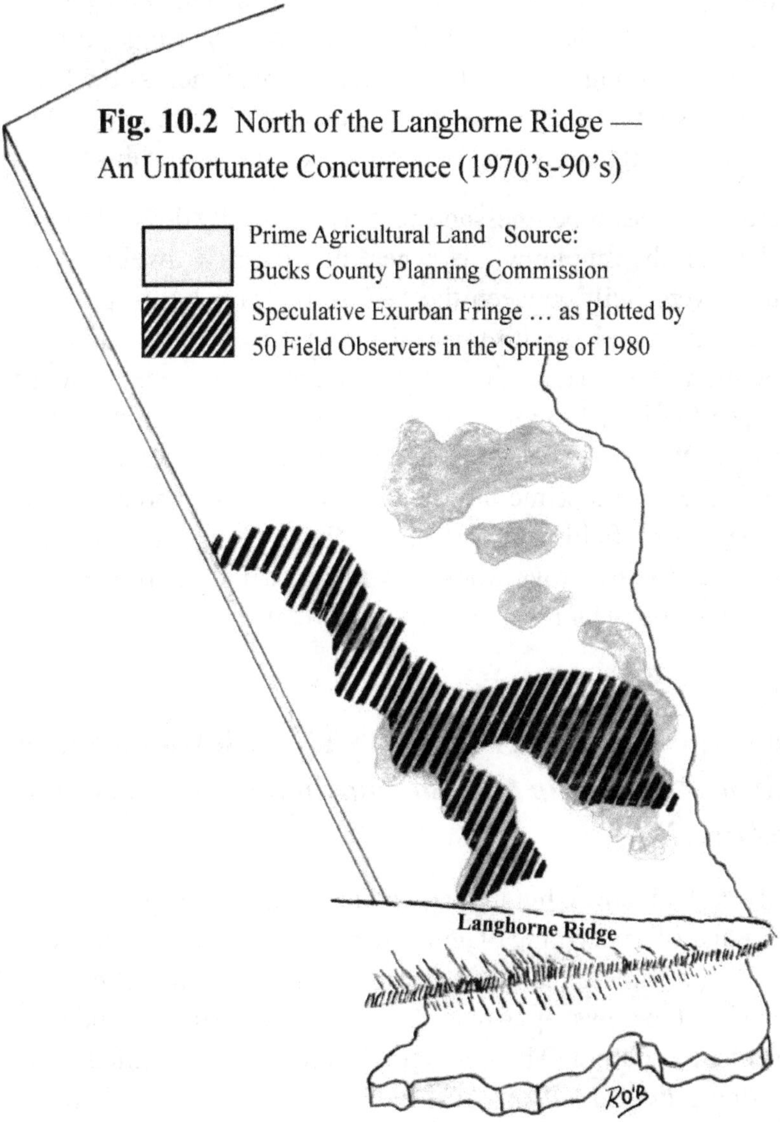

Fig. 10.2 North of the Langhorne Ridge —
An Unfortunate Concurrence (1970's-90's)

Prime Agricultural Land   Source:
Bucks County Planning Commission
Speculative Exurban Fringe ... as Plotted by
50 Field Observers in the Spring of 1980

Langhorne Ridge

RO'B

was seen, the presence of the speculative exurban fringe was acknowledged. The resulting map (the composite effort of fifty individuals who closely and repeatedly scrutinized the area both on foot and by car) shows the location of this very real, though temporary, fringe. It takes the shape of a two-pronged wave in Fig.10.2; it ripples across the lower part of the Triassic farmlands and covers much of Northampton, Warwick, Newtown, Wrightstown, and Lower Makefield townships.

There is also a somber message here. This visually defined "zone" stretches through the municipalities where half the new dwelling units in the county were built between the 1970s-90s. This built-up "zone" furthermore corresponded with most of the lower county's remaining prime agricultural land. Here, there is seen a most unfortunate concurrence between the best farm soil with land that lies in the immediate path of growth. What was good for the farmer, is now good for the developer. Half the state's prime farmland has been lost in precisely this manner. Abandoned fields and so-called "failed farms" are presided over by sad-faced scarecrows whose (hypothetical) tears trickle down into the rich, red soil. The losing game is not yet over.

Cartoon Caption: Mother Cow to Calf with Bulldozer on the Horizon: *"Hurry up and eat your lunch, Junior, before it's paved over"*

Only cartoon cows, but indicative of the way things go ... out on the cutting edge of everything. The local press favors a kind of genre photograph that it sometimes uses to fill space, or more altruistically, to jar what's left of the newspaper-reading public with visual reminders of the changes that are afoot. The photographs are invariable titled: "The Vanishing *Peaceable Kingdom*," "On the Edge of Town," or "Farming in Suburbia." A horizontal expanse of field is shown in the foreground with corn rows or "Cows grazing under Surviving Trees." A herd of milking cows, the locally popular black and white Holstein-Frisians, lie stunned and scattered in the field at various angles of repose. They look confused; they look like accident victims. They look out of place and

Fig. 10.3 Working the Soil. Author's sketch of Photo by Bill Johnson, *Bucks County Courier Times*, May 4, 1982, p.1.

not sure if they're even supposed to be here anymore. What heightens the sense of anomie is that several of them seem to stare at the horizon, at a cluster of new houses where a roofing crew with pick-up trucks and ladders is at work hammering. Here, a telephoto lens is especially useful because the livestock appear to be pressing against the sides of the houses. But then again, they actually are. One such classic news photograph (Fig. 10.3) shows a white-haired farmer in flannel shirt seated on a wooden grain drill. He works the reins of his two-horse team as the oat seeds are drilled into the furrows. His is an antiquated, animal-powered machine, an escapee from a museum of agrarian technology. The panorama of newly-worked fields gives way, on one side of the horizon, to a barn and silo held tight within the folds of the Triassic earth. On the other side, yet another housing development. It's also a rather prophetic image in that a cloud hangs over the farmer and his drill machine. For all those who believe in symbolism and sentiment, this is of course a dark cloud of foreboding.

Such news photographs show vanishing scenes; they show a fleeting glimpse of the last days of agriculture. They show farms that somehow managed to survive even this long. But now, flanked by the enemy and like General Custer's troops on the eve of the Little Big Horn, they know perfectly well what tomorrow will bring. Such scenes of imminent loss usually gather popular support for the man who so nobly plows the fields. The farmer is seen as the guardian of memory. And a memorable part of growing up appears to include one favorite barn, a barn at the end of an evening stroll where the sun went down through the hayloft opening. Also, the family farmer is thought of as the last steward of a "more honest and moral life" than that lived by the nonfarm population. According to a *New York Times*/CBS News poll, Americans still retain "an abiding Jeffersonian belief" in the virtuosity of farmers and farm life. The farmer is the keeper of cherished values, and those values spring from a closeness to the good, nourishing earth. And he fights the good fight every day, he fights the devil of development. Or so the myth goes. And when one of the earth's own outwits the devil, just as in earlier times, that little victory is woven into the fabric of local lore. Whether it's true or not, the Bucks farmer who was being driven under by taxes and so decided to bury his deceased wife (along with the family pets) on the farmstead thus guaranteeing his farm the tax-exempt status of "cemetery," was probably admired by many.

The farmers and their kin, perceived of as the last bastions of morality and strong family life in an age of immorality and loosened family ties, appear to be up against it. Despite a growing "Buy Local – Support Your Local Farmer" campaign, many farmers are hard pressed to merely survive. Taxes rise more rapidly than the value of their crops. Pressure from developers mounts and crop prices become deflated because of competition from other regions and from abroad. The farmer's plight also includes increased production costs (in equipment, fuel, fertilizer, and transportation to market, not to mention the forever escalating cost of farm labor). As all these things take their toll it is realized that food is not the only loss. The near mythological significance of the American freehold family farm (and nearly 90% of the Bucks' farms are of this type) is no less evident today than in the past. Where life is rooted to the soil and the sweat that pours out onto it, where life and work and the seasons are seen in harmony, here is the something solid and good that city and suburb lack. Here among the silos and barn ramps are the forces of decency and simplicity that counterbalance the greedy, dehumanizing rottenness of urban life, a rottenness that is spread via the suburbs by the developers. Ever since he absented himself from the rural byways and folkways, the devil had of course become urban, the evil one interviewed in Manhattan by Chambers and the evil behind the forces of urban outreach and overspill seen in the suburbia and exurbia of Schiddel and Spectorsky. As "estate homes," "executive estates" and gated "preserves" for active adults bury the nourishing red earth forever (forever?), lifestyles and rural intangibles are also lost. Myths so substantially built, die hard. (Developers attempt to perpetuate the myth that the farm is still somehow there even though 150 houses have sprouted in the fields by cleverly naming the development "Mirror Lake **Farms**" or "Hillcrest **Farms**." Although this assuredly fools no one, it probably soothes the conscience.) The twenty-one year old who says "I'd rather marry a farm girl because if I marry someone from the city or from Levittown, I know it would end in divorce," echoes the still surviving fiction that the farm population holds the higher moral ground. And perhaps among the "plain people" it actually does.

That young romantic had better find his farm girl quickly if statistics are any indication. The precipitous decline in the number of farms in Bucks County in the past century or more looks like this:[145]

1900 --	6,300
1954 --	2,730
1970 --	1,159
1980 --	990
2014 --	930

[145] USDA Census (a national farm survey conducted every five years and the Penn State Data Center.

Farmland acreage in the county declined by 50% after WWII, with over 70% of it converted to non-farm use between 1950 and 2000. Part of the remaining farmland is in the hands of speculators who may (temporarily) lease it back to the farmer. Only about 1% of the county work force is engaged in farming – this, in a county, made famous by its agricultural landscape. Not unexpected, but still rather discouraging. Here too, the discouragement is more profound than elsewhere because the county is one of the last repositories of wooden barns in America, one of the last visual reminders of Jeffersonian America; it is furthermore the first, last, and only *Peaceable Kingdom*. Surely, the devil himself must shed a tear, for he too was once an integral part of that once bountiful agrarian panorama.

B.C./A.D.

The devastating effect that rapid suburban and exurban growth can have on a community, a community that conflictingly finds its prime farmland to be the apple of the developer's eye, is seen in the twenty-six square mile municipality of Northampton Township. In the late nineteenth century, this area of the Triassic lowland was described by a local historian as an unbroken landscape of fertility, "the exclusively agricultural character of the region … not (being) favorable to the growth of towns." [146]

Named in honor of the parliamentary borough of Northampton-shire, it was first settled by English Quakers and later by a mix of Huguenot and Hudson Valley-Long Island Dutch. But the farms were large (200-300 acres) and the number of families always remained small; there were but forty households to share its broad green spaces in 1722 and little more than a thousand people by the 1840s. Throughout the nineteenth century Northampton remained a stable, slowly-growing

---

[146] J.H. Battle, ed. *History of Bucks County, Pennsylvania*, Philadelphia: A. Warner & Co., 1887, p. 422.

community of family farms, many of which had received their grants directly from William Penn and his heirs. After two hundred years of settlement and occupation, there were still less than two thousand people in the municipality in 1880.

At that time a few changes were beginning to make themselves apparent: a rail line and its "suburban" stations and summer bungalow colonies began to arrive. Yet it was every bit a part of the *Peaceable Kingdom* still. An historian described the area in 1887:[147]

Farming is the principal occupation, and the soil is fertile … The meadows produce luxuriant crops of hay, a staple product, much of which is hauled by the farmers themselves to Philadelphia. Since … (1876) dairying has also been pursued with profit.

A typical part of Northampton's countryside, the area around the village of Holland, is seen in Fig. 104; solidly farmed, it was well-drained and well serviced by the nearby mills. And here's the amazing thing: in the next seven decades the map changes hardly at all. By 1955, though the farmers' names had changed as had the size and shape of the farms, and though some small acreage had been set aside for woodlots, the area was still thoroughly rural. The original metes and bounds were still very much apparent. In all directions, and up and down the township, were corn and wheatfields, pastures dotted with Dorset and Suffolk sheep; there were blacksmith shops and wagon repair shops, corner stores, and still-functioning mills (incredibly, some mills still grinding grain into the early 1960s). And there were barns, the big banked barns, "our play castles and forts" on rainy days.

While the outwash plain was being Levittowned and built upon with industry, Northampton still remained (for a while) farm country. In the spring of 1955 the *Bucks County Traveler magazine* said:

You will discover typical Bucks County scenes, rolling farmlands, charming old houses, and distant hills, nationally publicized and unchanged by the years.

---

[147]Ibid. p.493.

But what had happened on the outwash plain in the 1950s was about to happen here. Innocence and tranquility would be elbowed aside. In the post-Levittown era, the county's greatest surge in growth targeted municipalities like Northampton and Warwick, just above the Langhorne Ridge. Driving across the area in 1961, J.R. Humphreys (*The Lost Towns and Roads of America*)[148] saw it this way:

> It was hard to stay for long in anything resembling country-side. Roads covered the land like vines, and houses were springing up everywhere ... we were in semi-countryside.

The following Census Bureau numbers and the map series in Fig.10.4 reflect the breakneck pace of rural to suburban growth, especially during the 1960s-1970s:

Northampton Township	Year	Population	% Increase
	1880	1,768	
	1950	2,248	27%
	1960	6,006	158%
	1970	15,807	163%
	1980	27,365	73%
	1990	35,406	29%
	2000	39,384	11%
	2010	39,726	0.9%

By the end of the twentieth century the growth frenzy had all but subsided in Northampton. The township had become 98% "urban" and 2% "rural" (U.S. Dept. of Agriculture). In the 1990s some 2,200 new houses were built, but this compared with over 3,600 in the 1970s and nearly 3,800 in the 1980s. A saturation point was nearing after several decades of turbulent growth. Gas stations, shopping and office plazas, schools and tract housing were scraped into being as fields, silos, and

---

[148] J.R. Humphreys, *The Lost Towns and Roads of America*, Garden City, N.Y.: Doubleday & Co., 1961, p. 47.

barn ramps vanished and ponds became retention basins. Next, developmental pressures would move north to Warwick Township.[149]

Although Northampton Township was said to be the fastest growing municipality in the entire state in these decades (with twenty six separate developments being built simultaneously in the 1970s), its story is far from unique. It typifies those places undergoing the total transformation away from farmland to a panoply of strip development in one generation. Growing up here in the 1960s-70s was "incredible" says one who did; "one day they weren't, the next day they were … $90,000 homes in 48 hours, (but) with no individuality … like covers from *Better Homes and Gardens* with sick-looking, scrawny trees, like Charlie Brown's Christmas tree."

"What happens" asks the local newspaper when, due to "the inevitable and evil result of development," the peaceful countryside "is yanked out of its quiet and bucolic existence and thrust abruptly into the helter-skelter, hectic life of a burgeoning bedroom community?" What happens when a community changes this fast, being forced to cope with over 1,000% growth in thirty years? Growth outruns any attempt at managing it and frustrates those who try to preserve that always elusive "character" of place. It's always a little, or in this case, a lot too late. Population overwhelms an area that doesn't have the infrastructure to absorb it. Narrow shoulderless roads that served well in the days of narrow hay wagons and infrequent stage coaches are burdened with rush hour traffic. Everyone drives because there are no sidewalks and, anyway, the shopping plazas are seldom built within walking distance of the developments.

---

[149] In the early twenty-first century Warwick would become the prototypical "exurban fringe." Located mid-county and just above Northampton, it's bracketed on the west by Bristol Road and crisscrossed by Old York Road (SR 263). Fewer than 1,000 people lived here in 1950, but the population climbed to nearly 12,000 by the millennium (having grown by 156% in the 1980's and another 100% in the 1990s). The township grew by 20% between 2000-10 to 14,437 (2010).

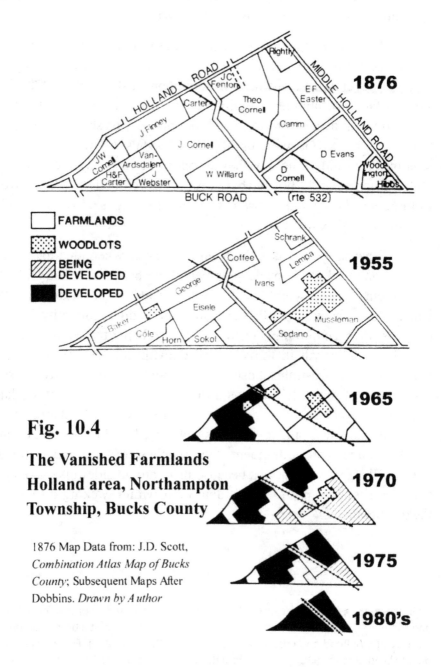

1876

FARMLANDS
WOODLOTS
BEING DEVELOPED
DEVELOPED

1955

1965

Fig. 10.4

The Vanished Farmlands Holland area, Northampton Township, Bucks County

1970

1876 Map Data from: J.D. Scott, *Combination Atlas Map of Bucks County*; Subsequent Maps After Dobbins. *Drawn by Author*

1975

1980's

The township's municipal services like water and sewer lines become overtaxed, necessitating the further taxing of residents. There's an alarming drop in water table levels; the more developments go up, the more the wells go down. Old wells that went down one hundred feet are replaced by new(er) wells that must be dug three hundred feet or more.

Surrounded by developments, the remaining farmers become fewer and fewer. "I really hate to leave," says one sixty-eight year old farmer ... "but I'm running out of land." "I'm glad it's over," says a seventy year old farmer ..."I'm ready for retirement." The farmers are crowded out by people fleeing other crowded places. With endlessly rising taxes, the 1,000 acre suburban farmstead becomes an unprofitable anachronism. The farm becomes an incongruous holdover in a world of split-levels and condos. The farm itself attracts arson, trespassing, and vandalism. Encroachment takes many forms: off-road vehicles roaring through the soybean fields, hunters (mistakenly?) gunning down prize heifers, littered cans and bottles jamming harvesting equipment, and theft of crops (one small revenge on the corn thieves is planting a row or two of field corn on the property margin ... the absconding thieves usually don't realize this type corn is inedible). Those who grew up in the area in the era B.C. (before the changes) and still live here A.D. (after the developers), echo the words of the planning commission: "Too much has happened too fast ... it's depressing here." And "I'm tired of looking at construction ... (my) quiet community has ... (turned) into an Erma Bombeck nightmare." With a cheerless melancholy, the local press periodically publishes photographs of the few remaining local farms with captions like these:

"Suburban sprawl confronts rural past."

"Disappearing from the scene, one of Northampton Town-ship's dwindling number of farms shines in the winter sun-light."

"The old farmhouse is surrounded by new foundations and building materials, as another agricultural tract gives way to residential development."

Now, there are few people left who even remember what the place looked like in the not too distant past.

Nothing Certain But Uncertainty

Farming is still a multi-million dollar business in Bucks County. Farms average about 80-85 acreage in size and many are still family owned and managed. Field grains account for more than half of what is grown on the rolling Triassic hillsides, with corn, hay, and soybeans being the top crops planted in the fine silt loam. Livestock, poultry-raising, and dairying are important as well.[150]

What directly ties the farmer to the suburbanite (and urbanite) are the more exotic, specialty items that surely guarantee a future for at least some family farms; these "alternate cash streams" include: pumpkins and gourds, hayrides (haunted or otherwise) and corn mazes, "pick-your-own" strawberries, "cut-your-own" evergreen trees, raw milk and ice cream, honey and jams, orchards for apples and cider and (increasingly) vineyards for wine, stables and tack rooms for recreational horse-back riding, farm ponds for fish propagation, woodlots to fuel all the new fireplaces and wood stoves in all the new (and old) houses, and turf for all the new lawns and golf courses. Then, there are the truly exotic novelties like bison (burgers), llamas and miniature horses. One of the niceties of life on the suburban fringe is the nearby presence of all this and more sold from roadside farm-to-market stands "just up the street" or from the rickety back porch of the farmer ... from beneath the blue porch ceilings "just down the lane." **"Buy Local"** – farming in some shape or form will survive, thus continuing to add to the amenity-rich base of Bucks out on the suburban, exurban, rural interface.

---

[150] Penn State Cooperative Extension, *"Fresh From Bucks County Farms."* This booklet is available at Penn State Data Center website and on the main page of the county web site (www.BucksCounty.org.).

Yet paradoxically, the suburbanite is thus both prospect and problem. The double-edged nature of the relationship becomes apparent when the people who buy from the farmers' fruit and vegetable stands on Sunday appear at township meetings on Monday to complain about the noise, dirt, and the smell of pig manure. The suburbanite brings the market closer to the suburban farmer, but at the same time is the cause of the higher taxes and mounting pressure to sell. Once established in the suburbs, and near enough to see a barn across the fields, a funny thing happens to the suburbanite: an "I've got mine Jack, so don't you come and spoil it" view takes hold. "Now, let's close the door behind us and keep the rest of them out" becomes his credo. It's the same xenophobic fanaticism that quickly seizes those who find the good life in really attractive places like New Mexico and northern California. The good life means nearness to nature, fields, and a less crowded and less polluted environment. It subverts one's purpose in moving to a place like Bucks County if, once here, the desired amenities people came to enjoy begin to fade away. So, those whose patios and driveways sit on former farmland, bemoan the fact that someone else's patio and driveway is going to sit on the next available parcel of farmland. "That farmer has no right to sell out," they protest. Yet, for over two hundred million years, the Triassic landscape has never been static, has never held people in place for very long; the devil of change never rests. That which propels the suburban fringe, by nature propels the exurban fringe.

Though suburbanites may find it increasingly uncomfortable as more and more fellow suburbanites crowd in around them, the spreading suburbs themselves are not perceived to be the problem. Wrath at what's done to the land, the farmers' diminished chances of survival, are blamed on the developer(s). The devil of development is clearly the evil. Though seen as "devils," there's little the developer does that's innately evil. By definition, they're "property investors" who buy up acres of land, then build houses and sell them. There's nothing pernicious in meeting the demands of the housing market and providing people with what they want. Even those opposed to massive and seemingly endless development realized there's another side to the story. Ambivalence shows through in one resident's words: "I don't like it. They keep building Wawas. I guess they're needed; it's for the better. And I do like the Wawa near me." There have been conflicting opinions about suburban growth for decades. Some developers may see themselves as the heirs to Bill Levitt; they help people realize the dream of home ownership and gain a piece of the good life on the good Triassic earth. However, not very many developers build as well and package their product in the same managed, pre-planned, and land conserving manner as Levitt. "Unfortunate," yes, but wicked or evil-inspired? Doubtful.

The wealthy exurbanite and the middle class suburbanite both condemn the developer. *"Save Farmland – We Can't Eat Townhouses"* is a bumper sticker just as likely to be seen on an Italian sports car and on a twelve year-old Chevy. The exurbanite wants to save a lifestyle based on much privacy and open space by preserving a protective buffer of farmlands. The suburbanite hopes to save his new found "country" style of living by saving those same farms. And in between them both, the farmer struggles to survive. This noble effort to keep the county green and open has led to a welter of legislative and other efforts at the local and state levels. The intent is to slow down the development process and better manage the direction and character of growth. The result is a gamut of laws, programs, and techniques designed to keep working farmers on the land for as long as possible. The variety of preservation strategies includes: tax-based land funds; bond supported land banks; development rights easements; transfer development rights; restructured property and inheritance taxes; agricultural districting programs; preferential assessment schemes; and cluster development. The complex inner (and inter) workings of all this can boggle the mind of anyone not having advanced degrees in land economics and zoning law.

In Bucks County the most effective way to save open space and preserve farming has been the publicly-supported Agricultural Land Preservation program. Following the loss of 70% of the county's farmland (which was taken over for non-farm uses), voters in 1989 authorized the county government to buy open space easements to ensure that farms would be preserved in perpetuity. Despite the county having some of the most expensive farmland in the state, the program has been a success. More than $145 million in municipal, county, and state tax monies has been used to preserve some 180 farms totaling 15,000 acres (or almost 20% of all county farmland). The county has 930 remaining farms on 75,000 acres of farmed land[151]

The program has worked well, and yet there is a more cynical view that sees it as too little, too late. The number of farms will still continue to dwindle and the corn stalk tassels that peak above the rooftops of the condos and townhouses may soon be harvested for the very last time. The big men (the developers) are too powerful and will win out over the little men (the farmers). Farming in "this earth rich county" has no future and is "on its way out." Discouraged and approaching retirement age, the local farmers labor beneath an air of uncertainty that hovers over their contested lands. The only certainty is more lonely barn ramps, and even these are not permanent.[152]

For a while yet, there will still be a moment at township meetings where lawyers, engineers, and elected officials gather to decide the status of the land, when a "representative of the past" raises his voice to say something like "I remember when my father carted hay along that road where you want to put ..." But, as the local reporter writes, "It's a perfunctory performance ... that has long since failed to stop the juggernaut ... it is a voice ...drowned out by bulldozers and hammers. The lament is fading, becoming passé."

None of this is to say that the area will no longer be farmed or that things agrarian will be mentioned only in the past tense. About 20% of the county's landscape is, despite the widespread changes of the last several decades, farmed. (This **is** down from 60% in 1950). The *New York Times* travel writer thinks the area still possesses a "rural splendor," an Old World ambience akin to that of the English countryside: "Bucks County has epitomized rustic charm for people seeking a rural

---

[151] *The Intelligencer*, August 19, 2015.
[152] The quoted material in this paragraph is from the Bucks County Planning Commission, *Farmers Survey*, 1978.

retreat ... (for) 300 years ... Much of the forty-mile long county ... remains as lush and serene as ever."[153]

And yet a closer look at the fabric of the land reveals the rents and tears, the frayed edges and untidy fringes of a place subjected to speedy and sometimes seedy growth. The countryside today is anything but English-looking. Change (meaning development) is accepted as the inevitable future. Yet this unremitting change is downright disorienting. An absence of just several weeks finds the native returning to the same place only to find a place that's strange and new: roads have been widened, asphalt covers the fields, and houses sit in farm pastures though the farms are gone. (The poor roads and potholes are forever!). You sense that it's probably the same place, but familiar landmarks and visual guideposts have been lost. It's like a space voyager traveling in warp time, returning to earth to find that he's changed but little, while the world about is hardly recognizable. That picturesque barn you hoped to photograph tomorrow, is gone tonight. The earthen ramp may last until the morning, when it too will be leveled and buried. Land altered so profoundly and quickly is even given its own classification by the Soil Conservation Service on (ironically) farmland maps: land with no soil left to conserve is "Urban Land" (Ub). In Ub areas "the soil material has been disturbed, filled over, or otherwise destroyed prior to construction" says the SCS. When traveling such disturbed and disturbing parts of the Triassic lands, the golden rule is to have the camera at the ready and be ready to photograph the place today. It will be "otherwise destroyed."

There is yet another subtle change to the landscape, a change so subtle that only an old folk devil walking the night roads and stalking the midnight fields would notice. Because of the onrush of development and the ever-growing outreach of urban and suburban rings and fringes, there is a reflected luminescence in the night sky, a perpetual twilight that has diminished the devil-dark, inky blackness of the nineteenth century sky to a bleached and pallid gray. It's ground-light pollution, and it softens the sharp edges of the darkness. The stars, once bright, now glow faintly in a matrix of cigarette ash. And the Milky Way becomes a sort

---

[153] Donald Jansen, The *New York Times*, September 20, 1981.

of dingy gray, almost wash day Milky Way. Over Bucks, the reflected light of the malls, the parking lots, the interstates, the millions of porch and walkway lights and street lamps, combine to create a zone of fluorescent gray-white that colors the horizon. This grades up into the heavens, turning the whole sky a mousy gray.

If the old folk devil were here today, perhaps he too would be sickened with and repelled by the consequences of "luminous pollution."[154] A Nubian black sky may still be found over the Adirondacks (less so over the Catskills and Poconos), the remaining farmlands of the *Peaceable Kingdom* are vaulted over by a gloomy grayish dome. This is surely as strong a purgative to earthly evil as a sky blue porch ceiling. As the bulls, goats, and horses of the heavenly constellations become pale and vanish, so too the farmyard animals down below. Serpens, the Serpent of the summer sky, even with more than a half dozen third magnitude stars, fades from the Bucks sky, and like the earthly serpent of old, is seemingly gone. Though ashen and hidden along the Atlantic Seaboard corridor, they're bright and strong in the dark Montana night.

---

[154] Light or "photopollution" is discussed in length at various online sites and blogs, including its effects on human health (headache, stress, fatigue) and animal ecosystems. Since the 1980s a "global dark-sky movement" has emerged to challenge light pollution in both city and suburb. More and more municipal governments are passing restrictive ordinances on types of outdoor lighting and the direction such lighting faces.

Fig. 10.5 On the Eve of Destruction. Farmhouse on Old Bethlehem Pike, Reiff's Corner, Hilltown Township. Now Demolished. *(Author's photo)*

CHAPTER 11

THOSE SIX PERCENT STEREOTYPES

*The quality of life in Bucks is good, Boyd said ...
Bucks already has a national image to work with,
and this image is positive. 'You think of Bucks and
you think of history, quaint towns, pretty countryside ...' he remarked.*

> –John Boyd, Princeton consulting firm
> president, quoted in "Sizing Up Bucks for New
> Business," *Bucks County Courier Times,* Novem-
> ber 29, 1981

*These are Porsches and Mercedes Benzes out
on the road ... This is Bucks County after all.*

> –Abbie Hoffman at Point Pleasant
> environmental protest, as quoted in *Bucks
> County Courier Times*, January 21, 1983

Scene

The hills above New Hope are drenched in winter sunlight. There, the master of the hunt leads a pageant of thirty riders, horses, and a dozen floppy-eared hounds, their noses to the ground, in pursuit of something even more elusive than the devil, the crafty red fox. With a shrill blast of the hunt master's silver horn, the cavalcade of male and female riders attired in black velvet derbies and sable leather boots, in yellow vests and dark blue and scarlet coats, follow the crying hounds through open fields and bracken, and along the high-banked country roads. The "hunt" goes on for perhaps fifteen miles, or until the "hunters" find that the hounds have chased the red fox into a burrow in the red earth. There, where the scent produced by glands in the animal's feet has led them, the hounds mark the ground with their urine. In truth, there may never have been a fox at all. No matter, for this is not blood sport. No fox need be killed. It is rather an English-like spectacle, a romp of color and noise, with characters who could be doing a remake of *Barry Lyndon* or *Tom Jones*, improbably crossing highways here in the Megalopolis. This stunning anachronism must surely convince the Sunday city motorist that this rolling Triassic countryside is indeed the playpen of the idle "uppah clahs" rich, the domicile of quality folks, the sandbox of WASP society. Bucks' country squire mystique is further confirmed when a local magazine recommends fox hunting as one of an "array of outdoor sports available to you."

More Scenes

From a prime time television special called *Bucks County U.S.A.* which aired on WCAU-TV in Philadelphia.[155] The host-narrator tools around Spectorsky's old "mink curtain" exurb in an open, chauffeur-driven Rolls Royce. He intends to show viewers all the magic of the county, the things that make it a very special place, things that entitle it

---

[155] The broadcast date was Friday, Sept. 8, 1977. It was a one hour show on Channel 10.

to be preserved as a national treasure. The host-narrator, a menswear designer and former *Playboy* magazine fashion editor, exudes all the smug arrogance and snobbery that money can buy, and that is expected of Bucks. His demeanor and manner of speech, his choice of quotes *("Bucks County is where God would live, if he could afford it")*, and his attire – a silk shirt with the two top buttons undone, allowing him to breathe a little less heavily; tight-fitting jodhpurs; and riding whip – all prove what the world already knows: that Triassic Bucks is indeed big bucks.

His video jaunt takes viewers on a visit to terribly talented and creative people to see them do typically Bucks countryish things: restoring old houses, painting and sculpting in their studio-barns, reminiscing about how much money they've made in life, and talking about their farms, horse pedigrees, and family trees. The show concludes with a lengthy segment featuring a dinner party at the host-narrator's estate where he explains his philosophies of food preparation (for example, how to make a mousse that doesn't collapse) and entertainment. He feeds and entertains millionaires, film critics, jazz pianists, and assorted faded luminaries. So, you see, a weekend afternoon in Bucks is for either this high style of home entertaining, or riding your horse to the chase, or both.

The obvious presumptuousness and pomposity of this TV special led one newspaper columnist to post the question, "This is Bucks County?" For many others who viewed it, and whose weekend afternoons consisted of walking the malls, drinking beer while watching football on the big screen at the neighborhood sports bar, or dealing with problems of static cling and ring-around-the collar at the local laundromat, they too questioned the validity of a show called *Bucks County U.S.A.* that didn't feature them doing their things in a very different Bucks.

This Five Percent of Life,
Exempt from Public Haunt

But *Bucks County U.S.A.* was in fact a perfectly good title for the program. Good and fitting because the scenes depicted the main components of a long-standing stereotype the county still possesses (or, as some might say, labors under). Bucks is ranked high in perceived exclusivity and big money (old and new) with the other geographic pieces of Spectorsky's northeast exurban fringe – e.g. Connecticut's Fairfield County and the Hudson Valley's Rockland County. Bucks is far from being one of America's wealthiest counties. There are scores of counties with higher per capita personal incomes and median household incomes, especially the Washington D.C. suburbs in nearby Maryland and northern Virginia. Many New Jersey counties also exceed Bucks in shear wealth.[156]

Of course wealth matters, but it was never just about the money. There was more to the stereotype. The *New York Times* travel writer put "taste" far ahead of "affluence" among the qualities exuded by Bucks County. The county's widely accepted image is that of a country gentry enjoying a private life on secluded and well-manicured estates with restored two hundred year-old farmhouses as their centerpieces. This gentry is professional, well-educated, overly refined, and, usually, New York connected. Everyone is supposed to know this, including the English traveler who, when hearing mention of Bucks, said: "Oh, yes, elegant and very beautiful." It was assumed that he had been to the Solebury – Makefield area, but when asked he replied, "No, never been to Bucks County." The county has a distant and distinctive stereotype. Seen from the outside and from afar, it literally drips with a cultured sense of style and leisure. It matters not that thirty people out of a population of two thirds of a million pursue the fox ... and no matter that

---

[156] Bucks ranks 77th nationally in Median Household Income, behind Montgomery and Chester Counties, Pa. It ranks 84th in Per Capita Personal Income according to census data for 2010 (U.S. Census Bureau, Washington D.C.).

the host-narrator speaks for a small clique of artsy patrician friends. These images of refinement and class support the stereotype.

The county works hard to live up to that stereotype. Property values and the prestige of an in-county address depend on it. Part of that stereotype, more manufactured than real, is an affected anglophilia; a supposed Englishness creates an air of doughy exclusivity. (This may seem unpatriotic or inappropriate in a county so intimately associated with the places where Washington and his generals slept and crossed the Delaware, but Bucks was a Loyalist hotbed. Many a fine old farm was hurriedly abandoned after the Revolution when its residents beat a quick path to Ontario or Barbados). The county's anglophilia is present, though never quite defined. It is regarded positively and is played up the *New York Times* restaurant reviewers and travel writers who boast of "the extraordinary similarity Bucks County bears to the British countryside ..." Local properties listed in the real estate sections of New York and Philadelphia newspapers conjure up the pastoral beauty of the South Downs and the rustic loveliness of Surrey. Surely, John Constable would have busied his paint brushes here and would have chosen to live in something like this:[157]

> Reminiscent of the Cotswolds and nestled into one plus acre of pine scented rolling woods in Solebury, this charming new three bedroom, two and a half bath 'Cotswold Cottage' offers gracious living ...

The developers take advantage of American anglophilia by attaching a feeling of Englishness to their products. So, not very British, non-fox hunting suburbanites find themselves living in Hampton and Wellington Manors, Headley Trace, Yorkshire Meadow, Yardley Hunt, and Polo Run (in house models named Afton, Oxford, Henley, and Stratford).

As with all stereotypes, there is some – perhaps much – truth. Bucks is certainly not the gentrified model of the English countryside it's sometimes thought to be. But part of Bucks **is** "country chic." In

---

[157] *The Advance of Bucks County,* April 2, 1981.

some shape or form, Spectorsky's "mink curtain" exurb still lives. Finding and hiring the right houseboy or pool boy still matters. Being seen and photographed at the right gallery openings, the newest late night nouveau lounges, poetry readings and coffee houses, and wine tasting parties and food festivals are of importance to some. In this area travel brochures emphasize antiquing "the old fashioned way." It's still possible to drive country roads in search of a dealer or restorer who lives down a hidden lane. Furniture galleries advertise the newest "authentic reproductions" of French period pieces. It is an area devoted to polishing and parading vintage autos and taking pride in well-stocked wine cellars, with exhibiting and comparing the children's pet horses. An area where the bumper sticker message "Have you hugged your horse today?" is a fairly common sight. An area where "farming can mean horse trailers parked along a mile of broad white-board fence. This horse country is not the magnificent panorama seen in Kentucky's Bluegrass region or West Virginia's Big Levels; but here too, as in those areas, the less aesthetic farm critters like pigs and chickens are frowned upon. In their absence, come the chestnut mares and bay geldings. It all falls short of a true equine aristocracy, but does create a local network of hunt clubs, tack and saddle shops, and dressage shows. There may be enough work to keep only two or three blacksmiths in business, but the farriers are never idle in Bucks.[158]

There are more screen, stage, TV, and sports celebrities tucked away per secreted square mile in Bucks than in any other comparable sized area on the East Coast. Here, on her day off, the Broadway actress might still come to dine and repose in a delightful country inn; with her kennel of pedigreed Belgian sheep dogs and a pack of male secretaries,

---

[158] Bucks County truly was, and is, horse country. Not just work horses and show horses, but race horses too. As early as 1810 Bristol hosted semi-annual horse races which attracted spectators and bettors from New York to Virginia. In Newtown, the second Tuesday in October (1811) "was made a day of frolic and horse-racing." Quite likely the towns had race courses even in the colonial era. In more modern times, Bensalem Township's Philadelphia Park Race Track became home to the Pennsylvania Derby. The Race Track stabled Kentucky Derby and Preakness Stakes winner Smarty Jones.

she may choose to romp through the "enchanted" scenery that is Bucks … gushing how perfectly delightful it is out in the country. Perhaps she'll soon decide to buy some part of it.

Yes, bit by bit and piece by piece, it all comes together – this later day version of Spectorsky's old exurb. It's still recognizable after decades of change, and its locale is still the almost New England-like hills and ridges 'round about' the village of New Hope. If not quite invaded, Bucks' gilded exurb has been touched with change. This comes in the form of tract housing, what are described as aggressively-mannered city people, power lines and pipe lines, and New Hope's (small) styrofoam and plastic fast food outer ring. Beyond that ring are the ostentatiously large estate properties, the long hidden driveways with the expensive foreign cars, and designer mailboxes rather than the Sears-bought metal bread loaf kind. Here one still finds all the manufactured countrified charm and rural elegance that leisure magazines just adore. Wood smoke and waterfalls. Pointed stone walls and stone terraces. Restored mills with massive stone grinding wheels whimsically propped against their sides like the extra parts of a Tinker Toy set all of whose pieces and parts didn't quite fit together.

Here, you've arrived. Here, in New Hope Borough and its surrounding townships (Solebury, Buckingham, and Upper Makefield) six percent of the county's population live the life the other ninety-four percent can only dream about. Yes, the exurb survives; but it lives in fear of subdivisions, big box stores, tattoo parlors, and sports bars. It lives in secret, in style, and in grudging esteem of those who may jealously spy its splendors on weekend afternoons, quickly glimpsing flickering images of real wealth through white fence boards and foliage at forty five mph. The devil, being a great believer in privacy, would surely find this exurb most sociable.

The old "Mink Curtain Exurb" is alive and well, as is the very privileged social scene portrayed in the vintage TV special. There is a

Fig. 11.1
BUCKS'
THREE
REGIONS

LAKES
REGION

CULTURAL
REGION

NEW
HOPE

From: *Visitors Guide to Bucks County,* Bucks County Conference and Visitors Bureau, Inc., Bensalem, Pa. 2006. *(Redrawn by Author)*

HERITAGE
REGION

continuity between these Bucks Counties and the one promoted for tourism today. As mapped in Fig.11.1 and as described in the *Visitors Guide to Bucks County,* Central Bucks (New Hope and its hinterland) is **the** "Cultural Region." Here is "where arts and culture abound." "Where arts and culture live large!" Here is "where a large artistic community thrives" amid all the glitter of galleries and studios, amid great and incredible shopping and dining experiences. By comparison, Upper Bucks (the "Lake Region") and Lower Bucks (the "Heritage Region") seem – not intentionally – diminished or somehow lacking in cultural appeal.

As the Charm Fades, Must Evil Come?

The county projects a widely accepted stereotype of high class, snooty, moneyed arrogance; and this is one of the things that most bothers young adults about the county (*See:* Appendix D). Much of this stereotype comes from the exurb's chichi epicenter, the village (borough) of New Hope. If there's any one place that comes to mind when Bucks County is mentioned, it's New Hope: "Isn't Bucks County in New Hope?" The little river village of 2,500 adds an element of funkiness, of sleaze, of devilishness to the stereotype. New Hope's allure is somewhere between the water-based uniqueness of a Sausalito and the aging, run-down seediness of a Coney Island. A Key West or Provincetown it's not. It is itself and uniquely so. It does do a reasonably good job of simulating Greenwich Village on the Delaware. Paradoxically, what it is, is a small country town, while at the same time the most urban, the most New York-like part of the county. And like many a gentrifying inner city neighborhood, its population is different: older (with 21% over 62 years), more diverse (7% Latino, mostly Mexican), better educated and with more college degrees, more heads of households living alone (41%), and more same-sex couples. So the Census Bureau says.[159]

What New Hope is depends on the season. Between the Memorial Day and Labor Day holidays the village's economy is pumped up with New York tourist dollars, especially on weekends. It's really the same gadabout geography excursion that brought Bohemian and Broadway types decades ago – i.e., a drive along venerable Route 202 to the clothing outlets at Flemington, N.J. ... and so why not another twenty minute drive to soak up all that historic ambience and buy a beaded sari in the overcrowded shops on Main Street in New Hope. The former artist and craft colony now lives on tourism. It's a tourist mecca generating income from its restored and reopened playhouse and its "cool" shops and bars. Summer is bread and butter time for the restaurants, the galleries and new age astrology shops, and the grownup lingerie boutiques. A pocketful of quarters is recommended to feed those parking meters until 9 p.m.

Like any tourist town from Lake George to Rehoboth Beach, New Hope too will always have its problems and its critics. When will the river flood again, filling the basements of shops and homes with muddy brown water? Will spikes in the price of gasoline keep the tourists away? Will the unavailability of reasonably priced and closely located parking spaces discourage tourism? Will the village's image and allure

---

[159] According to U.S. Census Bureau data, New Hope ranks #8 in the nation among places with the highest rate of same-sex couples, i.e., 59 per thousand households (or 6%). Provincetown, Massachusetts ranks #1 with a rate of 163 per thousand (or 16%). See: Sabrina Tavernise, *"New Numbering, and Geography, for Gay Couples,"* The *New York Times*, April 25, 2011, p. A1-A4.

be dampened by windows-full of the so-called "finer things," the gew-gaws and gimcracks that have pushed aside the genuine crafts and arts? Not to mention the million dollar condos and townhouses just outside of town. Will all the festivals (gay pride, indie film, jazz, wine and beer tastings, shad-on-a-stick, and the Revolutionary War) and fireworks be enough to keep people coming back for more?

And especially, what about the irritating and deafening parade of chrome? The borough is a magnet for hordes of leather- jacketed mo-torcyclists who roar through (and through) town spewing both gas fumes and noise. This has in fact been a bothersome situation for dec-ades from the bar-fly hippies of the '60s to the Hell's Angels and their biker chicks of the '70s (what would Satan make of that?) ... to the more current pack of over-the-hill riders who routinely ignore every attempt the town makes to tone it down for others. "Rev It Down" is the latest anti-noise campaign (*See:* Fig.11.2) launched by the Chamber of Com-merce. [160] The town's micro-geography may exacerbate the racket: nar-row sidewalks, closely spaced buildings and alleyways, and overarching trees that worsen the reverberations. It detracts from any attempt at con-versation by *al fresco* diners and is an insult to the casual, come-from-afar shopper. It's an indignity to the little river town; it deserves better. As expressed in a "Guest Opinion" column in the local press, "If you want peace and quiet, Philadelphia on a Saturday or Sunday morning is where it's at, not (noisy New Hope) Bucks County, and that just doesn't seem right to me."[161]

Given the all or nothing importance of tourism, townspeople are understandably very sensitive about the town's sometimes fragile im-age. When a local newspaper headlined an article "The No Hope People

---

[160] It's hoped that "Rev It Down's" genteel persuasion works: *"Motorcycle visitors are an important asset to the business community ... the bikes are a visual enjoy-ment that tourists and residents alike welcome ..."* (Chamber of Commerce) Say what?

[161] John Sikora, *"Noisy New Hope Belies Bucks' Peaceful Image," The Intelligencer,* September 10, 2012, p. A8.

Fig. 11.2

Bridge St. and the Delaware Canal in New Hope. "Rev It Down" poster campaign.

of New Hope,"[162] and depicted the town as a haven for "druggies," motorcyclists, prostitution, wealthy and not-so-wealthy drunks, and a mixed bag of street freaks left over from the '60s, residents were of course outraged at this piece of "slandering," "cheap shot" yellow journalism.[163] Drug deals in the parking lots at 3 a.m.? Displays of public love-making along the canal towpath at 4 a.m.? OK, but this is not to say that the same things don't occur in mall parking lots and on the sidewalks in other county boroughs. New Hope is probably not the "quaint country town of romantic retreat" described by a Philadelphia television station; nor is it that more pleasant place of memory remembered from childhood:[164]

> New Hope has become a caricature of itself. It is kitschy. It is cheap … It saddens me to see what New Hope has become. As a little girl I remember artists sketching at their easels along the sidewalks. Many of them were kind enough to give the ends of their pastels to a little girl who loved to watch them work … Now, I only pass through New Hope on the way upriver. I don't even stop to look around anymore.

But wait! Hold judgment. The "real" New Hope emerges only after Labor Day. This is backstage after the audience has left; this is the after-the-show show. No more showboating, the village now comes into its own. The "pleasant languor" of the past returns. That intriguing, indefinable whatever is back. The pace is slower, the streets are less crowded and quieter, and there's more of an opportunity to enjoy the ambience of old brick and stone. The artists and artisans who left for the summer are back again. Relieved of the blur of sandals and flip flops, the sidewalks are visible in all their variegated patterns of brick and block, cracks and slants among the zigzags that catch the late afternoon

---

[162] P.J. Davenport, *"The No Hope People of New Hope,"* *Bucks County Courier Times*, September 23, 1979.

[163] See "Letters: New Hope Residents Speak Out," *Bucks County Courier Times*, Accent magazine, October 7, 1979.

[164] Cynthia Dee Wilson, *"Problems Seen in New Hope,"* Letters to the Editor, *The Intelligencer*, September 1, 2006.

light before it dips beyond the Triassic hills to the west of town. The cafes and pubs are lively and, in a few at least, beneath a gallery of faded black and white autographed photos of no longer remembered celebrities, aspiring "writers" heatedly discuss intellectually stimulating, but never-to-be-published books while "poets" and "songwriters" wait on tables. Jazz played by striving, starving musicians provides the background as ceiling fans hum and *Cuba Libres* are sipped under the "marvelous" wall murals. Maybe it's the '60s outside; maybe the '20s. Inside, it's a bar in Key West, a basement apartment just off Washington Square. In its season, the village has, and has always had, atmosphere. While some of the genuine niceness has given way to a veneer of touristy glitz, New Hope does retain an allure. And too, a certain sense of style and differentness often remains.

When Benjamin Parry's mills across the river in New Jersey were destroyed by fire in the 1790s, he relocated to the Bucks County shore where the Aquetong joins the Delaware. There, he rebuilt his mills "with determination and **new hope** for the future." Today, the "enterprising and venerable" little village mixes equal parts moxie and hope, and in return hopes for a little respect. The good qualities sometimes elude the shallow, or at best, seasonal stereotype.

Ed's Big Joke

If you had asked Ed Koch, it was all one big joke. In a *Playboy* magazine interview he once expressed this opinion:[165]

> The country? Rural America? This is a joke! ... Rural America doesn't exist anymore, not even the farms. That day will never come back ... out in the country wasting time in a pickup truck? ... This rural-America thing – I'm telling you, it's a joke.

---

[165] *Playboy*, April, 1982, p. 70.

Ed Koch (1924–2013) will forever be remembered as the Bronx-born, outspoken New York mayor (1978-89) who may have lost his bid for governor because he antagonized the upstate "country" voting block that he thought didn't exist. The mayor might have pulled some weight in a place like New Hope, but little out in the "country," whether upstate New York or rural Bucks County.

Most of the remaining farms in Bucks are above New Hope and its surrounding "Mink Curtain" townships, up on the rolling red ridges and in the valleys settled by the Germans. Here, nearly half the land is still in family farms that lie amid a scatteration of vacation homes, cross-roads villages and small boroughs, and, especially, state park and game lands. There is no blend of red clay and redneckism here; no stock car races and six packs for breakfast found (by reputation) in northern Georgia. No foreign mission belt, no rubedom here. Bucks' backcountry is more subtle. It's a region of quiet, decent people (less than one per acre and many of German descent) who, in some cases, have worked the same patch of land for seven or more generations. Stereotypically (*See:* Appendix C), it's an area of hard-working farmers in faded blue bib overalls. They're religious (or at least more so than the downcounty heathens and hedonists) and rather conservative in their lifestyle and politics. And they all go to bed early; they sleep in beds in old stone farmhouses protected from evil by blue porch ceilings.

If there's any one thing that visually dominates the upper Bucks farmlands, it's the deep blue Harvestore solos, some as high as five stories. They're lined inside with fused glass and steel and they're usually chocked to the brim with corn feed for the dairy herd. The dairy herd means several dozen 1,600 pound Holsteins each of which consumes sixty-five pounds of feed and protein daily, washed down with twenty-five gallons of water. Like chickens, the animals are assembly line products most of whose lives are spent indoors beneath the horizontal stainless steel milking pipes. Better to control the diet and the quality of the milk. In cold weather, the herd provides the only source of warmth in the barn. Parked in attached sheds are the big orange and black Allis-Chalmers 6,080's and the black and red International Harvester 5,088's with wheels six feet high. So, no "sequestered vale of rural life" here. A grubby and muddy, but dedicated, farm life.

At opposite ends of the same county, it's more than an hour's drive from Levittown to the fields of Durham (*See:* cover illustration), Springfield, and Richland. It was only in jest, but a lower county newspaper writer referred to rural upper Bucks as just "coming out of the Dark Ages" because street numbers were finally being assigned to area houses. Distance in time does however distinguish the opposite ends of the county. While lower Bucks was being exurbanized and suburbanized, the upper county remained largely rural. Here the farmers embraced mechanization less quickly and more skeptically than elsewhere. Though mostly idle and rusting now, steel-tipped metal plows of the kind patented in the early 1800s can still be seen on the margins of the fields. Their retirement was perhaps recent.

Rows of corn and melons are plowed in with century-old wood-handled plows; and potatoes are rooted out with half-century-old potato-digging machines. This is not to say that the latest in agronomical tools and science is a stranger to the local farmers or that these farmers are unfamiliar with the prices and performance of the latest machinery. They're not. This is not old order Amish country where change is rejected out-of-hand. It's just that time, linear time and seasonal time as well, hangs heavier here. The passage of time, whether in seasons or years, is confronted more directly in the unbuilt upon Triassic earth and in the things that grow and die upon it. There are lessons here that even an Ed Koch could have learned.

Though far removed from the Megalopolitan trunkline, and somewhat protected by distance from the inroads of urban commutation and sprawl, the farmlands of upper Bucks are not entirely off the monopoly board. The building and opening of I-78 through the Lehigh Valley, and skirting the northern border of Bucks, created speedy access to New York City (The Phillipsburg-Newark Expressway) across northern New

Jersey. This is already impacting the upper county – growth has quickened and more pressure is put on the remaining farms and open space.[166] The demand for housing must be met, even if temporarily, by the increasingly ubiquitous mobile homes and trailer parks that sprout up in the fields and along the shoulders of the county and state roads that lead to the interstate.

Because of the proximity of the Lehigh Valley, malls (amid the stalls) and apartment complexes "grow in" from that direction. Linkages with the Lehigh Valley seem to encourage a kind of geographic schizophrenia. Life's daily details (doctor's visits, banking preferences, family ties, and cultural events) draw people out of county to Allentown and neighboring towns. This has actually created some "secessionist" feelings, though it's very doubtful anything would ever come of it. The "prestige" value of staying in Bucks County and having a Bucks County address far outweighs any thought of having an address in a less reputable county.[167]

All this reflects the bigness of Bucks. It's a county one-half the size of Rhode Island. It's also stretched-out and elongated like the Italian boot; similarly, it produces a strong north-south dichotomy in culture, lifestyle, and landscape. Upcounty, much of the acreage in townships is labeled "vacant land" on planning maps. This means "developable" land; this means that exurbia and suburbia loom large on the horizon. Developable parcels lie waiting in the fields and along county roads. These parcels will soon become "tracts."

For example, the Route 663 "corridor" west from Quakertown connects directly with the Pennsylvania Turnpike (I-476) in Milford Township. This highway corridor is less than four miles in length, but it's having the same impact on the upcounty rural landscape that the

---

[166] This is a more direct connection to Manhattan than the old(er) and more venerable Route 202. I-78 has helped revive Lehigh Valley cities like Easton and Bethlehem. I-78 is a major truck route that ultimately links the New York-Newark port and airport facilities with I-81 northeast of Harrisburg, Pa.

[167] With apologies to Northampton County, Pa.

opening of the turnpike had on the lower county in the 1950s (The Pennsylvania Turnpike was completed from Bristol to Valley Forge in 1954). Both opened full the throttle of growth. Milford Township grew by more than 20% per decade between 1980 and 2010 (when the population was 9,902). For years, a large sign stood in a field alongside Route 663 announcing "Bucks County – For Sale." Well, that field sold and a massive residential (1,000 "unit") and commercial project was approved. It will join the already existing raft of "Express" hotels and inns, gas stations and convenience stores. And sandwiched in between, a couple of farm stands selling raw honey, corn and pumpkins. "663" itself of course will have to be widened from two to five lanes. And so it goes — "progress" that is.[168]

The population of these upcounty farmlands, together with that of New Hope and its exurban fringe, amounts to only six percent of the county's total. And yet, it's a significant part of the stereotypical image purveyed in the old TV profile (*Bucks County, USA*) – locals who are either "creative … agricultural, or just plain rich." Here, the stereotype fits comfortably with the reality.

---

[168] The designated "663" first appeared in 1930 when the road was numbered and paved. Had it been numbered the "666" corridor, it would have been even more prophetic of the devil of development. "663" is also known as the "John Fries Highway," in honor of the man who led the Fries Rebellion of 1799. Fries (1750-1818) was an auctioneer of Welsh descent from Milford Township who led a Pennsylvania rebellion of his German neighbors against a new Federal tax on land and houses (assessed by the number of windows) to be paid in gold or silver and collected by ex-Tories. Arrested and convicted of treason, Fries was later pardoned by President John Adams.

FIG. 11.3 Old Stereotypes Survive:

The New Hope People (left), Upcounty Farmer (right)

"Creative ... agricultural, or just plain rich"

(See Appendix C for full citation)

CHAPTER 12

SUCH IS LIFE ...
IN THE "EDGE CITY"

On the Rampage, Pip, and off the Rampage,
Pip; such is Life!

–Charles Dickens, *Great Expectations*, 1861

There are only a small number of people who
care to look at the suburbs, where the action is.

–Peter O. Muller, "The Suburbs are Winning,
    Professor Claims," *Philadelphia Inquirer*,

July 17, 1978

Dull? What do you mean dull! We
had a gas riot here in '79.

–Levittowner

Mall: Five-hundred and fifty acres of asphalt-paved
parking space easily accessible via off-on ramps con-
necting with three interstate highways and the his-
toric and picturesque Old Ox Road ... Six fast-food
stand-up counters ready to serve the hamburger of
your dreams ... Your 14-year-old daughter's dream
of Paradise? Or your vision of Hell? Neither ... –
Russell Baker, "Heaven in Asphalt," The *New York*
Times, March 17, 1987

Golden Slippers
on Glacial Sands

Lower Bucks' outwash plain, that gravelly and sandy *"allée"* first settled by Europeans moving up the Delaware River and then the Neshaminy Creek and then across the Langhorne Ridge would, within two centuries, became a very essential part of the Megalopolitan mainline. The county Economic Development Corporation rightly boasts:

> Welcome to Bucks County, Pennsylvania, a premier location for business and industry located north of the city of Philadelphia, having immediate access to Interstate 95 and I-276, and being in the heart of the Boston to Washington D.C. corridor!

Today, this corridor contains some 60% of the county's population on 20% of the county's land. Nestled within this inter-urban zone are the "old" planned suburbs like Levittown and Fairless Hills. It's a vastly different world from the undulating washboard found on the other side of the Langhorne Ridge. The feel and texture of the land is not the same ... nor is the daily temperature range (it always seems to be a few degrees warmer and more humid on the outwash plain). It's different too in terms of population densities and even lifestyles. Mostly, this is "Edge City."

"Edge City" is a concept first identified and written about by Joel Garreau in his 1991 *Edge City: Life on the New Frontier*.[169] Garreau's classic example of an "Edge City" was Tyson's Corner in Fairfax County, Virginia. Close to Washington D.C., Tyson's Corner had evolved quickly and dramatically from cow pastures at a country crossroads to a sprawling suburban technology center with more office space than most downtowns in center cities. It developed incrementally around a mall (retail space and massive surface parking lots) and could not have been possible without the automobile. "Edge Cities" or suburban downtowns have become legion with more than two hundred having

---

[169] Joel Garreau, *Edge City: Life on the New Frontier*, New York: Doubleday, 1991.

been identified. They've captured much of the cultural vitality and economic muscle once identified with the older center city entertainment and business districts.

Lower Bucks County is a latticework of highways and rail lines, high population densities and a high number of apartment complexes, and a glut of big box stores and chain restaurants – all anchored by two grand (though aging) regional malls. In other words, the lower county from Bensalem and Croydon through Levittown and Fairless Hills to Morrisville has become the very personification of the great American "Edge City."[170]

The lower county "locates" itself between New York and Philadelphia and lies at the center of the great sprawling Megalopolis. And it will continue to sprawl because of the quick and relatively easy interstate and rail links between the county and both cities. New York is ninety minutes away; that's much closer than when the artists and writers wound their way down the back roads from Greenwich Village to New Hope. Commuters also connect with New York via I-78 from the upper county and via the New Jersey Transit and AMTRAK routes from the lower county.[171]

Lower Bucks, as an older urban/suburban outer zone is actually maturing in such a way that it needs the city that spawned it less and less. Philadelphia is there for concerts, museums, and sports events, but economically the area functions more and more as its own downtown. It creates jobs and services and provides living space. Bucks now supplies jobs for a majority of its own work force. This is no more apparent than in the lower county where the need to commute that thirty minutes

---

[170] Interestingly, Edgewood and Edgely are located in the lower county's "Edge City." Edgewood (*See:* Chapter 13) being a village between Langhorne and Yardley. Edgely is a village in Bristol Township and a station of the same name along the New York Division of the old Pennsylvania Railroad. (SEPTA today). Along the edge of the Delaware River, Edgely is cut through by the Delaware-Bristol Canal, Route 13, and the old Bristol Pike (*See:* George MacReynolds, Place Names in Bucks County).

[171] Eighteen people with ties to Bucks County died in the 9-11 terrorist attack on New York's Twin Towers and are remembered and honored in a Memorial Park (The Garden of Reflection) in Lower Makefield Township.

to Philadelphia is somewhat negated. While Philadelphia went through fifty years of population loss in the second half of the twentieth century, Bucks continued to grow (explosively). Much of that recent growth resulted from urban overspill or the flight from urban blight (gangs and drugs, stolen car rings, and apartment house burglaries). The eminent geographer Peter Muller offered this observant definition of adjacent northeast Philadelphia: "one-half million people waiting to move to Bucks County."

Despite the New York commuter linkage (via Trenton-Princeton), the lower county inevitably lives within the shadow of Philadelphia. It takes a strong dose of New York nerve to walk into the local convenience store and buy the New York Daily News or Post ... and sporting a Yankees or Mets baseball cap to boot. It does happen, or so they say. New York TV and radio (cable) stations reach here. But this is Phillies and Flyers country. Unlike the New York oriented cultural exurb around New Hope, lower Bucks is an extension of "Philly" culture. And a heavy duty and very visible one at that.

Happily, the total homogenization of the nation's cultural landscape never came to be. Regionalisms thrive; and there is a durable consciousness of and pride in the uniqueness of things local. Pockets of dialect along with other folkways persist in the more remote backwaters where a protective geography offers sanctuary. But regionalisms survive and flourish at the very heart of the Megalopolis despite standardization through the media and mass culture. Lower Bucks is stamped with the imprint of "Philly" culture, and that means fierce sports loyalties especially. At area sports bars, cheesesteaks and "hoagies" (never ever subs or heroes) are ordered up while rabid fans cheer on the local teams. Soft pretzels of course are always present. During commercial breaks talk briefly shifts nostalgically to politics and obituaries in the old neighborhoods – Fishtown, Port Richmond, Bridesburg, Torresdale, and Kensington. They may be living in garden apartments in Bucks, but their sentiments and thoughts are often with aunts and uncles, godparents and cousins who live in 80-family to a block row houses in the city's "great northeast."

Of the many cultural ties that bind the lower county to the city, none perhaps is as powerful as mumming. Philadelphia mums. It has done so since colonial times; it even has a Mummers Museum (1976). With many people now retiring to the Sunbelt, Florida and southern California have begun to mum. Lower Bucks mums! Communities send mummers "brigades" to march up Broad Street in Philadelphia on New Year's Day. In front of City Hall they engage in fierce competitions with brigades from other parts of the urban region. They are judged on the basis of their costumes, music, and drill performance. In the months leading up to the big day, all across lower Bucks elaborate satin suits with gold lamé cuffs, sequined gowns, and headdresses with faux ostrich plumes and bangles are assembled. At Christmas Eve house parties a calliope of sound from steel-stringed banjos, saxophones, accordions, and glockenspiels fills the air as mummers practice. On New Year's, those who aren't strutting their thirty five-pound costumes through the January cold, stamp their feet to keep warm along the line of march. From Levittown to Bristol, from Hulmeville to Bensalem, others are glued to the TV enthusiastically cheering on the county's string bands. Though this tradition is urban, it has become a much anticipated part of life in lower Bucks. It is however a tradition that doesn't travel well across the Langhorne Ridge and out across the Triassic lands. It helps set the lower county apart, holding it closely within the shadow of the city that mums, the Quaker city.

There is a stereotype that emerges from this city-spirited part of Bucks (*See:* Appendix C). It's that of the Bensalemites – many of them middle and working class former Philadelphians. Being contiguous with the neighborhoods in northeastern Philadelphia, the township has served as a "port of entry" into Bucks County. It's a comfortable enough transition given the similarities between lower Bucks and the city. There is little visual indication of where the city leaves off and Bucks begins.

From Market Gardens to Garden Apartments

You can start by saying that Bensalem Township recently made *Money* magazine's list of the one hundred best places to live in America (it ranked 85th).[172] The Parx Casino and Race Track were cited as one of the reasons why. Township officials were quick to add other reasons: good location, shopping, good planning and open space preservation, and especially good quality people who care about the community. Having said that, Bensalem also has a busy feel to it, an impermanent landscape of convenience and convenience stores (at least along the major roadways). It's a handy-enough springboard where almost ten percent of the county's population pauses while en route to some other place (usually further up- county). Foreign-born residents comprise more than 13% of the township's population; it's a mecca for immigrants from the former Soviet Union, India, South Korea, and Mexico ... all on their way up the economic escalator.

Bensalem's milestones are the ground-breaking ceremonies, the grand openings, and the less ceremonious going-out-of-business sales of individual stores, restaurants, and shopping centers. Yet hidden behind all the comings and goings are many families who grew up here when the land was farmed. And that's not that long ago. They remember "watching the sun rise over the strawberry fields and woods." And they remember watching from the windows of their parents' houses the road crews widening and paving the streets. They of course regret how quickly change has come. In the wink of a devil's eye! "Went to Vietnam, came back, and it was all malled over . . . my hunting places were gone." Some say things like this "... sixteen years ago, it was a great place to live and raise children; but now, there's no way I'd live there." It's the kind of place that finds itself vulnerable to the satirical pen of a local columnist who suggested a "Developers Hall of Fame" be opened here: "Wax renderings of every land developer who ever got rich in Bensalem will line the walls. A 30-foot mural entitled 'The Plundering of Bensalem' will be unveiled..." Why not "Hall of Shame?"

---

[172] *Money* magazine, September 2012.

For all the tremendous growth Bensalem has sustained (75% since 1970), there are surviving islands here and there that still reflect the past. There are ancient villages and hamlets pocketed away and hidden from view. There are reminders of the recent years when it served as a rural market garden (a vegetable and fruit shed) for the nearby city. The one-lane dirt roads have been made over into crowded four lane avenues and the drone of traffic is everywhere. But along the shoulders of those avenues, time has left its incongruities: tangled lots of weeds and vines where fields once were; small jungles of wild mulberry, the descendants of plants that escaped from local farmers who tried to cultivate the bush more than a century ago, hoping to compete with Japanese silk makers; a field or two that may well produce the last corn crop ever; vintage summer bungalows with white and pastel stuccoed walls and patched roofs; and much older, shaky barns. Ghosts from an era that ended decades ago and now find themselves uncomfortably sandwiched in between the hoagie houses, tattoo parlors, dollar stores and thrift shops, and the abandoned car dealerships.

It is a difficult place to take in; the eye is not allowed to rest. No one walks or sees the world on foot, though some dare try to be pedestrians. Sidewalks, where they exist at all, are but interruptions between driveways. For a few seconds one's senses are allowed a rest at traffic lights. Otherwise, Bensalem is a wash of roadside grit and grime, popped and jettisoned hub caps, delivery truck convoys. The loathing and scorn once reserved for Levittown is now heaped upon Bensalem. Its critics scolded Levittown for being too much in the grip of the automobile, but here – the landscape unapologetically caters to the every whim of truck and car: carburetor and transmission shops, body and muffler shops, and parking lots galore. Get your oil changed and tires balanced. Acres and acres of parking lots draped like aprons around the malls and plazas. Parking lots with a maze of oil splotches, yellow lines, and half-drunk cans of caffeine drinks standing alongside the yellow lines, alongside the plastic shards of taillight glass. Rows of speed bumps now replace rows of bumper crops.

There is in fact much history here. But demographically Bensalem is young, less rooted and more mobile. Bensalemites are younger in age (median age is 37) than the county[173] or state. One third (34%) rent apartments and have short term leases. In a reversal of when married couples with families used to live in the suburbs and singles lived in cities, Bensalem now has a high percentage of single-parent and non-family households. (Then again, Bensalem **is** the city). The township as city is also well-educated and well-paid (average incomes being considerably higher than county and state averages; the corporate, high-tech and white collar world has arrived). It all moves faster and faster: people, job changes, companies that come and go, mid-rise corporate towers that beg for tenants. The township has become the embodiment of what Pennsylvanian Vance Packard called "*A Nation of Strangers*" (1972). It's ironic in a way that in one of the nation's least mobile states, the township closely mimics the shallowly-rooted, impermanent, address-changing society Packard described.

A great many apartment house complexes were built in Bensalem in the 1960s-80s. Here again, the old theme emerges – the developers doing the devil's work. The apartment units were quickly built, and not always up to standard. There's a pretense of quality with mock colonial or classical facades and columns outside. But inside, walls and floors are often so thin and flimsy that neighbors can be heard putting on their socks. What seems like paper maché and cardboard construction can include faulty wiring, inadequate firewalls (lined with waxed paper), and doors that open the wrong way thus impeding an emergency exit. Fire is frequently the bane of apartment life. Fires that rage along roof ridges on winter nights, making people both homeless and propertyless because insurers won't insure what's in the gray cinderblock or brick-walled apartments. Embers drift up and snowflakes drift down, mixing in the ethereal night sky; teardrops and sooty water mingle and percolate down to replenish the ground. And far, far below it all, the once nourishing Triassic earth lies buried. Treetops compete with the burning

---

[173] The U.S. Census Bureau reports (2014) that Bucks County is "aging fastest in the region." 43.1 years is the average age in the county ... significantly older than Bensalem, Philadelphia (33.8), Pennsylvania (40.7), and the United States (37.6).

embers for a piece of the sky. Trees reach skyward, competing with utility poles and lines. Power company crews have bonsaied, dwarfed, decapitated and forced trees to grow oddly and laterally along the sagging utility lines. All beneath the same Bensalem sky where Ben Franklin flew his famous kite. All this in a place, "Bensalem," named (perhaps) for the seventeenth-century utopia of Francis Bacon's *New Atlantis* – a wholesome land of plenty where God's presence was surely manifest. [174]

Bensalem is an older suburb showing the wear 'n tear of a half century. The manor lands of the Penns and other colonial families are now covered with building complexes, identified by big single numbers and letters attached to their walls. Bensalem is linked together with neighboring municipalities via county roads and state highways now bottlenecked with a growing throng of cars and trucks. Street Road (State Route 132) slices through the township, carrying 54,000 vehicles daily; characterized by poor signage and aggressive drivers, it has the dubious distinction of being one of the most dangerous highways in America (*Time* magazine, 2014). Veteran U.S. Route 1, the old "Lincoln Highway" cuts through on its way from the Canadian border to southern Florida and, in Bucks, is paralleled by state Route 13. Lower Bucks is connected by the two. Route 13 traverses the county from Bensalem to Morrisville and was recently described by a local columnist as a "dreary landscape of gas stations, muffler shops, bars, fast food joints and hodge podge ..."[175] These highways (Routes 1 and 13) weave their way

---

[174] The derivation of the name "Bensalem" has long been subject to controversy. In Scotland, "ben" means hill, and thus "hill of peace" or "peaceful mount" seems possible, though the terrain here is basically flat. The township historical society believes that when Joseph Growden came to America he called his estate "Bensalem," as a probable "compliment to William Penn, a 'son of peace'." Maybe. But when Growden came over from Europe in 1682 he no doubt knew that Francis Bacon had called his popular new utopia "Bensalem" in 1627. Bacon's Bensalem sounds a lot like what Growden might have found here: "it was a land, flat to our sight, and full of woods . . . in God's bosom, a land unknown . . . "

[175] J.D. Mullane, "Tunnels Beneath Route 13", *The Intelligencer,* August 1, 2013, p. A3. When this "new" Route 13 was built in the 1950s it served the new Levittown and Levittown Shopping Center well. It has since aged,

through miles of older, blighted industrial structures and large wooded and weedy tracts that conceal behind their foliage remnants of a Cold War missile battery and the tarpaper and cardboard shelters that house homeless men. These highways are indistinguishable from thousands of other such "blue routes" that encourage an architecture of impermanence. These are the anywhere, everywhere highways described by John Updike in *A Month of Sundays:*

> ... a highway that, once threaded shadily through fields and pastures, was now straightened, thickened, and jammed with shopping malls, car lots, gas stations, hero sandwich parlors, auto parts paradises, driving ranges, joyless joyrides for the groggy offspring of deranged shoppers, gogo bars windowless as mausoleums ... drive-in insurance agencies, the whole gaudy, ghastly gasoline-powered consumerish smear, bubbling like tar in the heat of high summer.

Substitute "hoagie" for "hero," throw in a few topless lounges and massage parlors, add a couple of all-nite diners with green, rusting dumpsters in the back and that's very much the vehicular mainline that supports lower Bucks. It sits there in the pizza oven air of the Delaware Valley, garnished with a sauce rich in heat, haze, and humidity; the bad air is thickened with chemical smells and unseemly high ozone levels.

Such highway corridors are easily criticized. They're seen as just further examples of the typically loused-up and dreary ribbon of schlock that holds the Megalopolis together. A sin against aesthetics. A minefield of bad taste. Visual chaos ... and more. "...What is U.S. Route 1 between New York and Philadelphia but a topographical loony bin?" asks architect and planner Ian Nairn.[176] Yet, such highways are exactly what and where they should be, i.e., concentrations of commercial and industrial activity whose location maximizes the dictates of history and geography. Route 1's forest of advertising signs announce to the world

and not very well.

[176] Ian Nairn, *The American Landscape, A Critical View*, New York: Random House, 1965, p. 12.

that this is automobile row. Here, with immediate access to I-95's on-off ramps, dozens of wheelin' 'n dealin' auto retailers and repair shops provide jobs and services. To belabor the fact that it looks so messy, or that a muffler shop has replaced a dairy bar, or that a car wash has sprouted in an onion field, gives in too easily to nostalgia. Route 1 is America's vernacular highway, an autoscape lined with junkyards, gas stations, diners, and weedy lots. But it's little different now from how it was described by the federal (WPA) writers in their 1938 guidebook. It became what it is, and where it is, because there was a need for it. And that need is still best served here in lower Bucks.

A Closer Look: Shrinking a Landmark

In "Edge City" growth and change are on steroids; landmarks become lost landmarks in a nanosecond. Familiar roadside anchors are here today, gone tomorrow (morning). Just to name a few: the Greenwood Dairy Bar, the Ground Round Restaurant, the Neshaminy Mall Totem Pole, the Drive-In Movie (and even the flea market that had replaced it). All gone! Look what happened to Flannery's Airplane – it disappeared, only to return shrunk. *Cont'd.*

For 30 years everyone who drove along U.S. Route 1 through the Borough of Penndel made a mental note of Jim Flannery's Lounge and Restaurant because the aviation-themed eatery was built into the fuselage of a 125-foot long, four-engine airplane. The plane, a 1954 Lockheed Super Constellation, was operated for years by Cubana and then Capital Airways. A red, white, and silver gray landmark, it remained prominently parked high above the ground in Penndel from 1967 to 1997. Then, one day it was gone – dismantled and moved to a new home at an Air Force base museum.

More recently, a shrunken six-foot replica of the plane has come to sit atop a gas station – convenience store sign amid a tangle of overhead wires. Thoughtful, but not quite the same. *(Author's photos)*

"We Knew the 'Town' Would Last ..."

Once, an historic building stood along the shoulder of U.S. Route 13 near the Tullytown Station of the Pennsylvania Railroad. It should not have become another vanishing landmark; they should have placed an historical marker on it. It might have hosted tours of wide-eyes, reverential visitors on Sunday afternoons ... as it once did. There might have been long, long lines of people waiting to see the house within ... as there once was. Instead, "KEEP OUT" warnings were posted and it housed no one and admitted no one, and was noticed by hardly anyone. It had become difficult to even see the house from the passing highway; a half-cannibalized panel truck jacked up on cinder blocks screened the front of the house from view, while a lightless lamplight hung overhead.

This was the last surviving house model the Levitt & Sons opened to the public in 1951, and it was therefore the first and oldest Levittown house. This prototype was the ancestor of the 17,000 houses to come in Levittown, Pennsylvania. Thus, it surely deserved a place of honor in the Smithsonian between Archie Bunker's chair and the 1950s era ticket booth from Yankee Stadium. For quite a while, it sat totally forgotten at the far end of a trailer rental lot, amid a madness of six-foot weeds and a cracked sidewalk. The lawn was strewn with broken furniture and busted and rusted appliances. It was the shell of a building with shattered windows that were wired shut. It still looked sturdy enough and some of the history-minded Levittowners wanted to preserve it. But the house was set on fire in 1985 as part of a planned fire-fighting drill. "A piece of Levittown history ends in ashes" the newspapers intoned. "Only a chimney survived ..."

This house may not have survived, but Levittown surely did. And it does quite well. "We knew the 'town' would last" they said when the instant suburb celebrated its 25th anniversary in 1977. They celebrated 30 years in 1982 with a parade, a sky-diving exhibition, a drum-and-bugle marching competition, and a $50 per couple dinner dance with proceeds donated to the "Vest-a-Cop" program to equip the local police with bullet proof vests. Some "old timers" thought a dinner dance was a bit too formal for blue collar Levittown, and so arranged a "working-man's celebration" – a beef and beer party with a juke box reminiscing about the old days. The 50th and 60th anniversaries were celebrated with fond memories and memorable moments. At the 60th in 2012 the Smithsonian interviewed and recorded for posterity the thoughtful recollections of many of the original Levittowners. Maybe because of all the early criticism and wisecracks that Levittowners shrugged off, the "town" that shaped Bucks as perhaps the one local community with the greatest collective pride in its achievements. Therefore, it's the one with the best reason to celebrate.

In both the popular and academic literature of the past several decades, it's been fair game to crucify the American suburb for the evils it perpetrated on the nation's culture and landscape. The old suburban dream of a detached, single-family home is said to be fading. And thankfully so, say the critics. People are returning to the city to gentrify crumbly old neighborhoods, neighborhoods their parents may have fled for the suburbs in the 1950s and 60s. For the young, and even the elderly; the suburb has become boring, unable to fill their time and fulfill their needs. Activities for the young and social services for the old are readily at hand, and more concentrated in the city. America is living alone more now, a lifestyle better suited to small apartments and urban townhouses and lofts. No one can afford the price of a three-bedroom home anyway; nor can anyone really afford the upkeep, school taxes, and heating costs. Bankruptcies and foreclosures are taking over the suburbs, as one family after another is pushed over the edge by mounting fuel, utility, and trash disposal bills. The suburb is even described as "anti-woman" (a long-standing enlistee in the "war against women") because the sprawling, far-flung suburban landscape conspires against a woman's need for a female support system. In a 1980 magazine cover story, "Suburbia: End of the Golden Dream," the *New York Times* writer says it all. A cartoon depicted the typical suburban ensemble: lawnmower, tricycle, the four-member, two-child family – everyone smiling inanely on the lawn in front of their micro-castle, four bulgy-eyed and stuffed persons. Stuffed and mounted in a glass display case like the last family of passenger pigeons. The display case sits in a museum-like corridor; its label reads: "Suburbia, 1945-1975." Finis! The accompanying article says:[177]

> ... there is growing evidence that ... the suburban dream will not survive the generation that tried to realize it ... the suburbs are predicated on a way of life that is endangered in an era of two-paycheck families, childless couples and frequent divorce. And ... rising energy costs that threaten its very nature. The suburban era, in short, has come to an end.

Further in the article, the author, William S. Kowinski, arrives at the crux of suburban angst: "The energy crisis threatens suburbia's life blood, gasoline, at a time when the suburbs are already suffering from hardening of the arteries." Here, Bucks County's Levittown is singled out, since it was the site of "the first American gasoline riot." The local newspaper is quoted: "Liked trapped animals pushed against the wall, the gas-guzzling dreamers of America's Levittown have little left but frustration."[178]

In 1977 Howard Cosell both immortalized and stigmatized the Bronx in a way that would hurt for a good long while. Calling attention to a fire burning beyond the outfield wall of the old Yankee Stadium, the TV sportscaster intoned: "There it is ladies and gentlemen ... the Bronx is burning." Of course, much of it **was** actually burning in the 1970s. But to draw attention to the fact before a national TV audience and during a World Series game, glaringly validated how awful a place the Bronx was at the time.

Just two years later Levittown, Pennsylvania would get its two minutes (or two nights) of national infamy. Like the ballplayer who loses his chance for the Hall of Fame because of that one glaring error in the seventh game of the World Series, Levittown's place in American

---

[177] William S. Kowinski, "Suburbia: End of the Golden Dream," The *New York Times*, March 16, 1980, p.16.
[178] ibid.

culture, its success or failure as a social experiment, is conditioned now and maybe forever by one or two bad nights. Everybody saw it. Saw the instant replays on TV. The media fed it to a national audience and Walter Cronkite read it at the top of the evening news: "Dateline: Levittown, U.S.A. ..." It's an albatross, a leach that the community must live with, must live down. Most memories of it have dimmed, and most would prefer to keep it that way. Many make light of it now: "Yeah, I was there; took some pictures. But it wasn't much." Nothing but teenage boredom, firecrackers, and beer on a summer evening. Just Levittown. Sightseers mostly. People in t-shirts, shorts, and bathing suits sprung from their plastic lawn chairs and backyard bar-b-ques to see what all the commotion was. But for two weekend nights in June of 1979 it was a bloody battleground: riot casualties; an onslaught of victims; a gasoline battle; the night everyone went crazy – or so the media said. It was "a complete breakdown of law and order in Lower Bucks County ..." – so the authorities said.

Whatever triggered it – truckers protesting the price of diesel fuel, not Levittowners (though they readily joined the fracas) – is history now. And perhaps the whole event is best forgotten. A very brief aberration. A moment of frenzy in Levittown's decades-long quest for the "American dream." Yet, the question lingers. Why Levittown?

A random convergence of just the right conditions? The time, temperature, and tempers falling neatly into place? There is symbolism too: horse drawn wagons on dirt roads converging on a crossroads hamlet with the bucolic name of Emilie; a general store and blacksmith shop encircled by farm fields, chicken coops, and woods. And all within living memory. On this spot, ancient creeks run silent beneath the asphalt, stone foundations are entombed beneath the concrete. Name and form change: Emilie becomes Five Points; wagons become cars; and the smithy's shop becomes a gas station. Several gas stations. Function however remains the same: a crossroads cluster of services for the surrounding community, Levittown. The rapid journey from fields to suburb, all achieved on wheels. From chicken coops to buckets of Chicken Delight delivered (free) via the wheels of a Volkswagen bug. Anger and fear when the gas to turn the wheels runs dry. The gasoline-powered American suburb sputters.

The gas "riot" didn't happen in just any suburb, but in **the** American suburb. Levittown is to the metropolitan landscape what California is to other states. It's a bellwether of what is to come, a barometer of the future cultural environment. No place mirrors the suburban landscape as closely as Levittown and no place has absorbed as much criticism. In commenting on Levittown, Long Island on its 40th anniversary (comments that could just as easily apply to Bucks' Levittown) the *New York Times* described the community as having lost something of its "original spirit, even its raison d'être." Ironically, the middle age suburb was also accused of having become a part of the problem it once solved, i.e. Levittowns no longer meet the enormous need for affordable housing in their suburban regions. Even if they were affordable, who would want to live here anyway? Former New York Mayor and New Hope "darling," Ed Koch thinks such suburbs are no more appealing than the farmlands: "Have you ever lived in the suburbs? I haven't, but I've talked to people who have, and it's sterile. It's nothing, it's wasting your life."[179]

There will always be non-believers, yet Levittown seems to have instilled a sense of contentment in most who live there now. It may be a purely unscientific "most," but most regard Levittown as a safe enough, friendly enough, pleasing enough lifestyle still. The houses have more than held their value, many fall within the $250,000 to $350,000 range (depending on condition, remodeling, expansions, etc.).[180] Though doors are now locked at night and alarm systems in-

---

[179]*Playboy* magazine, April, 1982, p.70.

[180] Levittown house prices vary widely, depending on section, add-ons, and up keep. Most houses have been expanded over the decades to the point where from the street it's difficult to tell Jubilees from Pennsylvanians from Ranchers. It's hard to generalize, but prices range from $185,000-$250,000 for an expanded Cape to $290,000-$340,000 for a well-maintained Country Clubber. (*See:* Zillow, Weichert, and other realty websites).

stalled, an "up-state" sense of neighborliness is still mentioned as a positive quality. As one "old-timer" says: "I think it's all-right, and I think that's the way it will stay."

They either bought in or inherited, but some of the generation that grew up in Levittown has chosen to either stay or return. This second (or even third) generation can look back nostalgically on a younger Levittown: the community pools, soap box derbies, and little leagues; the man in the white coat who dispensed 15-cent "screwballs" from the yellow and white O'Boyle's Ice Cream truck; and when they were older, going to the Rollerama and the Langhorne Speedway --- and cruising the Parkway in souped-up cars. All in all, it was good to have grown-up in the all-American "dream" suburb. Writes one who did: "Levittown ain't Shangri-La by any stretch of the imagination. Never was really. Never will be. But I can think of a lot worse places to live."[181]

Downtown Bucks, by the Blue Water Tower

If life on the outwash plain is geared to gear boxes and gasoline, if the landscape is so given over to highways and acres of parking lots and used car lots, what provides the focal point? What counters the blur of movement and provides structure and order amid the visual chaos? What gives a sense of direction to such geographical disorganization, to this hodge-podge of concrete and asphalt? Where is the social cement? The center, or centers? The place where neighbors meet and talk? What lets former city people know that they're not aground in some made-over agricultural backwater, some sterile hinterland that Ed Koch agonizes over, that doesn't provide them with the goods and services they need? Where is your "downtown" when you're lonely and blue? When you just want to hang out and people watch? When you need a new pair of sneakers? At the volunteer fire halls? At the bowling alleys? Hardly! You know where the action is – the malls. Though aging now, they are

---

[181] Bill Newill, "In Defense of our Suburban Living," *Bucks County Courier Times*, March 23, 1980.

still the prime compass points, landmarks on the urbanized outwash plain. They are Levittown's and Bensalem's "downtowns." The down county downtowns.

When Levittown was built, it was given its own town center, of sorts – a sixty acre, $25 million one level "Shop-a-Rama" that opened in 1953; it was anchored by Pomeroy's ("the biggest department store between Newark and Philadelphia") and Grant's and Kresge's five-and-dime stores. The 65-store mall, with a tree-lined outdoor promenade, benches, and potted plants, was the super newest concept in retail marketing. A 1,200 seat movie theatre was built nearby to complete the package. Levittowners loved it and flocked to it in large numbers (the spacious parking lot always seemed full). The Easter Parade, along with countless other seasonal and community events, was held here. Levittowners now remember their first "downtown" fondly. Its lifespan would, however, be short.[182]

In 1956 the first fully-enclosed, climate-controlled "mall" was opened in a Minneapolis suburb. What has been called "the malling of America" had begun. Like an unstoppable storm front pushing out from the Great Lakes, it moved quickly to engulf the East Coast, Bucks' new suburbs included. The little (by comparison) Levittown Shop-a-Rama would be overshadowed by super malls. It would turn pale and wither as would dozens of Main Streets and State Streets that couldn't compete with the Soviet-scale shopping meccas erupting in fields all across the country. Russell Baker satirized the coming of these immense consumer Edens to the Megalopolis:[183]

Everywhere for miles around, giant menacing malls squatted sullen on the landscape. It was a severe blow to one's faith in the inevitability of happy endings. Would Marxism, in the final analysis, have been any worse than mallism? Does everyone know what a mall is?

---

[182] Shop-a-Rama would much later (2002) be demolished and replaced with several big-box stores (Walmart and Home Depot). *See:* Richard and Amy Duckett Wagner, *Images of America, Levittown*, Charleston, South Carolina: Arcadia Publishing, 2010, pp. 88-92.

[183] Russell Baker, "Pumpkinless Among Malls," The *New York Times, November 4, 1984.*

… fantastic asphalt abscesses with parking for hundreds of thousands of gasoline burners, chewing up meadows, forests, farmland. They harbor vital stores, restaurants that serve ancient food electronically revivified after years in the cryogenic vaults, and similar amenities necessary for a population of catastrophic size.

By the mid-twentieth century several giant regional malls had made their appearance in suburban Philadelphia. They were immediate successes, drawing hordes of sightseers as well as shoppers. Naturally, they were located near the turnpike and interstate junctions. Lower Bucks received its share – two such malls debuted, one alongside of Levittown and the other in Bensalem. They were the Oxford Valley and Neshaminy Malls. They were first generation malls that by today's standards are neither as grand nor imposing as the later day wave of three and four level super-spangled malls and "gallerias." In fact, they are rather incomplete and ordinary; many of life's essentials like the exercise gym, hardware store, and liquor store are absent from the color-coded location maps. They are quite lackluster oases too when compared with the womb to tomb California malls with their hospitals, day care centers, chapels, and mortuaries. Or when compared with Canadian malls and their ice skating rinks and ski mountains. Yet, Santa does arrive here and politicians come here to campaign. You can attend concerts and take community college classes for credit. You may still be able to buy postcards (remember postcards?) whose colors are faded from being on the store racks far too long, postcards printed years ago proclaiming "ultra-modern shoppers' spectacular" and "largest mall in the East." Postcards that with an embarrassing out-of-date look show '61 Chevy Impalas and Buick Electras in the mall parking lots. Though they may no longer be the super stars of the East Coast galaxy of malls, they continue to be an integral part of peoples' lives in lower Bucks. They are the county's "Edge Cities," its downtowns and Main Streets.

Levittown Shop-a-Rama (1953)

Oxford Valley Mall (1973)

Neshaminy Mall (1967-68)

Fig. 12.1 Vintage Postcard Views of
Lower Bucks' Malls *(Author's collection)*

Call it what you will – "Xanadu of the consumer culture, "the new social nexus of the highway generation," "the modern counterpart of the
village green," or simply the "OVM." The Oxford Valley Mall (1973)
is a merchandising temple that, with its baby blue water tower and adjacent eight-story glass office tower, towers above the low-rise landscape of the outwash plain, beckoning Levittowners and others to look
and shop at its 150 plus stores. It calls itself the "Mighty Mall" and is
currently anchored by Macy's, JC Penney, and Sears.[184] Like any respectable mall, OVM attempts to create and maintain a good Disney-
like environment: clean, airy, and antiseptic. Squads of uniformed
sweepers patrol its "streets" with brooms and dustpans, pouncing on the
offending piece of cellophane. The imitation tile floors of parquet and
imitation brick are passionately buffed of scuff marks and bloggers
comment favorably on the mall's cleanliness. Raked stone and gravel,
year-round greenery, and fountains that shoot two-stories high like rup-
tured hydrants create a peaceful mood. Though not quite the placidity
of a Japanese garden, mellow enough for most. Since the mall creates
a giant, hermetically-sealed bubble, the enticing aromas from the pre-
requisite food court (located where Woolworth's Five & Dime once
was), mix with the scent of cinnamon buns and roasted nuts, imitation
leather goods and holiday candles. This carefully maintained ambiance
pleases those who come to window shop, eat, or exercise walk in this
imitation downtown --- with a guaranteed free parking space. Though
in an age when everything and every place is instantaneously "re-
viewed" on the internet, it does have its critics – those who find it a little
empty, a little old, and not very big. Too much traffic from the nearby
and very popular Sesame Place. And the ATM fee is three bucks![185]

---

[184] Like all malls, OVM has had a sometimes bewildering parade of changing anchor
stores: e.g., Gimbels converted to Sterns and is now Sears; Wanamakers converted
to Hecht's which became Strawbridge's which was replaced by Boscov's which will
be demolished to make way for Target. *(See: Oxford Valley Mall, Wikipedia)*.
[185] These comments are from reviews posted on *Yelp.com/biz/Oxford-Valley-Mall*.

But, No Devils in Disneyland

Some may fret for the future of this part of the county, seeing it as a devil of a mess, malls and more malls all fused together by condominiums, apartments, and Levittown. But a stronger criticism of this mall or any mall is that its climatically-controlled, enclosed environment distances one from the unique and offbeat bits of culture and geography that mark the local scene, letting you know that this is indeed the land of William Penn, the Middle Atlantic Culture Hearth, the mid-section of Megalopolis and the Delaware Valley. The mall deceives and destroys, not so much the land itself, but an appreciation of it. Except for a few Phillies, Flyers and Eagles caps and jerseys, there's nothing to suggest among the acres of national brand name stores, that this is not suburban Milwaukee or Atlanta. There are no newsstands selling the local papers with news of the latest zoning battles in the townships or the latest archaeological dig plowed under by a bulldozer. The mall is the great homogenizer of national culture and, once in its cavernous interior, the reality of the world outside – an earthquake fault line and the unemployment line, Philadelphia's transported polluted air and the sea gulls that glide above the parking lots – is gone. Maybe this is the intention of those who design malls. The mall, as one writer called it, is "the post-urban cradle," a multi-sensory pacifier that, like Disneyland, allows for the suspension of reality for a few minutes or hours. A cavernous womb that like the Durham cave has no devil now. No noxious industrial stench. No super humidity in July and no bone-chilling winds to rattle the Christmas tree ornaments in early October. No mud, manure, nor pesticide-tainted air. Only the name "Oxford Valley" suggests that groaning farm wagons once struggled across a shallow creek near the sign of an ox on a local pub. And maybe their ghostly aura still does, out on the Triassic lands, only minutes and miles away.

Only minutes and miles away, down along that much maligned stretch of U.S. Route 1 to "where Philadelphia meets Bucks County," is Bensalem's Neshaminy Mall. Not quite as new looking or as large as the OVM, (only 120-plus stores) – Neshaminy is a one level enclosed mall opened for the Christmas season in 1968. For quite some time it had the feel of a large airplane hangar, or maybe a subway platform. It was illuminated by "horrible" skylights that cast an "eerie, ghoulish" glow on everything. The "New Neshaminy Mall" has changed ownership and been renovated several times; for example, large and colorful banners somewhat conceal and draw attention away from the gloomy ceiling. Its "sidewalks" were originally patterned with Belgian blocks, blocks that were given a circular shape at the center of the mall. It was a replication of a trolley turn-around at a busy (real) downtown intersection. With the upscaling this rather nice touch gave way to an earth-colored, non-symbolic Italian mosaic-tiled floor. The management promised that it would "knock your socks off." Despite the blog site criticisms[186] about the still cavernous and unfinished feel to it, and the SEPTA buses dumping off loads of "trashy" shoppers from Philadelphia, this is still a decent, if older, mall that retains fond memories for those who spent hours at the Space Port Arcade or browsed the stamp and coin store ("a shrine to forgotten hobbies."). The mechanical dioramas in Strawbridge's windows are not so fondly remembered: they seem to still haunt the kids of the 1950s–60s with their eeriness – macabre automatons with a herky-jerky motion that came to life every hour on the hour during the holiday season.[187]

The Neshaminy Mall is named for a nearby creek that bends sharply and forms a miniature gorge as it cuts its way through the hard rocks of the Langhorne Ridge. In turn, the creek is named for the American Indian tribe that once lived and hunted along that creek. Commendably, the mall commemorates the tribe through the use of American Indian motifs (e.g., signs with fluted arrowheads that say "This Way to the Mall.") Years ago there was a totem pole that stood just outside the mall and along the shoulder of Route U.S. 1. It was five stories high and floodlit at night; it featured animal faces and outstretched wings that beckoned motorists in from the highway. The local tribe probably didn't carve totem poles, and certainly not ones with the earth-tinted tans and

---

[186] *Malls of America blogspot.com/Neshaminy -Mall.*
[187] These "nightmare scenes" depicted key events in the region's colonial history, including Ben Franklin's kite flying electricity experiment here in Bensalem.

reds of the desert southwest. No matter – it's gone now, another victim of progress in the ever-changing landscape of "Edge City."

One American Indian is, however, still in residence, presiding over an oasis of tranquility in a corner of the mall. The local chief Tawanka squats beneath the frosted skylights, in front of the Macy's store sign with the red star. He is the centerpiece of a rather large tableau of rock and water. He is a larger-than-life metal casting[188] that may accurately portray members of the tribe … since he's near naked except for a breechcloth. This sinewy, very athletic-looking man sits atop a stone pile of hard rock quarried from the Langhorne Ridge. Water trickles from his hand to a sudsy pool below, but only when the water is activated. Near the pool of water stands a beaver from the days when wealth hereabouts was measured in animal pelts, buckskins, and clam shells. The animal appears to snarl … if that's what beavers do. The chief appears oblivious to it all, gazing ahead to where Buster Brown once sold moccasins to little braves. [189]   In the pool of water ("Neshaminy Punch"), coins accumulate on the bottom. It's actually quite a gentle scene – mall music plays and shoppers toss their spare change into the pool of water at his feet … hoping perhaps for a fate better than that of Tawanka and the beaver.

Such is life in lower Bucks, along the highway corridors of the Megalopolis, on the outwash plain of the Quakers, and down within the belly of the "Edge City."

---

[188] "The Neshaminy Indian" statue was sculpted by Henry Mitchell and presented to Strawbridge & Clothier, the mall's anchor store in 1970.
[189] Mall retail stores of course regularly come and go. In this volume's first edition, Chief Tawanka was flanked by Fanny Farmer candies and Buster Brown shoes. Currently, Lens Crafters and Auntie Ann's Pretzels have taken their place.

CHAPTER 13

JOURNEY'S END:
DIESEL AND ROCK
MEET STONE AND WOOD

... the night of urbanization falls on the rolling hills and gentle woods ... (they're) about to be engulfed by the concrete glacier of urbanization. The process cannot be halted ...

– Jan deHartog,
forward to *Upper Makefield Speaks*

Are those who move from the lower end just buying homes or are they buying a new lifestyle? Are they buying time, too, before the Great Megalopolis engulfs us all? Or is it an escape – a step back to the Lower Bucks that was?

--Kathy Finegan Clark, *Bucks County Courier Times* Accent magazine, May 22, 1977

Bucks County is the place to be.

– Bruce Toll, Luxury Home Builder quoted in *Bucks County Courier Times*, December 26, 1982

Observations at Five Hundred Feet

Climbing into the front seat of a Piper Warrior, climbing to five hundred feet above a small airstrip nudged against the side of the Langhorne Ridge, you then swing up over the Triassic lowland of central Bucks. You expect to see the worst. From all that's been read and said, you're prepared to see rampaging rivers of people and houses spilling out upon the farmlands. Those monster-sized planned and unplanned creations on the outwash plain have their army vanguard atop the ridge, and, like H.G. Wells menacing Martians poised atop the Hudson's Palisades, are ready to pounce upon the innocents below. It seems to be fated that this gentle Triassic lowland will be exurbanized, suburbanized, and urbanized in due course. "Engulfed" seems to be the way people see it happening.

It's become increasingly difficult to be poetically descriptive about this land. Sure, the river still has its poets, the hills have their balladeers, and covered bridges and banked barns have their artists (still), and the 900 or so remaining farms have their advocates. But is it all sunset aesthetics? One last teary-eyed burst of energy to preserve the beautiful before the "night of urbanization" has its way? In its prime, this rolling Triassic region was prime farmland, but as a "Pennsylvania sunbelt," it will soon be Levittowned, Bensalemized, malled (or mauled). The hungry lion of development will devour the countryside, taking the place of the amicable lion of the old *Peaceable Kingdom.* So it is said, and so it is feared.

When viewed from the window of the Piper Warrior, the Triassic ridges and valleys north of Langhorne are neither monolithic nor horrifying. If anything, they're surprisingly green and open. The surprise is akin to viewing the Megalopolitan corridor from the window of a jetliner. The expected carpet of concrete and asphalt is more a mosaic of open and vacant land, parkland, farmland, marsh and meadow, all scattered in between the urban and suburban nodes of activity. In Bucks, there are far more fields and woods than would be expected. About half the Triassic land in central Bucks is still green; it is farmed, it is rented by farmers, it is set aside from development … at least for now. Embedded within that country quilt of geometric shapes, like whitecaps and flecks of foam on a great Triassic sea, is a growing scatteration of housing developments and (mini)malls. All is impermanence and change; all is in the process of becoming something else. And all too quickly too. And all is weeds and fringes, the tattered edge of the "Edge City." But this is best appreciated with feet and nose to the ground.

Buckshot for Bucks

This is the real Bucks. No remote stereotypes, no touristy hype. No neat and clearly defined "suburbs" and "farmlands" packaged with sharp and sure edges. No memory-stern, antiquarian Bucks. In some ways, these Triassic lands are still a great inland sea, with all that humans have built but wobbly, ephemeral features on the surface of an ocean of deeply buried sedimentary rock. Gazing onto this imaginary sea, there are weed-choked shallows and fringes everywhere. It's all fringe and no center – the fringe of the metropolitan system, the suburban fringe, and the fringe of the farmlands. In some places it has the unfinished, scrubby look of the Canadian mid-north in Ontario and Québec provinces: idle farmland that hasn't yet decided on its future. It might go back to nature, to the black flies and weeds. It might become a lake country cottage with cross-country ski trails. Here in Bucks, it will probably never have that chance.

The writer James Agee, who once summered in a nearby farmhouse, eloquently described the fields of rural Alabama – and all the ways that people impressed themselves "upon the grieved membrane of the earth"[190] – by listing things observed in paragraph form. Had he written about the changeful landscape of Bucks, he might have catalogued: roads smeared with erosion's red-brown earth; roads with "farm equipment X-ing" signs; old roads that climb and then abruptly

---

[190] James Agee and Walker Evans, *Let Us Now Praise Famous Men.* New York: Houghton Mifflin, 1941.

dip, dangerous road dips that conceal oncoming vehicles until the last instant; roads that unexpectedly turn to an oil and chip pavement, then to gravel, finally to dirt; roadbeds grooved a good half inch by errant snowplow blades; potholes galore six inches deep or more; road signs inexplicably directing motorists to the Burlington-Bristol Bridge;[191] roadside ditches sparkling with glass and metal; roadside weeds humanely covering a litter of dead feral animals and household pets that may have hobbled here to die in the bedding of scrap wood and rusted barbed wire; many, many deer and the buzzards feeding on the carrion; and cruciform utility poles that serve to mark the graves; wooden poles pockmarked by woodpeckers; sagging wires and poles tilted east-southeast by last year's storms; fences similarly tilted, along with mailbox and newspaper tubes; "For Sale" signs accompanying everything from campers to boats for sale, houses and horses, snowmobiles and sod, farm fresh eggs (brown or white), bundles of wood and stands of cordwood split and neatly stacked in yards and waiting to be sold; yard sales; lawn sales; lawns landscaped with shrubbery and ceramic statuary: fawns, gnomes, St. Francis and jockey boys in whiteface and blackface the paint all peeling away; garages and barns; garages built like barns; barns that serve as garages; movie theatres with silos   built to look like barns; long, low dairy barns lighted for the evening milking; no barns but grassy barn ramps and stubbled fields of corn; baled and rolled up hay; and migrant farm workers, stooped and cheerless. And above it all: power lines that hum on light green stanchions that frame the horizon … while helicopters ferry interested buyers and builders over these roads and fields where surveyor's stakes with little red flags will soon appear.

This awkward mix of diverse and incompatible things suggests what might be called "buckshot" development. This unruly part suburban, part exurban, part rural use of the land occurs with no clear border

---

[191] This phenomenon is less common now than it used to be, but green signs advising drivers of distances and directions to the Burlington-Bristol Bridge were seen on even the most unfrequented backroads. What the attraction of this bridge was, or of Burlington, New Jersey was unknown. Nor was it known why someone wanted everyone else to drive there.

or boundaries. It results in clashing lifestyles and landscapes. Leapfrog suburban growth has resulted in a jigsaw of oddly-shaped housing tracts partially surrounded by farmlands, farmlands sandwiched in between parks and speculative land, and islands of industry shoulder-to-shoulder with apartment complexes and barns. And everywhere, that crazy glue that holds it all together, that everywhere present and inappropriately named "vacant" land. It's a mapmaker's nightmare; it's a zoning jumble.

This indigestible stew of mismatched and mixed together types of temporary land use is moreover flavored with disharmonies. Here where the spandex-clad and helmeted bicyclists (cycling while texting on a shoulderless road) must coexist with the steel-tipped work shoes and cowboy boots of the big rig drivers, the disharmonies are especially strong. It's not just that the cyclists are buzzed too closely by the "good 'ol boys" who seem to begrudge some sociological or income gap suggested by the mere act of bicycling. It's more than that. Local infrastructure has failed to keep pace with these diverse paths of growth. Roads are overburdened and sometimes too narrow; many bridges and narrow bridge abutments force autos to "play chicken" with oncoming monster trucks. Roads built for buckboards and stage coaches are now uneasily shared by immense quarry trucks and construction vehicles, lawn care and landscaping service vehicles, long flatbed trucks piled high with rolls of Pennsylvania-certified turf grass, the daily army of commuters and stop-and-go school buses, and the exercise joggers and bicyclists. Then, add to this mix the seasonal horde of sightseers who come to slowly soak up the changing foliage, the charm, and the history. (Leading one to wonder why paragraph-length historical markers sit on shoulderless forty five mph roadways, markers that simply can't be read without creating accidents caused by impatient drivers swearing and shaking their heads along with their middle fingers in the rearview mirror).

Everybody's whipping boy is the farmer, whose halting farm machinery is seen clogging the public highways. Caught in a mile-long parade of cars behind a wide-bodied hay wagon or a plodding tractor, drivers silently (some not so silently) curse the farmer. Off the roads as well, farmers are in other ways a pain in the burbs. The noise and headlight glare of harvesting machines intrude into the bedroom windows at 10 p.m. Cows moo for attention at 4 a.m. The stink of pesticide spray and pig manure, and the ubiquitous dust from plowing and planting, all make it hard for the suburban household to cope. Complaints are leveled against farmers who become the objects of "nuisance ordinances." Farmers in turn demand "right to farm" laws. Farm fields and equipment are vandalized and the farmer decides to sell. Ironically, suburbanites then accuse the farmer of "selling out" to the developers ... and round and round it goes.

Suburbanites become distraught when green fields and "vacant" land, passed over initially by the untidy, broken wave of development, finally gets developed. Advantageously, homeowners have to contend with fewer stray bullets zinging through the yard and walls from fewer hunters chasing fewer rabbits, turkeys, and deer. But eventually, a feeling of being hemmed in – again – stirs thoughts of moving, again.

For some (many?), a home in the suburbs is not the lifelong pride and joy it was to the Levittowners in the 1950s. It rather reflects the short-term, shallowly-rooted commitment the French traveler and writer Alexis de Tocqueville found in nineteenth-century America: "In the United States a man builds a house in which to spend his old age, and he sells it before the roof is on ..."[192] The home has become an investment whose sale (or resale) allows for the purchase of a bigger and maybe better house up the road, in the newer development. "Buy it and flip it" becomes the suburban mantra. How appropriate that the inventor of the Monopoly game was from Bucks County. Charles Darrow of Ottsville in Tinicum Township created the game in 1934, decades before the real game of buy and sell would commence in Bucks.

The messy overlap of suburb, exurb, and farmland on this temporary landscape produces its own fleeting vignettes: at the local bars, the murmur of stale soap opera dialogue while patrons absently glance at

---

[192] Alexis de Tocqueville, *Democracy in America*. 1835/40 (2 volumes), London: Saunders and Otley.

Fig. 13.1 Signs.
Roadside Signs of the Times

Jeopardy; a few farmers or farmhands in plaid shirts and overalls discuss the price for soybeans and sip from mugs of Rolling Rock or Yuengling beer; just beyond the neon signs and window curtains herds of dairy cattle graze on rented land. Soon, the rented land will support a shopping center with chain restaurant and trendy pub selling far more expensive micro-brewed brands of beer. Out in the night air, young suburban rednecks roar down country roads in customized, sport-striped pickup trucks; they vandalize rows of newly-bought suburban mailboxes, bashed to the ground with metal pipes and chunks of Triassic rock. Next day, it's left to someone else to pick the empty beer cans and vodka bottles from the roadside ditches. Some fun, eh?

Caught in this matrix of change in these sometimes messy fringe areas are the little places from former times, a couple of houses sitting at a crossroads with names only the oldest area residents might recall: Buckmanville and Bulltown, Chain Bridge and Chinquapin, Snoveltown and Timbuctoo, Stoopville and Tinkertown – now nameless clusters of buildings whose histories and uses are lost to memory. These and scores of other vanished and vanishing hamlets lie cut up and strewn about by the modern world. Also caught up and trying to cope with the tangle of growth and development are the somewhat larger towns and boroughs.

From Colonial Commons to "Cool" Town

Newtown is a case in point. One of the oldest town centers in Pennsylvania, this "ancient village" was bought from the American Indians in 1682 and laid out "in the depth of the Bucks County wilderness." It would be William Penn's "New Township." The early settlers lived in log huts until brownstone quarries and brickworks were opened. In the 1690s the townstead was gridded with a commons and sixteen wedge-shaped properties radiating out towards the fields that became farms with names like "Rural Retreat" and "Barn Brook," "Cottage Retreat" and "Spring Brook." During the Revolutionary War, the town commons was used for militia drills and farms were raided and plundered by the British army. Washington headquartered here, some of his troops skirmished and died here, and a group of captured Hessians was marched down the main street. Afterwards, Newtown went about the more prosaic affairs of a country town. It served as the "shire town" (the county seat) for more than a century; the court, court offices, and "gaol" were located here along with a bevy of public houses (pubs) for lawyers and locals. Edward Hicks painted signs for the pubs and the town gathered quite a reputation for its raucous mix of politics, horse racing, and fairs. This, along with being a stage and roadhouse junction, led to an active local temperance movement long before the days of Carrie Nation and Billy Sunday. Otherwise, the townspeople went about their daily business of tilling the "fine rolling land," while others manufactured carriages, wagons, and agricultural implements for the farmers. Hicks worked in one such carriage manufactory, decorating the sides of the carriages with farm scenes. The town's industrial sector included the usual complement of sawmills, tanyards, sash and door factories, bobbin and spool mills. Though agriculture was always the mainstay, the town had a degree of notoriety as a summer resort in the 1800's, becoming by 1905: "a pretty and flourishing village, the seat of wealth and culture, and possess(ing) all the appliances for comfort and convenience known ..."[193] These included Masonic and Oddfellows lodges, a fire company, a Building and Loan Association, cigar store and pool parlor, dry goods and notions shop, and a general store – all housed within Victorian buildings with mansard roofs, shaded with green and white striped awnings, and festooned on holidays with red, white, and blue bunting. It was a model main street (State Street, actually) that might have inspired Walt Disney. As late as World War II, the population had barely reached 2,000.

Most would agree that Newtown Borough is the reason for terms like "quaint" and "charming." It is a block after block mélange of restored colonial architecture and authentic Victorian structures built by retired farmers. Nearly all the buildings that were standing a century ago

---

[193] W. Davis, *History of Bucks County, Pennsylvania*. 1905. Volume I, p. 222.

are standing today; and since much of the "downtown" is on the National Register of Historic Places (as all the historic plaques attest), these buildings will be standing with much the same look a century from now. Antiquity creates its own pleasing aura: a walk through the town on a summer's evening is a stroll back through time. Much of the appeal is the street itself: the uneven, patterned brick sidewalks with enormous tree roots pushing through, making the bricks bulge; the flagstone walks and thirteen star flags; the foot-high curbs that better fit the height of stagecoach steps than car doors; the cast iron boot-scrappers and "Philadelphia mirrors"[194] on some houses; the concrete and metal curbside hitching posts; and the patriotically-painted hydrants. Gusty, narrow alleyways add even more character; sidewall windows and doors are all stoned in, lintels being the only telltale sign that there were windows and doors at one time. A two-story clock with stained glass face panels occupies one street corner and, in season, chimes Christmas carols. Faux gaslights, bicycle racks, sidewalk benches and flower pots, and little bistro tables with free Wi-Fi complete the picture. "A solid place to live" says one resident convincingly. Not surprisingly then, this "rural Bucks County burg" was chosen as one of the "(Ten) Coolest Small Towns in America" in a recent survey posted on Yahoo Travel. The reasons given; George Washington slept here (of course), the director M. Night Shyamalan filmed a few scenes here (*Signs*, 2002), and – most amazingly though incorrectly – "Amish Country Charm" was cited.[195] "(Most) of the convertibles around these parts are horses-and-buggies." An Amish Farmers' Market, yes. But "Amish Country" itself is more than one hundred miles to the west.

This brief history illustrates the fact that Newtown has as rich and colorful a past as any small town in America. With or without the

---

[194] Philadelphia or Franklin mirrors are mounted on the second floor outside wall and angled down so that who or what is at the ground floor doorway can be seen from the second floor window ... without the inconvenience of having to leave a warm bedroom only to be bothered by salesmen, panhandlers, or even uninvited relatives.
[195] "Budget Travel" on Yahoo, 2011. Newtown ranked #8 out of 10.
See: http://travel.yahoo.com/ideas/10-coolest-small-towns-america-045945954.html.

horses-and-buggies. Rightfully, the town is proud of its past and lets you know as you enter the borough: "Welcome to Historic Newtown. A Good Place to Live, Worship, Shop." The half square mile borough hasn't seen a working farm in an awful long while. So, no *Peaceable Kingdom* to be found here. A strange scene does however play out when borough streets, laden with heavy winter snows, are cleared by a parade of farm equipment that mysteriously appears to help collect and remove the snow. "It's weird" says one of the borough's 2,248 residents. That population is about what it was a half century ago, indicating that growth is something of a stranger here ... as it is in the older boroughs with older populations from Bristol to Quakertown.

In contrast with the borough, the surrounding twelve square mile township of Newtown has grown explosively. Two-thirds of the municipality was still categorized as "undeveloped" or farmed land in the 1980 Census. The growing pains were just beginning as Newtown Township added nearly 10,000 new people during the 1980s for an incredible 200% growth rate. And much more was to follow (*See:* Appendix B, "Statistical Bucks"). With a population of almost 20,000 by 2010, Newtown Township has what to realtors and buyers is that highly desirable demographic: affluent, educated, and young professional. What has happened here is the universal anywhere, everywhere development process described by Richard Lingerman in *Small Town America*:[196]

> ... their handiwork looked as inevitable as a force of nature, as though God had ordained that the American species should live in rows of little-differentiated houses surrounding and engorging small towns like a protozoa taking its dinner.

In the surrounded and "engorged" small borough of Newtown, small businesses were affected at two levels. Regionally, shops in the borough's business district were caught within the gravitational pull of the mighty mall(s); More locally, and on the borough's outer fringe, to

---

[196] Richard Lingerman, *Small Town America*. New York: G.P. Putnam's Sons, 1980, p. 458.

stay alive they had to compete with the mini-malls, office parks, health spas and gyms that sprouted in the surrounding township. They have managed to stay competitive by specializing in a more trendy, almost quirky line of merchandise not necessarily found in the big and small malls: New Age, Holistic Astrology shops selling healing crystals, chakra stones, organic incense, and Tibetan singing bowls; art galleries where fine arts consultants, appraisers, and sellers meet at wine and cheese soirees, and where you can frame your own artwork and purchase art supplies like calligraphic pens and inks; gourmet bakeries, ice cream, chocolate, and olive shops; and restaurants featuring gluten-free and ethnic menus with "awesome" dishes ... and even colonial period cuisine. Add to this the novelty floral and gift shops, the handicraft and craft boutiques, antique cubbyholes and "old world" gift shops, the salons and spas, along with the more traditional legal and financial services, and there you have it. It's an attractive commercial mix that seems to work nicely for Newtown, and along with the streetscape ambience and thick historical veneer, bodes well for the borough.

In the recent past, more of a problem for the borough's commercial and residential core was the fact that Newtown was used as a through route for much very heavy and noisy truck traffic. This resulted from the borough's location between a major interstate (I-95) and gaping rock quarries where Triassic argillite was blasted and extracted for decades. Argillite is a tough, firmly-cemented grayish mass of clay and quartz grains derived from lake-bottom muds that were exposed to and dried beneath the sun late in the afternoon of the Triassic period. Because of its hardness and grayish coloration, it can be mistaken for diabase. Because of this diabase-like hardness, it is valuable quarryable rock. It's quarried at several locations north of Newtown where it alternates in the stratographic column with layers of red shale and sandstone. It may be quarried for building stone; when dynamited and crushed it becomes rubble used for roadbeds. The quarried landscape shows enormous cavities, but only from the air (*See:* Fig. 13.2). On the ground, waste heaps of overburden are made into artificial hills and these "spoil banks" are then planted with runty trees to cover the bareness. Pre-dawn convoys of quarry trucks emerge out of a cloud of rock dust and wind their way through this damaged landscape on shoulderless, narrow roads that become a potholed Ho-Chi Minh Trail. The path of these trucks comes frighteningly close to young students waiting at the roadside for school buses. The trucks grind up the hills with indicator lights flashing and go roaring around the curves in a sooty cloud, mud guards slapping, sideboards rattling, and stone flying.

The argillite-carrying vehicles are a species all their own: forty-ton Mack trucks with massive bumpers, red, green, and silver cabs and bodies, and an assortment of air horns, dirt-splattered mirrors and lights. They barrel along the 33 foot-wide county roads towards Newtown spilling some of their 40,000 pounds of rock here and there. Sometimes entire truckloads spill. Police reports have called them "weapons on wheels." They move back and forth from the quarries to the interstate and to New Jersey all day, continuing until dusk. Because time is money and drivers do tailgate, the trucks sometimes appeared glued to the car bumpers in front of them. Motorists in 8-foot long smart cars who un-wittingly delay the truckers' speedy routine by attempting to soak up scenery or read roadside historical markers are no match for the quarry trucks.

The story of damage done by rock quarrying and quarry trucks is an old refrain in Bucks County. The painter Daniel Garber depicted the quarries along the Delaware River, hinting at the negative impact such activity had on the landscape aesthetic (in a way similar to the Hudson River Valley painters and their condemnation in words and on canvas of the quarrying at the Palisades and in the Highlands). In the last volume of his Bucks County trilogy (*The Good and Bad Weather*) Edmund Schiddel described the quarry trucks rumbling through New Hope in 1965: "… in this place that was so lovely and that's being ruined. **The noise!** Those quarries! Don't you hear them?" "And that constant stench from the road!"

It was a battle for Newtown. Convoys of quarry trucks poured through the borough (Washington Avenue) every weekday. The least offensive thing they did was add to the traffic congestion, tearing up corner curbs and pavement exposing trolley tracks from a quieter long

Fig. 13.2 Shovel and Quarries. (Left) Quarry shovel at Eureka Stone Quarry, Swamp Road, Wrightstown (*Author's photo*); (Right) Rushland Quarries in Wrightstown Township (*Google Earth* imagery, Copyright, 2013. Imagery date: 10/07/2011).

ago. Because the houses are closely spaced and fronted by venerable trees that overarch the streets and even touch above the utility lines, the street itself acted as a tunnel that trapped and exaggerated sounds and smells. Truckers might lay on the air horn when they saw a pretty girl walking along the sidewalk. But more jarringly, vibrating truck engines, cranking gears, and defective exhausts jolted the old houses, weakening the structures, loosening plumbing joints, causing leaks, and then electrical fires in walls and ceilings. As the sun filtered down through the diesel fumes, early morning joggers and walkers inhaled the same stuff that coated porches and house fronts with an oily soot, the stuff whose acrid and disgusting odor wafted up and into second floor bedrooms.

Feeling rather harassed, townspeople were tempted to think the devil himself rode in the diesel cab, dressed in a down vest and tractor cap, knifing a behemoth truck through an otherwise pleasant town. The damage and heartache done by quarrying both at and around the quarries and along the roads and streets used by the trucks was (and is) hugely disproportionate to the contribution made to the local economy: employment for less than one percent of the county workforce and less than one percent of the county's wages and salaries.

Relief did finally arrive. After truck counts were conducted and decibel readings scored in excess of legally and medically safe levels, the extent of the problem forced action. The political process (finally) responded and in 1991 plans were announced for the construction of a $16 million bypass to divert traffic away from borough streets. The four lane "funnel" (the Newtown Bypass) effectively separates most heavy traffic from the homes and businesses that line the now quieter and safer colonial-era streets. But the devil of growth and change is a relentless one, he's a mean creature who'd snatch a worm from a blind hen's mouth. And his assaults on civility and livability will continue.[197]

---

[197] That having been said, *Google Earth* "Street View" still captures images of quarry trucks lumbering through the borough, though admittedly with much less frequency. More troubling is the ongoing disruption caused by the equally noisy tractor-trailer trucks passing through at all hours of the day and night.

Through it all, and despite it all, the borough will of course survive, and survive with dignity and appeal. The Newtown Theatre is a good example of the way residents feel about where they live. This old "beloved landmark" dates to the time when Andrew Jackson was president, though movies themselves were first shown in the building as early as 1906 (thus making it the oldest movie house in America). Inspiring public oratory and campaign promises echoed from the rafters high above the wood balcony amid the glow of fireflies on summer evenings as Alf Landon (and others) appealed for votes. When this 300-seat icon was in danger of being taxed out of existence, the community rallied, expressing its outrage in letters-to-the-editor. Movie buffs were livid. Help arrived and the landmark was saved. The old electric floor fans were replaced with air conditioning in 2002 (for the movie premier of Shyamalan's *Signs*) and a new digital projector added in 2014. The theatre has "history and soul," and it's "not a generic box in a parking lot at the mall," says the president of the board of directors.[198] History preserved; battle won. It's (sometimes) like that in Newtown.

People rightly boast about living here, and not just because it implies money and/or status. The town may have more public spirited boosters than any comparable small community in America. Life here can easily become a pleasingly crowded datebook of civic-minded events, historical society gatherings, market days and antique fairs, house and garden tours and open houses, library fund raisers and sidewalk sales, car shows and "brew fests." While everyone may have their own personal version (or vision) of what the town should be now and in the future, and what balance should be struck between a true historical aesthetic and a commercial/business environment, nearly all agree that the town should not become "just another New Hope." The devil is thus kept at length. Indeed, the devil and his doings are denied in a manner much befitting a place so much at the center of Quaker tradition.

---

[198] Andy Smith as quoted in *The Intelligencer*, July 29, 2014.

The Unfinished Manuscript of the Land

In *The Quality of Life* James Michener wrote about how difficult it was to preserve the historical character of a place, a place overwhelmed by a Niagara of population growth and subject to "accelerating change."[199] Difficult but necessary. One such place is located adjacent to Newtown in Lower Makefield Township. It's a pre-Revolutionary village that's been bombarded with growth and change for years, actually for decades. Yet it survives and retains its (sometimes confusing) identity. It's a ragged crossroads collection of two dozen houses that, when I first encountered it back in the 1980's, seemed rather scruffy and muddy with broken and rusted things scattered about. It was a place that seemed to have even misplaced or forgotten its name – or several names.

Quaker settlers arrived in the 1680s and took up land grants awarded to them by William Penn himself. For a time, the place was called "Stradlington" for the village blacksmith. Later, it became "Biles Corner" for the local doctor who operated a stagecoach tavern at the crossroads. Then, when little cottages and even a hotel were opened for summer boarders from the city, it became "Summerville." Boarding houses were built after the Pennsylvania Railroad's Reading Line station was opened. At different times later on it was called "Edgewood" or "Woodside." After the 1890s it began to decline, yet retained its farm economy and rural character. During the twentieth century the name "Woodside" was still being used on some maps, but at some point local historians decided that it would be "Edgewood" … forevermore.

So, what do people who live here now call it? The people who've moved into the dense and encircling web of surrounding developments may not know or really care. "Woodside? It's an intersection, period!" But one longtime resident, standing on her porch steps with her words all but lost in the noisy swoosh and rattle of cement mixers and flatbed trucks carrying bulldozers, said: "I think they call it Woodside. Used to be Edgewood. I'm not sure now; there **are** some woods left."

---

[199] James Michener, *The Quality of Life*, Philadelphia: Girard Bank, 1970, no page number.

Rapid change creates the burden of place name confusion. But there is visual confusion as well. Woodside/Edgewood may exist only as a blur on the other side of the windshield. A 60-second blur with little opportunity to stop and park and look. A few ancient stone and wood structures obscured by signs that promise "New Condominiums. Coming Soon." A large billboard barks: "Exciting Things Are Going to Happen." Exciting things means another 190 new condominiums. A derelict gas pump with the price frozen at twenty-six cents a gallon. Nearby, an old general store with broken windows and a lawn covered with tall weeds and discarded mattresses. The store still has its blue porch ceiling that speaks of a simpler folk world when what was evil could at least agreed upon. Beneath all this and almost invisible is the fine silt loam once regarded by local farmers as some of the very best soil on the Atlantic Seaboard.

There's more than just confusion in this swirl of twentieth-century change. There is a sense of loss, laced liberally with nostalgia for what was lost. That longtime resident, standing on her porch amid the welter of change, lives in a house built and once owned by the dairy company that owned the town. The dairy herds are gone of course, but she can still point across the roofs of the condominiums to where her husband was born. She can also point to where the blacksmith shop used to be and to where the schoolhouse was before it burned down. Then time and memory give way to bitterness: "Greed! It's all greed," she says, "The greedy developers have taken it all. They fill up those houses with New York people, I hear. Who else can afford them?" In the end, she admits to having had a good life here in Edgewood (or Woodside). But "now it's nearly over, and they can do what they want with the place."

There will be no endings, no final paragraphs. Personal ones perhaps, but not for this place, or any place. It's endlessly reborn, coming back in different shapes and forms, with one name or another. Hopefully, enough of the past gets preserved. What's there today is simply the uppermost level of an archaeological dig where the ashes and potsherds, the gas pump and blue porch ceiling, the detritus of one generation gets stacked upon that of earlier generations ... to be tenderly peeled away by future archaeologists.

As a postscript, the next chapter in Edgewood village's story is far happier. In the 1970s the integrity of the village was threatened by the construction of I-95 on one side of it. Also, the relentless sprawl of developments, strip malls, and office parks was closing in. In response to these "menaces," Lower Makefield Township created the Edgewood Village Historic District in 1979, thus bringing the buildings under local protection. And in 1980 the crossroads village merited inclusion on the National Register of Historic Places. (*See below:* Fig. 13.3).

Fig. 13.3 Historic Village of Edgewood ... at the intersection of Langhorne-Yardley Road and Edgewood Road *(Author's photo)*

Not far from here is "Journey's End." It too is heavy with history and some mystery; but no real end at all. When a settler named John Palmer and his young bride arrived in Bucks County in the 1680s, they came with little more in their pockets than a 500-acre land grant signed by William Penn. In their first seasons in the New World, they did as other settlers did in this valley, they sheltered themselves in a cave. Eventually, they built a small fieldstone house to accommodate what would be a family with fifteen children. Their new home in a new world, at the far end of a long sea voyage from England, was named "Journey's End."[200] It was very appropriate because it symbolized the successful search for a hoped-for haven, a place to put down new and permanent roots. It was the treasure pot at the end of one family's rainbow. The house they built still survives, though hardly anyone knows where it is or what it looks like. It weathered the centuries and now survives in a faded hamlet. It exists, at least at this stage in its history, as a garage to house someone's car. Someone else's dreams, someone's end of journey, shelters nothing more than someone else's car. But from the farmlands of the *Peaceable Kingdom* to the housing tracts of the late twentieth century – and beyond – the larger journey never ends.

---

[200] As we conclude Chapter 13, it can be noted that coincidentally "Journey's End" is likewise the 13th episode (of Series 4) of the popular British science fiction television show *"Doctor Who."* The episode was broadcast in 2008 and involved people who had spent many years seeking a new home; they were welcomed by the mountains and rivers, but more recent developments were forcing them to leave. Just coincidence!

CHAPTER 14

POSTSCRIPT:
RAINY TRIASSIC NIGHT

He could not see the land as it was, he could not smell the land as it smelled; his feet did not stamp the clods or feel the warmth and power of the earth ... He did not know or own or trust or beseech the land ... The land ... gradually died; for it was not loved or hated, it had no prayers or curses.

– John Steinbeck, *The Grapes of Wrath*, 1939

*In the first place you can't see **anything** from a car; you've got to get out of the goddamned contraption and walk, better yet crawl, on hands and knees, over the sandstone ... When traces of blood begin to mark your trail you'll see something, maybe. Probably not.*

– Edward Abbey, *Desert Solitaire*, 1968

*Don't it always seem to go
That you don't know what you've got
Till it's gone
They paved Paradise
And put up a parking lot.*
– Joni Mitchell, *Big Yellow Taxi*, 1970

The Japanese are said to believe that thoughtful activities such as thinking and writing are facilitated when it rains. No doubt something in those acid rain-soaked ions somehow stimulates the brain. Here, in the gut of the county, it's raining bullfrogs and heifer yearlings. Or so the old farmers might have said. Or they might have said something like this: "It's raining pitchforks with the tines at both ends." It's a hard, chill rain that brings a chilly loneliness with it. Thoughts turn to dead parents and lost friends. It's a night that might even break a devil's heart.

Buckingham Mountain and other nearby hills appear to float upon the Triassic lowland; the misty rain makes them look like miniature, bluish Alleghenies. I sit in the eighteenth-century farmhouse with the brass door-knocker depicting the devil incarnate. The house with the red basement fireplace ... now surrounded by puddles of rain water. The house along the high-banked road that Old Splitfoot paused in front of, when he walked out of the county so long ago. Raindrops strike the eaves and window panes and dribble down the stone and lime-washed walls, soaking into the red earth. Raindrops splatter red mud along the base of the walls; the bottom foot of the wall is cracked, moss-covered, and permanently stained tan. The house and the earth seem joined. The evening air smells of fish and ocean water, which sometimes happens this near the coast. Familiar daytime shapes dissolve into the gathering night, into the wet and rainy night; the ordinary becomes mysterious and ...I feel deeply contemplative.

A Zone of Contention

The rain engorges the many creeks that flow across the lowland and feed into the river. For a few hours only the water level rises above the banks carrying a rush of tumbling, foaming water that washes across the ancestral roads in red-brown sheets as steam rises wraith-like from the cooling asphalt. This sudden, temporary rush of water creates the illusion that these creeks are what they once were: dependable and ever-present sources of water power. But to think that today's sorely diminished creeks, creeks so feeble they could barely spin a pinwheel, are in any way equal to the ancestral creeks that easily turned thousand-pound stone waterwheels is a sad delusion. Thirsty exurban wells and a man-designed system of holding reservoirs and storm sewers deny them their natural flow.

It's like that too with the devil, and with the whole concept of evil. He **seems** to be present to many people; at times, he **seems** to go about his typically nefarious business as in the past. Surely, suggests a letter writer to *Time* magazine, the computer is the devil in disguise. Or, in disguise, does he work in the nearby nuclear power plant? A *Time* cover artist shows the devil's face, hollow-eyed and gaunt, rising in a mushroom cloud above a blasted red earth. Again, the magazine's movie critic writes of the devil and his role in the decay of "old-fashioned moral standards" in an era of "lean, mean, rapier-clean business practices" as portrayed on the screen.[201] A television evangelist says that he wrestles with the devil on his living room floor. In Rome, Popes talk more and more about "this dark and disturbing spirit" who acts with "treacherous cunning."[202] Today's omnipresent devil would appear to live a busy life. The life of a very active senior citizen. Since seniors are the fastest growing population sector in the county and "gated communities for active adults" are the fastest growing type developments, the old devil would no doubt feel right at home in Bucks.

Expressions of what's evil or demonic take on more local, particular guises in Bucks. These include a variety of abstract forces and a multitude of more solid forms: rich and snobby people, poor people, burglary and arson ("the devil made me do it" defense), cemetery vandalism, crooked politicians in cahoots with the crooked developers, cancer-causing agents in the air and in the drinking water and too little water, people from the city (any city will do), and the scourge of drugs. Has respectable old Quaker, Mennonite, and exurban Bucks become

---

[201] *Time* magazine cover "Thinking the Unthinkable", March 29,1982; Richard Corliss, "A Season of Flash and Greed," *Time*, December 14, 1987, p.82.
[202] Similar such language has been used from Pope Paul VI to Pope Francis.

one of the nation's drug capitals? Has evil finally triumphed? Every week the local press reports on "cocaine dens" set up in the kitchens of the old farmhouses; and local authorities stake out secluded driveways where the drug is "cooked" in the backs of window-darkened vans.

In other ways too, evil makes its presence known: 3-letter chemicals appear in the groundwater; radon gas seeps up through the rocks of the Reading Prong (much as the old folk devil once did); and Satanical graffiti is scribbled on abandoned buildings along Routes 1 and 13. But inarguably, everyone's favorite devil(s) are the developers and all their minions. There's a strong and pervasive disgust with the land developers, their bulldozers, cement mixers, and quarry trucks ... and, not to be forgotten, the compliant politicians who conspire to help transform this beautiful county into a "badly congested and overbuilt hell."[203] The words used to describe what the developers have done are unequivocal: "Those who rape the land (and then "develop" it) are the devils within the county." They, in turn, enable the "rich snobs with their McMansions" to invade the county. The population is ten times what the infrastructure can handle and "it's only getting worse. The suburbs are now the urbs." One young critic summed up "amazing" Bucks with this unhappily iconic image: "Last week I saw a tree get hit by a BMW outside the Walmart supercenter."

Criticism of the evils the developers have inflicted on the county is tinged with much nostalgia for a recently vanished (and still vanishing) farmscape. For many, the "good old days" were the days of their youth in the 1970s-80s; they still have fresh memories of running through the corn rows on nearby farms and school trips to the pig farms in Bensalem. Included are memories of cows grazing in fields as seen from school bus windows – in fields where two hundred townhouses called "Sweetwater Farms" now squat. It's more than just a sweet nostalgia for the fading away of "Old Bucks County." There are elements of approbation and utter disgust as well. The fact that big box stores and half-vacant strip malls sit on land once cultivated by family farmers is

---

[203] This quote and much of the quoted material in this chapter is drawn from the survey presented in Appendix D.

troubling. Part of your personal history seems to have been taken away and you want to scream: "Enough is enough." The widening of Street Road (Route 132) is recalled with mixed fascination and horror – watching men and machines work into the evening with the dawning realization that "everything would go wild" because of that widening. All too quickly a congested corridor of convenience stores, shopping plazas, gas stations, and a racetrack and casino(s) has "butchered" the familiar farms and woodlands. "The Toll Brothers[204] took over and then everything went downhill" – change the name of the developer and this becomes a reoccurring theme. Most people do however realize the inevitability if not the desirability of change … and that they themselves are the problem: "It's sad to see all the changes, but (it's) understood that you're part of those changes."

Yet, is any of this the "ocean of physical and moral evil" the church defines?[205] A cosmic perniciousness? The antithesis of good? When it comes to people and land, is there a sinful and malevolent violation of morality operating in the county? The county looks the way it does because the untidy aesthetics is a consequence of decades of shoddy and unorganized growth. This, no matter how diligently planners have tried to deflect, direct, and contain that growth. It is, in other words, the typical American fringe, the no man's land between city, suburb, exurb, and farm. Though nowhere is it the "sordid, degraded, vilified" Middle Atlantic landscape described by Henry Miller in *The Air-Conditioned Nightmare*.[206] Bucks may be almost as good as its reputation says it is. It may be as nice a place to live as any other, and many county residents really wouldn't want to live in any of the other 3,000-plus counties. But the atmosphere is seen as soured by "money-grubbing

---

[204] Toll Brothers, "America's Luxury Home Builder," is usually the first name that comes to mind when people in Bucks County think of developers. The Horsham, Pa.-based company's website mentions a commitment to "preserving our natural environment." Online critics will beg to differ.

[205] For example, kinds and degrees of evil are defined in the *New Catholic Encyclopedia*, Washington D.C.: Catholic University of America, 1967, Volume 5 … on page 666 (Honest!).

[206] Henry Miller, *The Air-Conditioned Nightmare*, New York: A New Direction Book, 1945, p. 37.

corruption" and by developers who say "Well, we're sorry" after they've hatched their mistakes, after they've uprooted 200-year old sycamore trees and demolished equally ancient buildings. People do complain about the "greedy developers, (who) with the blessing of our elected officials, have long since destroyed any historic value our township ever had." They feel this way not because of post-millennial angst, but because they can see these things happening every day. By the millennium, Bucks County had become a highly contested landscape caught between the forces of tradition and modernization. A balance was sought between nature and history on the one side, and development on the other. And in the end, no one was pleased.

Possession: The Devil of It

One thing more needs to be considered. For the many who hope to enjoy the county's undeniable attractions there is discouragement in that so much of everything is posted. The land, the landscape, is placed off-limits because nearly every tree, every utility pole, and every fence is posted. A common complaint is this: "There used to be so much open space to enjoy in Bucks. Not anymore. It's 'Stay Out', 'Private Property'… It's all 'No this and no that'. It's all coming to an end." Is this then the nature of things?

The county today is a difficult place to walk about, to photograph, or to absorb oneself in by getting close to the land. It's no longer the kind of place to gadabout, to go wandering in. There's no place, save the malls, to walk the blues away. It probably began to be like this many decades ago when the run-down and abandoned farms were bought up in the early days of mink curtain exurbanization. Eventually, the open countryside disappeared along with places from which to view it. Some of the nicest vistas became private, and those places described and painted by earlier generations became inaccessible. As the wife of one of the New Hope painters remembers: "… as more and more property was bought up it was increasingly difficult to find subject matter without trespassing…we began traveling for the sake of new subjects."[207]

What's missing is the opportunity to rummage around historic caves and quarries, to follow clues to caches of long-lost pirate and outlaw treasure, and to chip away at Triassic rocks in search of fossils and dinosaur tracks (which should rightly be regarded as part of the county's natural endowment, along with rich farmland and scenery).[208] The chance foray up onto the green, wooded seclusion of the diabase hills is taken away. Views of the hills are difficult because the quarry trucks own the roads and there are no shoulders to safely walk or bike on. Scenic Bucks has no scenic parking areas where a camera can be used. The hasty impression from the automobile window is the usual way people "see" Bucks. Views from the hills are impossible because even "vacant" or undeveloped land is posted. Resultantly, Bucks looks like this:

> *Private: No Trespassing*
> *Patrolled: Keep Out*
> *No Entry Allowed*
> *Positively Private Drive*
> *All Persons are Strictly*
> *Forbidden to Trespass*

The variations in the posted warnings are endless and confirm what Calvin Trillin once said in *The New Yorker*: that "in a soft economy, the one safe investment is a company manufacturing 'No Trespassing' (signs)."[209] Some signs have a one-two-three punch to ensure that the

---

[207] Emily Leith-Ross as quoted in *Upper Makefield Speaks*, p. 47.

[208] It's no one's fault of course, but the county and its history (and its geologic faults) are even difficult to observe because road cuts are rare and roads follow the rock formations rather than slice through them at revealing angles as happens in the western states.

[209] Calvin Trillin, "Lower Bucks County …," *The New Yorker*, November 15, 1969, p. 169-75.

command is clearly understood: "Posted, No Trespassing, Keep Out." Befitting the county's arts and crafts reputation, some hand-lettered signs are quite fanciful. Others, reflecting the literary character of the county, are wordier, more expressive:

> *All Persons are Hereby Notified and Warned Not to Trespass on These Premises. This is Private Land ... You are Warned that No Person may Trespass for Any Reason!*

To preserve their messages against the ravages of time and nature, some signs on trees are covered in plastic. Plastic bags are draped over the signs; sometimes a bag will split open and fill with dirty brown rainwater. And it looks like the tree's enema bag.

Although the deterrent language used on the signs evokes fears of being shot, pursued by a farmer with a pitchfork (or trident), or mauled by a pack of hunting dogs, this is no redneck boondocks. Here in the land of country squires, violators are attacked by lawyers; fines, prosecution and imprisonment are used to remind the passer-by to keep passing by. Like the old German farmers who used a battery of warning devices to keep evil away, the property owner may depend on more than strongly-worded signs to preserve privacy. High fences, tall trees and densely-planted hedges are useful for preventing glimpses of the front lawn or the house itself. If however spied, the lawn is seen to have lawn statuary: silver or blue, sun-reflecting Victorian gazing balls, brown and yellow sunflower pinwheels, iron-rimmed wooden wagon wheels with their lower half buried in the ground, and ceramic mushrooms sheltering a family of gnomes under their umbrella-like caps. These, along with the security company signs, protect the home turf. Or so a visitor from a more superstitious culture might conclude. (Lawn statuary is generally frowned upon in the older, wealthier "mink curtain" exurb; here, it may be regarded as a tacky, middle class display of poor taste best confined to the lower county). The more refined exurbanite might however choose to decorate with pieces of Asian stone sculpture or Oriental shrubbery. A pair of pink flamingoes might also be OK – assuming they're original late 1950s collectibles from a local auction house.

It was probably predictable that it should be this way, given the fact that from the very beginning the ownership of property and the use of property qualifications for voting were more important in Pennsylvania than elsewhere (for example, New England).[210] This refrain from an old hymn has few subscribers here: that we are but strangers on this earth and that it is a place not our own, unlike our rightful in the "heavenly country." Again, Calvin Trillin: "… Americans may have a special feeling for property, the way the Irish are said to have a special feeling for poetry, and the French for wine."[211] The presumed inalienable right to not just land, but very private, posted, fenced-off land is humorously expressed by Ambrose Bierce in *The Devil's Dictionary*:[212]

> LAND, n. A part of the earth's surface, considered as property. The theory that land is property subject to private ownership and control is the foundation of modern society … Carried to its logical conclusion, it means that some have the right to prevent others from living; for the right to own implies the right exclusively to occupy; and in fact laws of trespass are enacted wherever property in land is recognized. It follows that if the whole area of terra firma is owned by A, B, and C, there will be no place for D, E, F, and G to be born, or, born as trespassers, to exist.

The attitude that "This land is mine, so don't even consider stepping on it, touching it, or looking at it" is of course not unique to Bucks, though it may be more pronounced here than elsewhere. But is this touchiness, this exclusionism wrong? Evil? Definitely not! After all, people have worked hard for what they have (or, at least some have) and trespassers do gun down animals, cause vandalism, and fill the roadside

---

[210] *See:* E.Digby Baltzell, *Puritan Boston and Quaker Philadelphia*, p. 120.
[211] Calvin Trillin, op. cit.
[212] Ambrose Bierce, *The Devil's Dictionary*, p. 101.

ditches with assorted trash and discarded fast food packaging. But when trespassing with a camera, easel, field guide to the birds, or simply with one's eyes brings a quick dash from the house and a gruff "Who do you represent?" or "What do you think you're doing?" it reveals a serious paranoia. The simple physical and mental pleasure of walking and the psychic relief of just looking at something green and open is now so difficult to come by; that's maddening. It makes a fist, a boxing glove of the brain.

We can no longer indulge our vagabond instincts since roads, even those out beyond the suburbs, are shoulderless traffic-hardened arteries where life's passing parade (with all the clowns and floats) zips by in a blur at fifty five mph. Nor are cross-country field excursions possible as they are in Britain with its 5,000 miles of foot paths (and despite fierce trespass laws). Out-doors magazine writers and bloggers may raise the idea of recapturing "the lost art of walking," and in other places – like (ironically) urban neighborhoods -- that may be possible. But not here. There are no wild lands left free of private ownership or government management. Most of the outdoors is someone else's property … and is treated like a jealously-guarded mistress.

In Bucks, the last wilderness vanished when the first wave of up-county German farmers broke through the woods and found their downcounty counterparts from the British Isles edging in from the other side. Many of the early redemptioners, after three years servitude, found "everything already belonged to somebody else"[213] – and simply left.

The last of the countryside (defined as rustic or pertaining to things rural) went at no specific date in time, but was certainly all but gone not long after the devil departed in the 1880s. Ever since, the county has been a "zone of contention," a speculative gameboard on which the land is prized only for its dollar value. The county is 610 square miles of prime time real estate, caught between the metropolitan outreach of New York, Philadelphia, Trenton, and the Lehigh Valley.

---

[213] As quoted in Dorothy Stockton Cameron, *History of the Presbyterian Church of Deep Run, 1725-1975*, p. 22.

Nature, the kind that transcendentalists and "romantic" travelers swooned over, went with the last passenger pigeon. The fight now is to preserve farms, not countryside or nature. But farms are factories stacked with chemicals and skillfully managed from the barn-side computer and operated as an "agribusiness." All parties contest the future of the "farmlands." None of this has anything to do with "countryside," nor is nature in its purest sense party to it. Landscape architect Grady Clay:

> There is hardly any real country left, especially east of the Mississippi if one defines "country" as a territory devoid of urban influences; and the so-called edge of the city has become a complex zone of contention ... The rightful place of nature in this scene (is) subject to disruption by expanding urban energies.

By the end of the twentieth century the older industrial cities of the Megalopolis had become badly beat up and run down, fountains and bottomless pits of blight and then abandonment. People were left far removed from anything green and open that might have suggested something of beauty or spiritual value. They were distanced from the cycles and seasons of the natural world found only in the countryside. Scenery and aesthetics had been replaced by an appraiser's-eye view that saw only market value and capital investments. Progress, growth, and development(s) have all distanced people from what used to be called "countryside" ... an increasingly charmless countryside with a monetary value assigned to every acre and every vista. The landscape became private, locked up ... and admonished us to go away and stay away. Peripatetic walking shoes and the serendipity of cross-country hikes were dead upon the Triassic earth. Shot dead for trespassing! Victims of a vain effort to find, touch, and feel the good red earth. A writer in the *New York Times*, commenting on the lost countryside in the New York exurbs, summarizes the essence of it:[214]

---

[214] Anatole Broyard, "Is a Boy Better Off Out Here?" The *New York Times*, February 18, 1979 (New Jersey section), p. 6-7.

We say that we live in the country, but exurbia is not country ... In my darker moods, I feel that I inhabit a void with trees. Few of us live off the land or have any necessary relation to it. We learn no great moral lessons from the land ... We merely reside here, in a benign exile from the city, in a landscape that strikes us as so undifferentiated that we feel impelled to punctuate it with pools and tennis courts.

Or, consider Patricia Toft, a letter writer to the local newspaper; she describes a dream that has fallen apart:[215]

The residents of Bucks County are up to here with corporate centers, shopping centers, mini malls, large malls and the like. When are the county and township officials going to say stop? Most of us moved to beautiful Bucks because it was quiet ... We don't need to be two minutes from the nearest pizza place ... No longer can we entertain out-of-towners for a ride in the country. There is no country.

Yes, Patricia, there is no country. But, there is more ...

As Time Goes By

These observations are based neither on a preference for some supposed rustic Eden nor on a sickly sweet nostalgia for a past that was never personally lived and probably didn't exist anyway. There's more involved. Human and behavioral scientists say that we are a nation afflicted with personal disconnectedness, loneliness, and chronic social emptiness. These conditions are supposed to stem in part from our high rate of geographic mobility and other related "ills" and are evidenced in

---

[215] Patricia Toft, letter to the *Bucks County Courier Times*, October 16, 1985.

the faulty relationships people have with one another. That same disconnectedness seems to characterize the relations people have – or don't have – with the land they live on and the landscape they live in. The visual relationship and deep spiritual bond between people and the earth they walk upon, or rather drive across, has been lost. How can you feel spiritual towards, or deeply attached to a place that changes so fast? That you can't recognize from day to day? James Howard Kunstler remarked that so much of the American landscape has become like that in *The Geography of Nowhere*: suburbs and exurbs afford "no escape from other people into nature; except for some totemic trees and shrubs, nature has been obliterated by the relentless blocks full of houses."[216] Ecologist and author Barry Lopez put it this way: "...we've traded in a fraternal or companionable relationship with the land for an economic one – the land as thing ... if we do not retrieve... some more gracious relationship with the land, we will find our sanctuaries, in the end, have become nothing more than commodities...landscapes related to no one."[217]

Much of Bucks County has become a hardball speculative fringe that cannot be touched, felt, or appreciated with the senses. In this cynical era, land is esteemed not for its intrinsic historical or ecological worth, but for its monetary value.[218] But land values do not foster a sense of mental wonder (Do they?); they offer no spiritual comfort, and speak nothing of nature and calendar cycles. The only thing learned is this: we have further distanced ourselves from primordial things, things that our long ago folk beliefs informed us of and bound us to. Genuine folk fears and fantasies no doubt put us into a greater communion with the natural world than a lifetime membership in the Sierra Club. Even with all our

---

[216] James Howard Kunstler, *The Geography of Nowhere,* New York; Simon & Schuster, 1993, p.105.

[217] Barry Lopez, "Treasured Places," *Life*, 1987, p.40-41.

[218] This may not be a uniquely modern attitude toward land. The historian Richard Hofstadter found that American farmers of the early nineteenth century developed an attachment not to the land itself, but to land values. When land values rose, they sold out and moved on. So much for the ancestral sod! See: Hofstadter, "The Myth of the Happy Yeoman," in *The Age of Reform*, 1955.

modern gadgets designed to keep us connected to the earth's grid (GPS navigation, Google imagery, maps, and directions) we've lost our way, becoming hopelessly disconnected from our surroundings.

Henry Miller once wrote that an area like the Bucks' countryside was terrifying: "Topographically the country is magnificent ... and terrifying. Why terrifying? Because nowhere else in the world is the (separation) between man and nature so complete."[219] How complete? Arthur Shenefelt, who was once appointed by the county government to study the growing problem of traffic congestion, described the county as "a world-wide point of focus for economic influence and development." He further and correctly described Bucks as a "national crossroads and international hub area." He concluded that because of continued growth along the Megalopolitan mainline (the I-95 and U.S. Route 1 arteries) and the more recent surge of the Princeton-New Brunswick high-tech corridor, the days of cows and barns were passé. Said Shenefelt:[220]

> ... our cows graze at exactly that point on the entire earth's surface marked for heaviest density traffic, north/south – east/west. since 1929.

Yes, that complete a distancing between people and countryside. And terrifying. Terrifying in that by breaking our ties with the land we set ourselves adrift from what was once a source of psychic healing. The nineteenth century artist Thomas Cole wrote of the earth's ancient "power to mend our hearts." But not when a once-nourishing earth is chained, posted, and kept away from us. It cannot touch our hearts and we cannot touch it.

Ironically, the most inviting and unposted areas of the land are the cemeteries. Here, there is no distancing us from the most natural of facts. Where else does the so obvious amalgam of humanity, time, earth, and biological cycles touch our minds so directly? Until dusk that is. As the

[219] Henry Miller, op. cit., p. 19-20.
[220] Arthur Shenefelt, "Is Bucks a Victim of Time and Place?" *Bucks County Courier Times*, March 17, 1986.

sun goes down, no stargazing and no folk devils pondering inscriptions on crumbling tombstones. The intimacy of the nightscape, the sensuousness of the evening, and the feel of the moon tugging on the blood tides in the veins, are all denied. It's closing time.

When the daily rituals of folk life were practiced, when the land itself was imbued with power, beauty, and superstition, when people painted their porch ceilings blue, these things were done with an actual purpose in mind. The devil was in the earth and it was a time of earthly evil, but an evil that was known. And an even more powerful God was present too; at times the land was therefore bountiful and good. Now, the folk devil has departed and, contrary to rumor, he never did return. Perhaps he still rides the Montana winds, while the red basement fireplaces sit purposelessly in Bucks. Decade by decade and subdivision by subdivision, life in the county has become further removed from any real contact with the earth, further removed from any strong feelings for it. We have nothing more to say to it because we don't know where it is; we have no strong feelings for it because we do not experience it – not necessarily possess it physically or legally – but do not even experience it visually. And the land has nothing more to say to us. Once it was conquer me, hate me for my evil, love me for my undulating curves and the reflection of God within me, touch and be tempted by me, be intimate. That capacity to speak has been smothered by asphalt and concrete. The passion has gone out of the relationship and the telephone has stopped ringing. All is entropy and atrophy, an emasculated landscape drained of its pagan energies, drained of value both profane and sacred. And that's the devil of it.

In his 1980 *Bucks County Idyll*, Robert J. Seidman described "Big Bucks County" this way: "Man's hand had been everywhere here -- (Everything) hummed of careful breeding and whispered the soft rustling sound of money." But something was missing. "That's what's been missing. They've bred out all the wild and the mystery."[221] John Updike's Reverend Tom Marshfield thought that "athletic fields and

---

[221] Robert J. Seidman, *Bucks County Idyll*, New York: Simon & Schuster, 1980. P. 34-35.

golf courses excepted, the out-of-doors wears an evil aspect…" But evil exists only when man imparts it to something he feels strongly about. Evil, as well as good, speaks of powerful forces and creatures that visibly or invisibly inhabit the world, yet this land has fallen silent and speaks neither of virtue nor badness. The land gives us only a silence, like the eternal silence of the infinity of space that rolls above the Triassic earth. It's a total silence, the alien indifference that St. Francis found in the cave. No angry darkness, but the cool, silent nothingness that exists at the rear of the Durham Cave. Nor, should we expect anything more. Though not writing specifically about Bucks County, Alan Lightman of M.I.T. wrote in a *New York Times* Op-Ed piece ("Our Lonely Home in Nature"):[222]

> We feel betrayed. We feel betrayed by nature … all the evidence suggests that nature doesn't care one whit about us … In the 20th and 21st centuries … nature is neither friend nor foe, neither malevolent nor benevolent.

The devil's favorite ruse is making people think that he isn't present at all … when he really is. His best disguise is no disguise. Nothing. Maybe this is what the old folk devil meant: "the devil that's seen is better than the devil that ain't." The devil of it is that feeling of nothingness, the lukewarm void left by a disconnection with the land. Seriously or playfully, the land was once clothed in a wardrobe of evil to make a work-a-day farm world more understandable, more manageable. Then, artists came to regard it aesthetically, imparting a beauty to it. Now, the evil is gone, and as time goes by, the soul is gone and the beauty fades away.

---

[222] Alan Lightman, "Our Lonely Home in Nature," The *New York Times*, May 3, 2014.

Iron and Stone, Earth and Bone ... and the Rain

The rain beats down on the old stone farmhouse, finger-tapping on the roof; it bounces and beads on the slate shingles, forming puddles around the foot of the red basement fireplace. Fifty feet away, across the yard, rain comes down on the same farmhouse, the same in every detail except size and that it's made only of wood (Fig.14.1). Badly rotting wood. It's a miniature version, a scaled-down replica of the larger house, built by the hands of a bygone craftsman. The house was built for purple martins, although they're no longer common in Bucks County. Early settlers valued the presence of the martins, welcoming them with ready-made nesting places: hollowed-out gourds and raised boxes on poles fifteen feet high. The German farmers built hoods above their barn doors and house windows, with holes for the martins to enter and nest. The fast-flying birds worked off their keep by devouring flying insects and protecting the barnyard fowl from predatory hawks and crows.

Fig. 14.1 A House for Martins. Buckingham
(Author's sketch)

A house for these beneficial birds was built when they were common to the surrounding farmlands, and when they perched on the utility wires along the roadsides. These steel-blue or purple-colored birds winter in Brazil and return to Pennsylvania in early April. But there are unexplainable gaps in their migrations. In some years, even for long stretches of years, they seem not to return at all or, if having returned, choose another nesting place. The house awaits them and is repeatedly washed by the rain and dried by the sun. No other birds will use it. Its windows are round, dark eyes that open onto the rooms inside, the individual nesting apartments. The two-by-four foot house sits atop a pole in the backyard, like a beacon out on the remorseless Triassic sea. Its future will be that of the larger house. That house may be sold, its fields subdivided, and the road widened. If the martins ever do return to look for their house, they too may feel a sense of disorientation and impermanency.

Like their ancestors the dinosaurs,[223] who they evolved from at this same place but in late Triassic times, these shrunken feathered dinosaurs have ways of disappearing too. They're not required to tell us why, and they don't. We know why the passenger pigeons left. While shotguns were a more common means of expression in an agrarian world (and still are among some redneck exurbanites), it's a bit more subtle today. With a shriveled farmscape, with few barnyards or barnyard fowl left to protect, the martins too – indigenous to agricultural environments – become victims of habitat destruction and over-development. With the vanishing birds, forerunners of evil and harbingers of good, the biodiversity of the Triassic earth is further diminished.

---

[223] Paul Olsen, renowned Columbia University paleontologist, writes conclusively that "Birds are the direct descendants of dinosaurs --- a stroll in New York City really does look different knowing that those are small grey dinosaurs walking and flying all around!" http://www.1deo.columbia.edu/edu/dees/courses/v1001/dinosaur
The journal *Science* reported (August, 2014) that a suborder of dinosaurs called theropods survive to this day as birds. These "shape-shifters" just kept "shrinking and shrinking and shrinking for about 50 million years" said the scientist. (Michael S.Y. Lee of the University of Adelaide, Australia).

The rain and the dark help conceal what has become this urban fringe. Tonight, the fringe has a reprieve from the future. It is not bothered by the usual and daily growth surges. The realtors and builders dream of tomorrow's big moves while the quarry truck drivers and bulldozer operators, weary from their labors of shoving and hauling away the Triassic earth, huddle in the relaxing neon-lit glow of the barroom. Down Megalopolis' long corridor, Philadelphia will edge a little closer tomorrow, bringing more people, gridlock, and falling water tables. From the other direction, New York's outreach will lengthen deeper into the hills of northern New Jersey, its power flowing along the interstates and state roads lined with corporate headquarters, more and more of whose young go-getters will drive home along the narrow and overburdened farm roads and "cow paths" to their mini-estates in Bucks. Soon enough, they and others – more than 100,000 others – will grow the county's population further.[224] But all this awaits tomorrow. Tomorrow will again bring with it the relentless assault on what's left of the rural.

Tonight, stasis and equilibrium. Tonight, a log burns steadily in the fireplace of the old stone house. Save for the sound of the rain, the rooms are as quiet and empty of sound as those in the martin house. It would be tempting to relieve the silence with good music, but listening to the silence is also good. On nights like this such pertinent questions come to mind as where the birds go when it rains. And what did the dinosaurs do, certainly too large to find shelter, when the rain poured down on Triassic nights eons ago? And who else lived here reflecting on the rain one hundred, two hundred years ago? When I first came to this house, I researched it well. I thought it would be comforting to find a continuity, a long genealogy of a single farm family whose deeds and misdeeds might be read in the township histories and deed books as well as in the wide and worn wooden floorboards. Stability? Not here. And maybe not anywhere. Again, Grady Clay: "... it is foolish to yearn for

---

[224] The Delaware Valley Regional Planning Commission projects a population increase for Bucks of 132,000 in the years between 2013–35. Maybe more, a lot more. Then again, maybe not. The U.S. Census Bureau reports that few new residents are now being added to the county's population (*See:* Appendix B).

a settled stability of scene that never existed."[225] Since it was put together with stones and lime from the nearby fields around 1745, the house has changed hands dozens of times. Families came and stayed awhile, and then, like pocket combs and matchbooks, just vanished. Ownership changed every decade or so. That one in five Americans change address every year is a statistic the twentieth century shared with previous centuries. All these comings and goings, the parade of people quickly changing costumes from period to period, have brought many changes to the house as well: rooms have been enlarged, walls removed, staircases built, wings added, and the basement fireplace closed. The architectural historian who visited the house said that it had a very complex past and that it would give up its secrets only reluctantly. So too with its human history.

It seems almost pedestrian to lament the fact that people, so many people, pull up stakes and move on to parts unknown. Pulling up the old survey stakes and "making tracks" is, after all, one of the main dramas of American life. Gone are all the people, following their dreams west through the wind and water gaps of the Appalachians and along the interstates to the Sunbelt. Gone are the passenger pigeons, the farmlands of the *Peaceable Kingdom*, the barns and barn ramps, the eight-square schoolhouses, the expressions of a folk culture. Gone are the martins and gone too is the devil. Gone! From the rain-splattered panes of the farmhouse window, the high-banked road is empty. Nothing. Nothing but rain pounding away at the ocean bed of another time, breaking down and eroding the Triassic soil, carrying the past away in muddy brown torrents. One almost wishes for some earthy evil, some substance of feeling, to come walking back out of the dark-recesses of human experience, to come hobbling down the road in a wet and tattered black coat. With a flash of his polished teeth, he might say, "Hey, I'm back again! Feel the fear and hate me, and again try to protect yourselves against me. I bring back mystery, excitement, and threatening energies to the land. The shadow of God has returned. The magic is back." But, of course, it's not.

---

[225] Grady Clay, op.cit, p.16.

Down on the great outwash plain of lower Bucks, sheets of rain drive along old U.S. Route 1. And on a big black Suburban parked outside an adult book shop, the bumper sticker reads: "Another Shitty Day in Paradise." Paradise? And why not, for according to the county histories, this area near Route 1 was once called "Eden."[226] But where in the garden is the corrupting devil now? In truth, no devil, no garden. Maybe all the shit, as the folk Germans believed, does keep him away.

In the Durham Hills the great earth cave sits empty and silent. The fluttering of wings and the high-pitched call of the little brown bats is heard no more. The tens of thousands of bats that had hibernated in the cool moist air of the cave for uncountable generations are now nearly extinct. "Total Devastation." "A sad ending for the bats of Bucks," somberly intones the local newspaper (The *Intelligencer*, April 1, 2013). The insect-eating "farmer's friend" is gone, gone along with the passenger pigeons and the purple martins. The bat is thought to be the victim of a puzzling disease spread perhaps by mankind's carelessness.[227] At the rear of the now-deserted cave, a dark pool of water collects beneath the Durham Hills. Here, where it all began, no endings, no answers, and certainly no bats. Just what is and will always be: the cool, wet, and timeless stillness of the cave.

In the rain, one thing remains. In an upcounty graveyard, a rusting six-foot trident, like a beacon in the night, stands abandoned. (Fig. 14.2) Throughout the night, raindrops, acid raindrops strike the trident and the nearby gravestones, further dissolving peoples' identities. The

---

[226] Eden: Name given to the South Langhorne Post Office in 1882 (A. Henry Fretz, *Bucks County Place Names*, Harrisburg: Pennsylvania Dept. of Internal Affairs, Monthly Bulletin 21:2, 1953, p. 31). "The name Eden was not generally adopted by the residents (who retained the use of 'Attleboro') as a town name ... The name 'Penndel' was just adopted in 1948." (George MacReynolds, *Place Names in Bucks County*, 1953).

[227] The disease is called "white nose syndrome" and causes a white fungus to form around the nose (a fatal infection) that results in the loss of body fat needed to survive the long winter hibernation. It's theorized that the fungus spread from Europe on the equipment and clothing of American cave explorers. Thus, a downside to globalization.

Fig. 14.2 Trident, Raindrops
(Author's photo)

raindrops, like teardrops, strike the tines and drizzle down the trident's ancient shaft, entering the red earth and filtering to the water table below the bones of the early settlers. Still further down, the rain slowly dissolves the dinosaur footprints.

The pitchfork-like trident, a farmer's tool whose Old English linguistic roots actually gives us the word for "evil," came to symbolize much of what the county was. It was a hard-worked land that people felt attached to and to which they imbued a sense of mystery and magic. The trident spoke of generations of Celtic and New World restlessness and an American nostalgia for an agrarian past (See, for example, the symbolism in Grant Wood's *American Gothic* (1930)). It speaks now of a simple sadness for all that's lost when this one and only *Peaceable Kingdom*, once so deeply and iconically rural, is overwhelmed by growth … and changes so very quickly.

APPENDICES

APPENDIX A

In the black & white satellite view below, Bucks County is seen in the context of the Middle Atlantic region between New York City and Philadelphia. Allentown and the Lehigh Valley lie to the north (upper left). New Jersey and the Atlantic coast are to the east. This is the heart of the Megalopolitan corridor. Scale is approximately sixteen miles to the inch. (Or eighty-one miles from New York to Philadelphia "as the crow flies").

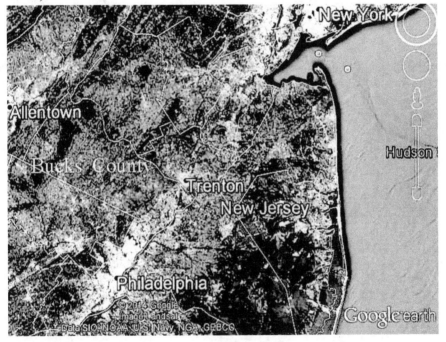

Google Earth Image (Copyright 2014)
From Landsat satellite. Image date: 4/9/13.

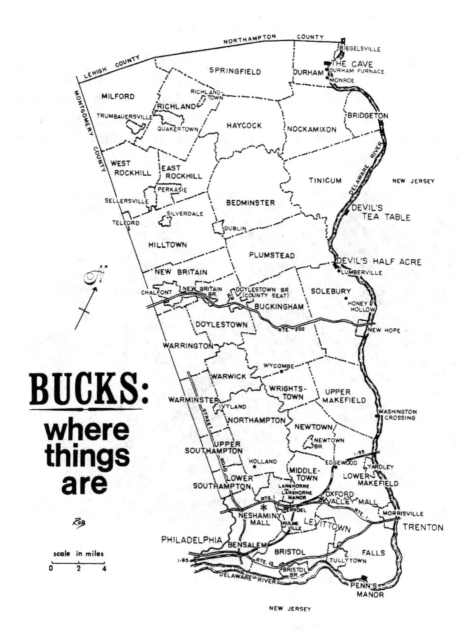

BUCKS:
where
things
are

ℛ𝑜𝐵

scale in miles
0   2   4

APPENDIX B

STATISTICAL BUCKS

County Population Growth (U.S. Census Bureau)

Year	Population	Growth	Period	% Growth
1790	25,401	--------	--------	---------
1800	27,489	2,088	1790-1800	8%
1810	32,371	4,882	1800-1810	18%
1820	37,842	5,471	1810-1820	17%
1830	45,740	7,898	1820-1830	21%
1840	48,107	2,367	1830-1840	5%
1850	56,091	7,984	1840-1850	17%
1860	63,578	7,487	1850-1860	13%
1870	64,336	758	1860-1870	1%
1880	68,656	4,320	1870-1880	7%
1890	70,615	1,959	1880-1890	3%
1900	71,190	575	1890-1900	1%
1910	76,530	5,430	1900-1910	7%
1920	82,476	5,946	1910-1920	8%
1930	96,727	14,251	1920-1930	17%
1940	107,712	10,895	1930-1940	11%
1950	144,620	36,908	1940-1950	33%
1960	308,567	163,947	1950-1960	113%
1970	410,056	108,161	1960-1970	35%
1980	479,211	62,483	1970-1980	17%
1990	541,174	61,963	1980-1990	13%
2000	597,635	56,461	1990-2000	10%
2010	625,255	27,620	2000-2010	5%
2014	626,685 (+0.6% over 2010)			
2035	753,784 (projection, DVRPC)			

Bucks' Municipalities (Townships/Boroughs)

Lower Bucks	Pop.2000	Pop.2010	% Change
Bensalem	58,434	60,427	+3.4
Bristol Boro	9,923	9,726	-2
Bristol	55,521	54,582	-2
Falls	34,865	34,300	-1.6
Hulmeville Boro	893	1,003	+12
Langhorne Boro	1,981	1,622	-18
Langhorne Manor	927	1,442	+55
Lower Makefield	32,681	32,559	-0.4
Lower Southampton	19,276	18,909	-2
Middletown	44,141	45,436	+3
Morrisville Boro	10,023	8,728	-13
Penndel Boro	2,420	2,238	-4
Tullytown Boro	2,031	1,872	-8
Yardley Boro	2,498	2,434	-2.6
Total Lower Bucks	275,614	275,434	-0

Central Bucks	Pop.2000	Pop.2010	% Change
Buckingham	16,442	20,075	+22
Chalfont Boro	3,900	4,009	+3
Doylestown Boro	8,227	8,380	+2
Doylestown	17,619	17,565	-0.3
Ivyland Boro	492	1,041	+112
New Britain Boro	3,125	3,152	+1
New Britain	10,698	11,070	+3
New Hope Boro	2,252	2,528	+12
Newtown Boro	2,312	2,248	-3
Newtown	18,206	19,299	+6
Northampton	39,384	39,726	+1
Plumstead	11,409	12,442	+9

(Continued)

	Pop.2000	Pop.2010	% Change
Solebury	7,743	8,692	+12
Upper Makefield	7,180	8,190	+14
Upper Southampton	15,764	15,152	-4
Warminster	31,383	32,682	+4
Warrington	17,580	23,418	+33
Warwick	11,977	14,437	+21
Wrightstown	2,839	2,995	+5
Total Central Bucks	228,532	247,101	+8

Upper Bucks	Pop.2000	Pop.2010	% Change
Bedminster	4,804	6,574	+37
Bridgeton	1,408	1,277	-9
Dublin Boro	2,083	2,158	+4
Durham	1,313	1,144	-13
East Rockhill	5,199	5,706	+10
Haycock	2,191	2,225	+2
Hilltown	12,102	15,029	+24
Milford	8,810	9,902	+12
Nockamixon	3,517	3,441	-2
Perkasie Boro	8,828	8,511	-4
Quakertown Boro	8,931	8,979	+1
Richland	9,920	13,052	+32
Richlandtown Boro	1,283	1,327	+3
Riegelsville Boro	863	868	+1
Sellersville Boro	4,564	4,249	-7
Silverdale Boro	1,001	871	-13
Springfield	4,963	5,035	+1
Telford Boro	2,211	2,207	-0
Tinicum	4,206	3,995	-5
Trumbauersville Boro	1,059	974	-8
West Rockhill	4,233	5,256	+24
Total Upper Bucks	94,489	102,780	+8.7

APPENDIX C

Old Stereotypes ... Just for Fun!

I debated whether or not to include Appendix C in this edition. It appeared in the 1988 edition and was based on a survey conducted in 1980 and published by the *Bucks County Courier Times* in its October 4th, 1981 *Accent* magazine (*See illustration*). After all, it is rather dated (a third of a century, and counting). So, I decided to use it ... It has value as a time capsule of late 1970s-early 1980s popular culture. More importantly, it remains one of the most satirical, self-deprecating pieces of humor about the county and the types of people living in it.

Students at the local community college taking a course in Bucks County geography were given a novel assignment. After defining and discussing "stereotypes," students were asked to describe the "typical" people who lived in several areas of the county. Most had never been "up-county" (or even to New Hope for that matter) and yet created colorful word portraits of people in those areas. I then translated the words into sketch illustrations.

The newspaper story was titled *"Bucks County Stereotypes: Students Make Fun of Themselves"* and the staff writer was Janet Falon. The story was reprinted in the first edition with permission from the *Courier Times*.

Second Generation Levittowners

DRESS: Female, if over 35: vinyl K-Mart slippers, large pink plastic rollers, discount designer clothes. If under 35: her brother's Flyer's jersey, jogging shorts, knee-high sweat sox and sneaks. Male: army jacket, t-shirt with name of bar in Wildwood, khaki pants, black Converse All-Stars with orange laces, hair parted in middle, reflective shades, and (optional) cycle helmet under arm.

CAR(S) TYPICALLY DRIVEN: Parents: '63 Ford or Chevy wagon with body cancer that Reedmans won't even consider. Kids: Mustang GTO with mag wheels.

BUMPER STICKER: Parents: Walt Disney World. Kids: "Grass, A... or Gas if You Want a Ride."

LAST BOOK READ: Paperback: Readers Digest. Hardbound: The Best of Readers Digest.

HERO: Parents: U.S. Steelworker. Kids: Bruce Springsteen.

VILLAIN: Parents: The IRS. Kids: parents. Everyone: Trenton.

AUTHORITY FIGURE: The Lawn Doctor.

COLLEGE OR EDUCATION: Levittown Beauty Academy or Pennsbury High 12th Grade (Home economics major).

RELIGION: Retired Catholics.

POLITICS: "Buy American."

DRINK: Parents: Bud or Miller Lite in cans followed by Maalox. Kids: Molson Imported Golden.

FAVORITE PASTIMES: Parents: coupon clipping and flea markets. Everyone: hanging out at the mall. (Discount drug store for parents and games arcade — Space Invaders, especially — for the kids).

FAVORITE TV PROGRAM: All the "soaps," especially "General Hospital" (having replaced "Eight is Enough").

HOUSE LOOKS LIKE THIS: just like the neighbors; i.e. a double carport with a Jubilee attached.

WALL CALENDAR: From the local funeral parlor.

HABITAT (CAN BE MOST FREQUENTLY SEEN): Coming and going to the mall by day, the bars and bowling alleys by night.

LIFE'S DREAM: For some, to become a financial burden on their children; for others, none ... they've reached the ultimate!

DRESS: Female: Heavy make-up, red nail polish, stained Grateful Dead t-shirt, cut-off rolled-up Jeans, high heels from Woolco. Male: cowboy shirt for going-out, but daily, mechanics uniform with "Joe's" auto body logo, cigarette pack (Camels) rolled up in sleeve, tattoo on arm, blue work pants with cuffs, wallet chained to pants.

CAR(S) TYPICALLY DRIVEN: Somebody's else's souped-up pick-up truck with one burnt-out headlight; or, if wealthier, a customized van with dents and baby seat in front.

BUMPER STICKER: Rear: "Hey Iran, Up Yours." Front: a Bucks County Community College parking sticker.

LAST BOOK READ: Phillies Yearbook or Sears Catalogue.

HERO: The Phillies Phanatic.

VILLAIN: Anyone doing under 55 mph on Street Road

AUTHORITY FIGURE: The man who runs the local state store

COLLEGE OR EDUCATION: Occasional night classes at BC3.

RELIGION: Only when claiming charity on tax return.

POLITICS: "Vote' Who Me?"

DRINK: Whiskey with a six pack (cheapest brand) for the guys. Kahlua with cream or Amaretto for the gals

FAVORITE PASTIMES: Making ends meet during the day and getting burnt-out at night.

HOUSE LOOKS LIKE THIS: A garden apartment with wax paper insulation in the walls and cardboard thin floors, furniture. Imitation Sears-Roebuck.

WALL CALENDAR: A smudged Miss Piggy calendar two months behind.

HABITAT (CAN BE MOST FREQUENTLY SEEN): Working on the car or sitting in the car in front of the 7-11 or Dunkin' Donuts.

LIFE'S DREAM: To move up to Levittown after hitting the Daily Number.

Bensalemites

New Hope People

DRESS: Female: "punk" hairdo, sequined Jordache t-shirt, heavy on the jewelery, leopard pants with skinny belt. Male: Ralph Lauren jeans, pastel colored Izod Lacoste shirt, gold neck chain, one earring; (M&F) earth shoes or docksiders and gold insignia rings.

CAR(S) TYPICALLY DRIVEN: Weekends: new pick-up truck with "Support the Arts" bumper sticker; weekdays: Mercedes 280SE with "It's Fun to be Wealthy" bumper sticker.

LAST BOOK READ: Their own or "Antiquing as an Inflation Hedge"

HERO: Mink

VILLAIN: If straight: Trespassers; if gay: James Michener.

AUTHORITY FIGURE: Mayor Koch.

COLLEGE OR EDUCATION: Princeton (or anything with Ivy, really!).

RELIGION: Merrill Lynch

POLITICS: "Stop the Pumping Station"

DRINK: Perrier with a twist, or an imported white sweet wine, or vermouth on the rocks; local vintage used only in party punches.

FAVORITE PASTIMES: Having a bash (catered, of course), name-dropping, and looking in the mirror.

FAVORITE TV PROGRAM: For the record: only watches PBS. In fact: "Fantasy Island" and "Bosom Buddies."

HOUSE LOOKS LIKE THIS: A small castle with solar panels on large fenced-in estate with lots of "No Trespassing" signs; house loaded down with antiques and houseboy.

WALL CALENDAR: Bucks County Conservancy's Architectural Heritage with guild meeting dates neatly penciled in.

HABITAT (CAN BE MOST FREQUENTLY SEEN): On TV, in plays, or at New York parties

LIFE'S DREAM: To remodel the barn into a cute arts 'n crafts studio

DRESS: Male: Green or beige Sears workpants or bib overalls caked with dirt, long underwear, flannel shirt (torn at elbows), red handkerchief (used) in back pocket, "John Deere" or "Agway" tractor cap. Female: Same.

CAR(S) TYPICALLY DRIVEN: Beat-up 1950 vintage pick-up truck with mud guards and trailer hitch

BUMPER STICKER: "Save Farms — We Can't Eat Townhouses" or "Wash Me" scratched in dirt

LAST BOOK READ: Farmers' Almanac

HERO: Rain (having replaced John Wayne and John Boy Walton)

VILLIAN: The unholy trinity. Gypsy moth, drought, and the developers (unless, of course, the price is right)

AUTHORITY FIGURE: "Nobody Can Tell Me What To Do"

COLLEGE OR EDUCATION: DelVal

RELIGION: The National Rifle Association

POLITICS: The Moral Majority.

DRINK: Raw milk from the bottle in the morning (or morning after) and Rolling Rock or Gennie in 16-ounce returnables in the afternoon and evenings

FAVORITE PASTIMES: Watching it rain while drinking Rolling Rock or Gennie

FAVORITE TV PROGRAM: "Dukes of Hazard" (having replaced "The Waltons").

HOUSE LOOKS LIKE THIS: Rundown stone farmhouse in need of paint with broken fly-encrusted screens, pick-up truck parked on gravel in front.

WALL CALENDAR: Agway Feeds with picture of bull

HABITAT (CAN BE MOST FREQUENTLY SEEN): Just standing around the fire house, local bar, grange hall, or at church social.

LIFE'S DREAM: Ultimately, to secede from Lower Bucks County, but for now, a vacation in Kutztown

Upper Bucks Farmer

APPENDIX D

Bucks County Survey and Postcard Project

Greetings from Bucks County!

DEAR MOM,
CAN'T WAIT FOR
You TO SEE OUR
NEW TOLL BROS
HomE !

74799-8

Post Card

Name: JESSICA MADDEN

Date: 10/31/07

PLACE STAMP HERE

(2006-2014)

    They've lived in Bucks County for an average of twenty-one years and their average age is 21 years. Daily, they drive the county roads to work and to classes at the community college campuses. Between 2006-14 these students were surveyed as to their likes and dislikes about the county. Of those surveyed, 34% identified with (were born in/grew up in) Lower Bucks; 38% with Central (middle) Bucks; and 16% with Upper Bucks. Another 12% lived nearby, either in Philadelphia or other neighboring counties. They expressed their opinions in writing and were furthermore asked to write a mock "postcard" to a relative or friend telling them something interesting about the county. They were asked to be creative, humorous, and – most of all – candid in their comments. They did; and they were!

    All of those surveyed gave the author permission to use their observations. Many of the opinions expressed and comments made have been woven into the preceding chapters. The survey results were tabulated and appear in the two never-before-published tables on the following pages.

Survey Results: Table 1 — Most frequently mentioned things liked BEST about Bucks County

Lower Bucks	Central Bucks	Upper Bucks	All Surveyed
Location: proximity to places	Open spaces/farms	Open spaces/farms	Location: proximity to places
Good schools/college	Location: proximity to places	Scenery/landscape	Open spaces/farms
Historic places	Historic places	Historic places	Parks/nature
Parks/nature	Parks/nature	Parks/nature	Scenery/landscape
Open spaces/farms	Scenery/landscape	Location: proximity to places	Good schools/college
Shopping/restaurants	Good schools/college	Small town atmosphere	Historic places
Scenery/landscape	Shopping/restaurants	Good schools/college	Shopping/restaurants
Nice, friendly people	Small town atmosphere	Nice, friendly people	Nice, friendly people
Family/community	Low crime/feels safe	Low crime/feels safe	Small town atmosphere
Suburban look/feel	Nice, friendly people	Good weather/ Seasonality	Low crime/feels safe
Low crime/feels safe	Family/community	Family/community	Family/community
Delaware river/canal	Lots to do/attractions	Shopping/restaurants	Suburban look/feel
Small town atmosphere	Suburban look/feel	Peace(ful) and quiet	Delaware river/canal
Lots to do/attractions	Good weather/ Seasonality	Clean/unpolluted	Lots to do/attractions
It's Home	Peace(ful) and quiet	Delaware river/canal	Good weather/ seasonality

Also mentioned were: jobs, fishing and hunting, country roads and covered bridges, farm markets, antique shops, the arts/museums, diversity of classes and ethnic groups, the race track and casino ..... and Wawa convenience stores.

Survey Results: Table 2   Most frequently mentioned things liked LEAST about Bucks County

Lower Bucks

Crowded/
    too congested
Sprawl/overdeveloped
Traffic
Nothing to do/boring
Loss of farms/
    open space
Cost of living
Too many strip malls
Taxes (school)
Crime/gangs/drugs
Trashy/dirty/rundown
Weather/too cold
The Police
Flooding
Lack of public
    transportation
Real estate prices

Central Bucks

Sprawl/overdeveloped
Traffic
Crowded/
    too congested
Nothing to do/boring
Cost of Living
Loss of farms/
    open space
Taxes (school)
Lack of public
    transportation
Snooty/Stuck-up people
Too many strip malls
Bad roads
The Police
Crime/drugs/gangs
Weather/too cold
Real estate prices

Upper Bucks

Sprawl/overdeveloped
Traffic
Taxes (school)
Bad roads
Cost of Living
Crowded/
    too congested
Loss of farms/
    open space
Nothing to do/boring
Lack of public
    transportation
Local politics
The Police
Too many deer
Weather/too cold
Snooty/Stuck-up people
Too much Construction

All Surveyed

Sprawl/overdeveloped
Traffic
Crowded/
    too congested
Loss of farms/
    open space
Nothing to do/boring
Cost of Living
Taxes (school)
Bad roads
Lack of public
    transportation
Too many strip malls
The Police
Weather/too cold
Snooty/Stuck-up people
Real estate prices
Trashy/dirty/rundown

Also mentioned were: too-fast paced, boarded-up empty stores, light pollution (at night), air and noise pollution, lack of good-paying jobs, the casino, too close to the city, too many trucks and "crazy" truckers, too many tourists, too many "uppity yuppies" and their Starbucks, too many Canada geese, no sidewalks, too much roadkill, and far too many banks, pharmacies, and old people.

Sample *"Greetings from Bucks County"*

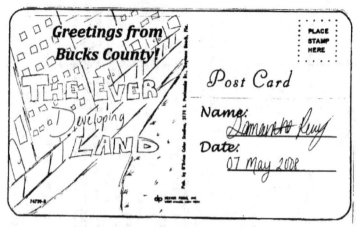

"I'm sitting in traffic on (Rte.) 313 because of all the yuppies that moved here, so I'm spending my free time to write you a postcard." – Josh Nevells

"The farms are all being built into neighborhoods ... (come) say good-bye to the farms ..." – Lauren Miller

"I don't know what to say ... You have to go further north anymore to get away from (all) the city people. They are like a disease ..." – Bryant Watts

"The roads are crowded, the people are rude. The south is dirty, and the north is country. Taxes are high, utilities ridiculous." – Josh Minnich

"This is Tom telling you to come see Bucks before there's nothing left to see!" –Tom Wilkinson

"They call it 'Bucks' because you need lots of bucks to live here or even just to visit." – David Wiest

"Pennsylvania has a whole lotta nothing ... except (for) Bucks County." –Jacquelyn Nowalinski

"It's so much nicer than Brooklyn." – Jennifer Gonzalez

BIBLIOGRAPHY

Adams, Harry C., ed. 1996. *Wanderings Through Historic Hilltown With Edward Mathews*. Bedminster, Pa.: Adams Apple Press.

Ashton, John. 1896. *The Devil in Britain and America.* London: Ward and Downey.

American Society of Planning Officials. 1970 (Winter). *The Urban Fringe: Techniques for Guiding the Development of Bucks County*. Chicago: Volume 4:1 (pamphlet).

Baergen, Rudy. 1981. *The Mennonite Story*. Newton, Kansas: Faith and Life Press.

Baltzell, E. Digby. 1979. *Puritan Boston and Quaker Philadelphia.* New York: The Free Press.

Battle, J.H., ed. 1887. *History of Bucks County, Pennsylvania*. Philadelphia: A. Warner & Co.

Bodnar, John. 1974. *Ethnic History in Pennsylvania, A Selected Bibliography*. Harrisburg: Penn. Historical and Museum Commission.

Blanshard Jr., Paul. 1954. Boom Times for Bucks Farmers. *Bucks County Traveler* (2-part article), January, p.9ff; February, p.15ff.

Bowen, Genevieve, ed. 1951. *Our Bucks County*. Doylestown,Pa.: Bucks County School Director's Assoc.

Bray, Jane W. 1967. *A Quaker Saga*. Philadelphia: Dorrance.

Brodsky, Harold. 1973. Land Development and the Expanding City. *Annals of the Assoc. of American Geographers* 63 June: p. 159-66.

Buck, William Joseph. 1855. *History of Bucks County.* (Published? Printed for the Author?).

Buck, William Joseph. 1887. *Local Sketches and Legends Pertaining to Bucks and Montgomery Counties, Pa.* Printed for the Author.

Bucks County Bicentennial Committee. 1976. *Official Historic Guide for Bucks County.* Morrisville, Pa.

Bucks County Historical Society. 1908-1940. *A Collection of Papers, etc.* Riegelsville, Pa.: B.F. Fackenthal, Publisher. Volumes 1-8.

Bucks County Planning Commission. No Date. *The Villages of Bucks County, A Guidebook.* Doylestown, Pa.

_____. 1970. *The Urban Fringe, Techniques for Guiding the Development of Bucks County.* Doylestown, Pa.

_____. 1976. *Bucks County Population Projections.* Doylestown, Pa.

_____. 1977. *Comprehensive Plan, Bucks County, Pa.* Doylestown, Pa.

_____. 1977. *1975 Land Use Report.* Doylestown, Pa.

_____. 1978. *Farmers Survey.* Doylestown, Pa.

_____. 1979. *Agricultural Preservation in Bucks County.* Doylestown, Pa.

_____. 1985. *Natural Resources Plan.* Doylestown, Pa.

_____. 2007. *Bucks County Agricultural Land Preservation Program.* Annual Report. Doylestown, Pa.

Bucks County Planning Commission. 1970's-80's. *Planning Progress.* (Various Numbers) Doylestown, Pa.

Bucks County Schools. 1977. *Bucks County Chronicles.* Doylestown, Pa.: Intermediate Unit #22.

Burke, R.T.A. et.al. 1946. *Soil Survey of Bucks County, Pennsylvania.* Washington D.C.: U.S. Dept. of Agriculture in cooperation with Penn State College, School of Agriculture. Series 1936, No. 25.

Bush, George S., ed. 1996. *The Genius Belt, The Story of the Arts in Bucks County, Pennsylvania.* Doylestown, Pa.: James Michener Art Museum.

Cameron, Dorothy Stockton. 1976(?). *History of the Presbyterian Church of Deep Run, 1725-1975.* Printed by Ross Painter, Hilltown Township, Pa.

Carus, Paul. 1969. *The History of the Devil and the Idea of Evil.* New York: Bell Publishing Co.

Chiccarine, Jerry A. and David Luz. 2007. *The Upper Perkiomen Valley.* Charleston, S.C.: Arcadia Publishing (Images of America Series).

Clark, Kathleen Zingaro. 2006. *Bucks County* (Images of America). Charleston, S.C.: Arcadia Publishing.

Clark, Sara Maynard. 1957. The Night the Devil Came to Bristol. *Bucks County Traveler.* Nov: p. 38-39.

Clay, Grady. 1973. *Close-Up, How to Read the American City.* New York: Praeger Publishers.

Council on Environmental Quality. 1975. *The Delaware River Basin, An Environmental Assessment of Three Centuries of Change.* Washington D.C.: U.S. Government Printing Office.

Craig, Robert W. 1988. *Temples of Learning: Octagon School-houses in the Delaware Valley.* N.Y.: Columbia University MS in Historic Preservation.(Avery Classics Thesis Pres.).

Davis, Bertha, Olive Steele and Charlotte Cutshall. 1980. *Postcards of Bucks County, Pennsylvania as Printed by the Arnold Brothers.* Washington Crossing, Pa.: Washington Crossing Card Collectors Club.

Davis, William W.H. 1905. *History of Bucks County, Pennsylvania.* (3 Volumes). Pipersville, Pa.: A.E. Lear.

Delaware Valley Regional Planning Commission. 1980. *1980 Census of Population.* Trenton: Regional Information Services Center.

Diamond, David. 1982. The Levittown Generation Turns 30. *Philadelphia Inquirer Magazine.* Dec. 12: p.31 ff.

Dwyer, Bill and Givens Crews. 1953. Has Big Steel Hurt Our County? *Bucks County Traveler* (Two-Part Report, October-November: p. 9ff; p.12-13).

Dyke, Linda F. 1989. *Henry Chapman Mercer, an Annotated Chronology.* Doylestown, Pa.: Bucks County Historical Society.

Frost, William J. 1973. *The Quaker Family in Colonial America.* New York: St. Martin's Press.

Garreau, Joel. 1991. *Edge City: Life on the Future Frontier.* New York: Doubleday.

Gaustad, Edwin Scott. 1962. *Historical Atlas of Religion in America.* New York: Harper & Row.

Geyer, Alan and William H. Bolles. 1979. The Devil in Pennsylvania. *Outstanding Scenic Geologic Features in Pennsylvania.* Harrisburg, Pa. Dept. of Environmental Resources.

Glassie, Henry. 1968. *Pattern in the Material Folk Culture of the Eastern United States.* Philadelphia: University of Pennsylvania Press.

Graeff and Hostetler. 1956. Pennsylvania German Culture. *Mennonite Historical Bulletin,* XVII, Apr: p.1-4.

Gurney, Joseph John. 1860. *Observations on the Distinguishing Views and Practices of the Society of Friends.* New York: Samuel S. and William Wood.

Halverson, Deborah. 1982. On Quaker Soil. *Early American Life.* June: p.33-37.

Hanauer, David. *David's Photographic Tour of Bucks County, Pennsylvania.*www.davidhanauer.com/buckscounty/ about/indexhtml.

Harris, Rev. W.S. 1904. *Sermons by the Devil.* Harrisburg, Pa.: The Minter Company.

Hemsing, William Souder. 1987. *Diaries of* ... Souderton, Pa.: Indian Valley Printing Ltd.

Herman, Andrew Mark. 2000. *Lower Bucks County* (Postcard History Series). Charleston, S.C.: Arcadia Publishing.

Hill, Napoleon. 2011. *Outwitting the Devil.* New York: Sterling Publishing Company.

Hoffman, W.J. 1888-89. Folk-Lore of the Pennsylvania Germans. *Journal of American Folk-Lore.* Part I, p.125-35; Part II, p.23-35.

Hughes, Robert. 1975. Imperturbable Innocence. *Time.* May 12, p.62. (A review of the Edward Hicks Retrospective at the Crispo Gallery, New York City).

Ikeler, Bern. 1952. P. Alston Waring: Productive Acres. *Bucks County Traveler.* February: p.21-23.

James, Stuart. 1961. *Bucks County Report.* New York: Midwood (Tower) Publications.

Jamson, Donald. 1981. What's Doing in Bucks County? The *New York Times*, September 20.

Jones, Louis C. 1952. The Devil in New York State. *New York Folklore Quarterly.* VIII:I, Spring, p.5-19.

Keats, John. 1956. *The Crack in the Picture Window.* New York: Ballantine Books.

Keister, Douglas. 2004. *Stories in Stone, A Field Guide to Cemetery Symbolism and Iconography.* New York: MJF Books.

Kenderdine, Thaddeus S. 1901. *The Kenderdines of America,* Doylestown, Pa.: Doylestown Publishing Co.

Kimball, Penn. 1952. "Dream Town" – Large Economy Size. The *New York Times* Magazine. December 4.

Kirchhoff, Adam. (No Date) *Pennsylvania German Legends.* www.kutztown.edu/academics/liberal__arts/anthropo.

Kowinski, William. 1978. The Malling of America. *New Times.* May 1. P. 31-55.

Kitchen, Mr. & Mrs. Norman. 1976. *Newtown Then* ... Newtown, Pa.: Bucks County Assoc. for the Blind.

Kriebel, Howard W. 1904. *The Schwenkfelders in Pennsylvania An Historical Sketch.* Lancaster, Pa.: Pennsylvania-German Society.

Kunstler, James H. 1993. *The Geography of Nowhere, The Rise and Decline of America's Man-Made Landscape.* New York: Touchstone Book, Simon & Schuster.

Lemon, James T. 1972. *The Best Poor Man's Country: A Geographical Survey of Early Southeastern Pennsylvania.* Baltimore: John Hopkins Press.

Leopold, Aldo. 1981. Tribute to a Feathered Tempest (Passenger Pigeon). *American Heritage.* December. P. 32-33.

Levittownwebsite: http://home.comcast.net/~levittownrelics/facts/index.

Lingerman, Richard. 1980. *Small Town America.* New York: G.P. Putnam's Sons.

Long, Amos. 1972. *The Pennsylvania German Family Farm.* Breinigsville, Pa.: The Pennsylvania German Society.

Lynch, James J. 1952. The Devil in the Writings of Irving, Hawthorne, and Poe. *New York Folklore Quarterly*. Summer, VIII:2, p. 111-31.

MacReynolds.George. 1976. *Place Names in Bucks County*. Doylestown, Pa.: Bucks County Historical Society. (First edition, 1942).

McNealy, Terry A. 1970. *A History of Bucks County, Pennsylvania*. Fallsington, Pa.: Bucks County Historical and Tourist Commission.

Magda, Matthew. 1998. *The Welsh in Pennsylvania*. (The Peoples of Pennsylvania, Pamphlet No. 1). Harrisburg, Pa.: Pennsylvania Historical and Museum Commission.

Masello, Robert. 1994. *Fallen Angels and Spirits of the Dark*. New York: Berkley Publishing Group.

Michener, James. 1961. *Report of the County Chairman*. New York: Random House.

_____. 1970. *The Quality of Life*. Philadelphia: Girard Bank.

Miller, Alan, ed. 1950's. *Bucks County Traveler*. Doylestown, Pa. (Various magazine issues, especially from late 1950's).

Miller, Henry. 1945. *The Air-Conditioned Nightmare*. New York: A New Direction Book.

Morigi, Gilda. 1973. *The Difference Began in the Footlights: The Story of the Bucks County Playhouse*. Author.

Muller, Peter O., Kenneth Meyer, and Roman Cybriwsky. 1976. *Metropolitan Philadelphia: A Study of Conflict and Social Cleavages*. Cambridge, Mass.: Ballinger Publishing Company.

Muller, Peter O. 1981. *Contemporary Suburban America*. Englewood Cliffs, N.J.: Prentice-Hall , Inc.

Noll, E.P. 1891. *Atlas of Bucks County, Pennsylvania*. Philadelphia: E.P. Noll & Company.

North, Sterling and C.B. Boutell, eds. 1945. *Speak of the Devil*. New York: Doubleday, Dorant Company Inc.

Nutting, Wallace. 1924. *Pennsylvania Beautiful (Eastern)*. Framingham, Mass.: Old America Company.

O'Brien, Raymond. 1988. *Bucks County, A Journey Through Paradise, From the Peaceable Kingdom to the Suburban Dream*. Dubuque, Iowa: Kendall/Hunt Pubs.

Pennsylvania, Department of Agriculture. 1897. *Second Annual Report*. Harrisburg, Pa.

Pennsylvania State Data Center. 1982. *1980 Census of Population, Economic and Social Indicators*. Harrisburg, Pa.

Pervy, Charlotte Stryker. 1948. *The Bucks County Scrapbook of Old Roads and Towns*. Doylestown, Pa. Author.

Pullinger, Edna. 1973. *A Dream of Peace: Edward Hicks of Newtown*. Philadelphia, Pa. Author.

Rhoads, Ann F. and Timothy A. Block. 2000. *Natural Bucks County, Guide to Public Natural Areas*. Doylestown, Pa.: Bucks County Commissioners.

Richie, Margaret Bye. 1980. *History of Bucks County Architecture*. Newtown, Pa.: Sandra L. Chase.

Ruth, John L. 1985. *A Quiet and Peaceable Life*. Intercourse, Pa.: Good Books. (Originally 1979).

Ruth, Phil Johnson. 1987. *Seeing Souderton, The Borough's Story in Photographs, 1887-1987*. Souderton, Pa.: Moyer Packing Company (MOPAC).

_____. 1988. *A North Penn Pictorial*. Souderton, Pa.: Clemens Markets.

Ryder, G., ed. (No Date) *Letters to and From Caesar Rodney, 1756-1784.*

Seidman, Robert J. 1980. *Bucks County Idyll.* New York: Simon and Schuster.

Schiddel, Edmund. 1959. *The Devil in Bucks County.* New York: Simon and Schuster.

_____. 1965. *The Good and Bad Weather.* New York: Simon and Schuster.

Scott, J.D. 1876. *Combination Atlas Map of Bucks County, Pennsylvania.* Philadelphia, Pa.: Thomas Hunter.

Scott, J. Ernest. 1908-09. *Old Shad Fisheries on the Delaware River.* Doylestown, Pa.: Bucks County Historical Society Papers. p. 534-41.

Smith, C. Henry. 1907. *Mennonites in History.* Scottdale, Pa.: Mennonite Book and Tract Society.

Soil Conservation Service (SCS). 1975. *Soil Survey of Bucks and Philadelphia Counties, Pennsylvania.* Washington D.C.: U.S. Department of Agriculture.

Spectorsky, Auguste Compte. 1955. *The Exurbanites.* New York and Philadelphia: J.B. Lippincott.

Stilgoe, John R. 1984. The Suburbs. *American Heritage.* February/March. p. 21-37.

Teller, Walter. 1963. *Area Code 215, A Private Line in Bucks County.* New York: Atheneum.

Thrower, Norman. 1966. *Original Survey and Land Subdivision.* Washington D.C.: Assoc. of American Geographers (Printed by Rand McNally & Co., Chicago).

Tolles, Frederick B. 1960. *Quakers and the Atlantic Culture.* New York: MacMillan Company.

Trego, Charles B. 1843. *A Geography of Pennsylvania*. Philadelphia: Edward C. Biddle.

Trillin, Calvin. 1969. Lower Bucks County, Pennsylvania ... Buying and Selling Along Route 1. *The New Yorker*. November 15, p. 169-75.

Vlach, John Michael. 1981. Quaker Tradition and the Paintings of Edward Hicks, A Strategy for the Study of Folk Art. *Journal of American Folklore*. Vol. 94, April-June, p.145-65.

Wagner, Richard and Amy Duckett Wagner. 2010. *Levittown* (Images of America). Charleston, S.C.: Arcadia Pub.

Walker, Frederick. 1952. Industrialism in Bucks County. *Bucks County Traveler*. October, p. 8-11.

Waring, P. Alston and Walter Magnes Teller. 1943. *Roots in the Earth, The Small Farmer Looks Ahead*. New York: Harper and Brothers Publishers.

Wenger, John C. 1937. *History of the Mennonites of the Franconia Conference*. Telford, Pa.: Franconia Mennonite Historical Society.

Wiegner, Douglas. (No Date) Schwenkfelders, Who Are They? http://pages.prodigy.com/JPBCOSA/schwenk.

Willard, Bradford et.al. 1959. *Geology and Mineral Resources of Bucks County, 1944* ... Harrisburg, Pa.: Topographic and Geologic Survey (Pennsylvania's Mineral Heritage).

Woods, William. 1974. *A History of the Devil*. New York: G.P. Putnam's Sons.

Yoder, Don. 1965. The Devil in Pennsylvania. *Pennsylvania Folklife*. Winter, p. 36-52.

Young, Art. 1893. *Hell Up to Date, The Reckless Journey of R. Palasco Drant* ... Chicago: Schulte Publishing Co.